*Hidden Beast 2*

# Hidden Beast 2

by Ellis H. Skolfield

Toshiba 1200H and 1200HB computers
were employed in the preparation of the manuscript.

Manuscript and graphs were initially produced on a
Toshiba ExpressWriter 311.

Most Bible quotes are from the King James Version.

A few are from the New American Standard Bible
THE LOCKMAN FOUNDATION
1960, 1962, 1963, 1968, 1972, 1975, 1975, 1977
and are quoted by permission.

Cover art by Mary Ziegler

ISBN 0-9628139-0-7

PUBLISHED BY FISH HOUSE
Printed in the United States of America

# Acknowledgements

My heartfelt thanks to friends who have helped along the way in the production of this book. Without their continuing encouragement Hidden Beast would never have been written. To the brethren who supported us with their prayers and tithes. To one special brother who kept pushing and prodding, and almost daily took me out for breakfast to get the latest printout, but would not let me use his name.

To the churches where I have taught or worshipped, and who for good or ill have influenced what is written here. To the pastors and elders who read the manuscript before production, and wanted either to burn it, or urge me on, depending on their doctrinal position.

To Ray Taylor, Blair Kneram, Dino Fonda, Ralph Lyman and others who would visit, or call (sometimes long distance) to fellowship. To the brethren who gave us the word processor on which it was written. To my dear patient wife who spent many late hours correcting the manuscript for grammar and clarity. To Loren Williams for his editorial help, but whose good advice I was sometimes too hardheaded to take, and to Arthur Holt for his meticulous proofing. To Carol Shearn for typesetting the manuscript.

Most of all, praise and thanks to the Lord Jesus who spiritually sustained me, and kept me going through the dry times: those times when the enemy tempted me to quit. To our blessed heavenly Father, who through His Spirit permitted me to see the immeasurable gulf which separates His Word from some of the distortions and subtle half truths of the enemy. "Thank you, Oh Lord of Hosts, for your protecting hand."

## *Behold...*

The days come, saith the Lord GOD,
that I will send a famine in the land,
not a famine of bread, nor a thirst for water,
but of hearing the words of the LORD:
And they shall wander from sea to sea,
and from the north even to the east,
they shall run to and fro
to seek the word of the LORD,
and shall not find it.


Amos 8:11-12

# Preface

The prophetic concepts contained in *Hidden Beast 2* are far from new. In fact, many of them have been in the true church of Jesus Christ for over 300 years. Events in the Mid-East are now validating these earlier end-time views and throwing today's popular views into question: particularly the newer views which hold that most of Revelation will be fulfilled in a Great Tribulation still to come.

The Anabaptist, Thielman J. van Braght, has given us an outline of some of these early principles, even declaring that REV 12:6-11 was in the process of being fulfilled in his own time! That extraordinary insight (among others) has been passed down to us through *Martyrs Mirror*: a monumental 17th century chronicle of the persecution of the saints, from the days of the apostles through the Reformation:

"From Adam to Noah, from Noah to Abraham, from Abraham to Moses, from Moses to Christ, from Christ to the end of the world, God ordained, for each of these periods, different customs, as regards to the external divine service of this church; also different signs, seals, and appurtenances; though **it is, was, and shall be, the same church, the same people, and also the same God whom they served, still serve, and shall serve unto the end.**[1]

"And that thus the Son of God died, and tasted death and shed his precious blood for all men; and that he thereby bruised the serpent's head, destroyed the works of the devil, annulled the handwriting and obtained forgiveness of sins for all mankind; thus becoming the cause of eternal salvation **for all those who, from Adam unto the end of the world, each in his time, believe in, and obey Him,** GEN 3:15, 1JO 3:8, COL 2:14, ROM 5:18.

"After the Ascension of Christ, the very numerous church which was at Jerusalem dispersed, on account of persecution, through the land of Judea and Samaria, except the apostles; so that this distinguished church, which, it appears, was the chief one on the face of the earth, had to sojourn secretly in a strange land, ACT 8:1.

"Afterwards when the emperor Domitian had banished John, the holy apostle and evangelist, for the Gospel's sake, on the island of Patmos, the Holy Ghost revealed unto him the future state of the Church of Christ, namely, that she would have to flee into the wilderness, on account of the persecution of Antichrist,and there be fed by God, **a thousand two hundred and threescore days, which, reckoned according to prophetic language, means as many years,** REV 12:6-11.

"Whether we begin to reckon these years from the death of the apostles; or with the year 300, when the so-called patriarchs had their origin; or with the year 600; or a little later, **when Mohammed rose in the east among the Greeks,** and the pope in the west among the Latins, and raised no small persecution against the defenseless and innocent little flock of the church of Christ, so that all who did not wish to be devoured, either in soul or in body, had to hide themselves in deserts and wildernesses; **let it be**

---

[1] Boldface is not in the source document, but is the author's to draw your attention to a central thought.

reckoned as it may, say we, a very long period is to be understood by it, which has extended to this, or about this time..."

Thielman J. van Braght
July 31, 1659AD

From pp 21, 25, and 40 of *Martyrs Mirror*.

From the above it is apparent that the reformation church understood the three following principles: (1) That the 1260 prophetic days of Revelation 12:6 were to be understood as 1260 years which spanned at least part of the Christian Era. (2) That regardless of historic position, every true believer is a member of one universal church which transcends time. (3) That regardless of the method of worship which God ordained for a given time, every saint is saved by faith in God through the finished work of Jesus Christ on the Cross of Calvary. *Hidden Beast 2* is built on these historically accepted foundational concepts.

# Contents

# *Introduction*

To Be Read

---

About two thousand years before Abraham, there was a beautiful civilization flourishing in the Tigris and Euphrates valley. The city of Sumer was at the height of its splendor. They even had artisans working in precious metal who invented the electric battery. Archaeologists believed this battery was used to gold plate objects made of base metals. The Sumerians also had horses and chariots and fine cool houses. They invented board games with which to while away their leisure hours. Written languages, fine textiles, lovely pottery, sculptures of gold and silver (inlaid with lapis lazuli) have been found in the what remains of the pre-flood cities of the Middle East.

But there were no temples, no idols, and no cult sites. In fact, no indication of any kind that the Sumerians, or anyone else in the pre-flood era, worshipped anything at all. A handsome, intelligent, people who worshipped nothing.

From then, to this very day, there has not been a major civilization that worshipped no god at all. Not one. But now, the natural sciences, evolution, and humanism have again displaced the worship of all gods, including the God of Heaven. The God who created us all has been replaced by theories that man believes to be more "rational." The concept of a Supreme Being is presumed to be a primitive idea that man has outgrown.

That is what the Sumerians thought, too. Then came the flood:

> LUK 17:26-27  And as it was in the days of Noe, so shall it be also in the days of the Son of man. **They did eat, they drank, they married wives, they were given in marriage, until the day that Noe entered into the ark, and the flood came, and destroyed all...**

> 2PE 3:6-7  Whereby the world that then was, being overflowed with water, perished: **But the heavens and the earth, which are now, by the same word are kept in store, reserved unto fire against the day of judgment and perdition of ungodly men.**

A flood will not end our age,  Our age will end in fire. But when will that fire be?  Now, the Christian Era has also run almost two thousand years; and two events, unique in history, have taken place in our times.[1]  Following a centuries long dispersion among the nations and a holocaust in which they were almost eliminated from Europe, in 1948AD the new nation of Israel was established.  Then in 1967AD, the Jews again ruled in Jerusalem for the first time in 2573 years. From a human standpoint, both were impossible; and yet these two events happened, just as the Bible predicted.  These fulfillments of prophecy give us time-pins to which we can tie other prophecies about the end of all things.

For instance: We are now in the End Time.  That is not conjecture, but a scripturally provable fact.  The time of Gentile domination of Jerusalem and the Holy Land ended in 1967.  In LUK 21:24 Jesus said: "...and Jerusalem shall be trodden down of the Gentiles, until the times of the Gentiles be fulfilled."  So we are now in a time after "the time of the Gentiles," and Daniel defines that time as the "End Time."

---

[1] B.C. used to mean before Christ, and A.D. (Anno Domini) used to mean: In the year of our Lord. Historians who do not accept the Lord have changed that.  B.C.E. now means Before Common Era, and this new C.E. (Common Era) is the old AD.  As a party of one, the author refuses to accept these new names!  So throughout the book BC and AD are used in the good old fashioned way, and the meaning of C.E. has been changed to Christian Era. The author does not use "Church Age" because of the doctrinal views some denominations have attached to that term.

What can that mean to us? It's business as usual, isn't it? No it isn't. The troubles which now face the world far transcend anything we have ever faced before; and they won't go away. They are beyond our ability to correct, and are worsening, and becoming more complex, by the day. Middle East wars, and conflicts on every hand, irreparable damage to our environment, a world food shortage, natural disasters; and now we have weapons capable of destroying the whole planet. Satan has been cast to the Earth and loosed upon it, REV 12:9.

We are in a world situation without hope, were it not that God has a plan. A wonderful plan to save sinful man from this doom of his own making. God's plan has taken 6000 years to unfold, and only now can we begin to understand some of it.

To comprehend His plan, we first need to recognize that the Bible itself is the foundation of our faith, and not our traditions. Doctrines and traditions have a way of changing over time. Denominations are founded, and new songs are sung. Then they (and the views they supported) are abandoned; and all that is left are a few crumbling bricks, and some half-buried gravestones. That is the story of the church throughout the Christian Era.

This book is outside those traditions. It is written to those who hate the closed minds and hardened hearts to which, over the years, we have all fallen heir. The author includes himself. It is to those who are more concerned with truth than with conformity. To those who believe that "all our righteousness is as filthy rags." It is to those who are tired of being "approved of men," and want to please God only. If that is you, then this book is for you:

> REV 2:17 He that hath an ear, let him hear what the Spirit saith unto the churches; **To him that overcometh will I give to eat of the hidden manna...**

Without getting into a lengthy explanation of what was going on in the church at Pergamum: God's Word is our spiritual manna, our heavenly food. Here, the Lord promises insights into unseen truths if: (1) we study the Bible and, (2) do not rest in the traditions passed down to us. Traditions and devotional platitudes don't address today's problems. They don't deal with the immorality and apostasy in the churches, the drugs, the atomic weapons, the terrorists, the wars, and the rise of new Islam. But, God's Word does![2]

With the advent of the new nation of Israel, and Jerusalem now under Jewish control, the Lord has opened His Word anew. These monumental events have made it possible to look at the prophetic books in a new way; and the picture is not as pretty as we would like. There are some tough declarations in the Bible about the times ahead. As a result, there are some sober things written here. Some folks can't believe that judgment is coming on the church, even when Scripture declares it:

> 1PE 4:17-18 **For the time is come that judgment must begin at the house of God:** and if it first begin at us, what shall the end be of them that obey not the gospel of God? And if the righteous scarcely be saved, where shall the ungodly and the sinner appear?

> 2PE 3:11-12 Seeing then that all these things shall be dissolved, what manner of persons ought ye to be in all holy conversation and godliness, **Looking for and hasting unto the coming of the day of God, wherein the heavens being on fire shall be dissolved, and the elements shall melt with fervent heat?**

These verses are yet to be fulfilled, but their day will come. The events leading up to that day, and how we are to prepare for it, is our central subject. Hidden Beast 2 is divided into three books. Many chapters have illuminating graphs, charts, or time-lines. These charts re-quote the Scriptures used in the text and have other useful information. They are keyed to the text, and appear at the end of each book.

---

[2] As spoken of here, "traditions" are those church dogmas, doctrines, and practices which are not recorded in Scripture. Positions derived by the interpretations of men. Just before they went into the promised land, Moses told Israel, "What thing soever I command you, observe to do it: thou shalt not add thereto, nor diminish from it," DEU 12:32. That same principle applies today.

BOOK 1

# The Day Years

The temple mount as seen from the north. The Mohammedan Memorial "The Dome of the Rock" stands in its center as it has for almost 1,300 years. Circled in the lower right is a little unimposing cupola, "The Dome of the Tablets." Late archeological evidence indicates that the Holy of Holies in the Solomonic and Nehemiahan temples was located here, some 330 feet northwest of the dome itself. The dome is situated in what was once the court of the gentiles.

# Chapter 1

# *Tortoise And Hare*

To know where we are going, there are a couple of technical matters we need to address first. Understanding Bible prophecy depends on knowing historic pins, and on using sound interpretive methods. Let's begin on square 1.

God's total message to fallen man is contained in the Bible. "Thus sayeth the Lord" appears over 3000 times in the Old Testament. Jesus openly declared His deity, and then proved it in the resurrection. Scholars tell us that the resurrection of Jesus Christ is one of the best verified facts in all history. The Bible tells us of all these things, and states that the Scripture was written by men directly inspired by God:

> 2TI 3:16 **All scripture is given by inspiration of God**, and is profitable for doctrine, for reproof, for correction, for instruction in righteousness...

> 2PE 1:21 For the prophecy came not in old time by the will of man: but **holy men of God spake as they were moved by the Holy Ghost.**

However, Scripture was not given to man all at one time. It was written over a 1550 year period, from about 1446BC to about 95AD. Though the Bible contains isolated words and a few short passages from other Middle Eastern languages, it was primarily written in two languages. The Old Testament was written in Hebrew, and the New Testament was written in Greek. All of the Bibles in common usage today are translations from existing manuscripts written in those original tongues.

God's plan, as recorded in the Bible, embraces many writing styles, including prose and poetry, some literal, and some figurative:

(1) Most Scripture is written in **Plain Language**. The historic books, poetic books, the gospels, the epistles, and major prophets like Isaiah can, for the most part, be understood literally. They need no interpretation, and are to be accepted verbatim.

(2) Some of Scripture is **Visionary and Allegorical**. All the way back to Joseph's time, biblical visions used allegorical language, GEN 37:5-9. Peter's vision of the sheet full of unclean beasts is a New Testament example of an allegorical vision, ACT 10:9-23. An allegory is usually an imaginative little tale on one subject, used to illustrate a different truth. Unless the message was intended to be hidden, biblical visions (sometimes called apocalyptic visions) were interpreted by the prophet himself.[3]

Using an earthly writer's tale as an illustration, Aesop's Fables are allegorical. One of his little fables, the "Tortoise and the Hare," is familiar to us all. In that story, Aesop's hidden message is that slow and steady is better than brilliant but unpredictable. Reading an allegory is like receiving a message in code. The encoding makes the message no less meaningful, if you know the code!

Some scholars believe that none of the Bible is figurative, that all should be interpreted literally. They have not looked carefully at the prophets, or at Jesus' parables. Both are full of figurative language, and all of Jesus' parables are allegorical. Here is the point: It is just as wrong to insist on a literal interpretation of figurative language, as it is to allegorically interpret literal language. That is so important it should be restated:

**(1) An allegorical interpretation of literal language will lead to faulty doctrine!**

**(2) A literal interpretation of figurative language will also lead to faulty doctrine!**

---

[3] A classical allegory is a story which contains figurative language, but figurative language can be used outside the allegorical setting. A technical point of interest to English buffs. In the interest of simplicity, when figurative language is referred to in this book, it is called allegorical language, regardless of the setting.

Both errors lead to fallacy. For instance, if we had concluded that Aesop was writing about real turtles and real rabbits, we would have missed his message entirely. The same is true of biblical allegories. If we fail to interpret God's allegories allegorically, we will totally miss the Lord's message. Interpreting Bible allegories literally, and vice versa, is one reason there are so many bizarre end-time doctrines around.

So how do we know the difference? How do we know when some passage of Scripture should be allegorically interpreted?

The Bible itself tells us. Biblical allegories contain signposts which tell us they are figurative. Signposts like: the kingdom of heaven is "like," or "like unto," or "as," a wedding feast, or a mustard seed, or a pearl of great price, or a king going to a far country, or a sower going forth to sow, and so on. Now the kingdom of heaven is not really a wedding feast, a king in a far country, a mustard seed, a pearl, or a sower. It is only figuratively likened unto one.

Only a small portion of the Bible is figurative, but it is of major importance to us, because most end-time prophecies are written in figurative language. Apocalyptic books like Daniel and Revelation are visionary and full of allegories. These prophetic books are written in symbolic language because their messages are hidden, not because they are unimportant. There are beasts with many horns, and horses of various colors, trumpets and scrolls, seals and bowls. If we study the surrounding verses carefully, these objects and creatures are obviously symbols of something other than what they seem. What can these spiritual symbols signify to our material world?[4]

The Lord did not have the prophets record these symbolic pictures to keep their meaning from us, so in the fullness of His time, there must be a biblical way to unravel these mysteries and understand these hidden messages from the Lord. Now here is another important point:

---

[4] The word "apocalyptic" is usually defined as a visionary or symbolic style of writing. Many books in the Bible contain apocalyptic elements, but Ezekiel, Daniel and Zechariah have major passages written in that mode. Revelation is almost totally apocalyptic in style.

**If Bible prophecy is not to be understood by real people, in a real world, fighting a real battle against a real enemy, Satan... if it cannot be related to history in real time, then it is meaningless!**

Since all scripture is profitable, 2TI 3:16, that is obviously not the case. Prophecy should have a historic fulfillment to which we can relate, and should have an impact on our lives. But Bible prophecy is so complex, where do we even begin to crack the code?

On a spiritual level, by recognizing that unless the Lord takes the prophetic veil away from our eyes, we will see nothing; and by putting our study in His hands. Then on an interpretive level, by identifying the writing styles of the prophet we are studying, and placing ourselves in his historic shoes. We need to stand in the same time and place as the prophet, and look at what he has written from his perspective. For instance, the prophet John tells us that Revelation is not all futuristic:

REV 1:19  Write the things which thou **hast seen**, and the things which **are**, and the things which **shall be** hereafter;

Note the tenses of the verbs:

(1) "...hast seen," Past!
(2) "...are," Present!
(3) "...shall be hereafter." Future!

If we place ourselves back when Revelation was written, circa 95AD, we see that Revelation contains the past, present, and future of mankind **from the time of the prophet**. Revelation tells us of events in the Old Testament Era, events in the time of Christ, and events in the Christian Era. To understand Revelation, we need to separate what has been already fulfilled, from what is still to come. OK, but how can we do that? By applying the biblical rules for interpreting allegorical language.

The book of Revelation is written as a series of 12 visions, in 22 chapters. All are primarily allegorical. That can be proven from the text itself. Besides using the allegorical signposts of "like" and "as," etc., Revelation also shows it is pictorial in a way which appears in only one other book in the Bible: Ezekiel. The key phrase used in Ezekiel to identify figurative language is, "in the spirit." By using that expression, the prophet is telling the reader straight out that he is having a vision.

"In the spirit," or a similar phrase, appears four times in Revelation. "Like" or "like unto" appears 23 times. "As" appears 59 times. That adds up to a total of over 80 allegorical signposts in only 22 chapters! The beauty of this is, the Lord has given us a whole Bible full of examples of how to interpret biblical allegories. If we can read, and know how to cross reference, we can apply His rules. Allegorical interpretation is not guesswork if we use the guidelines the Lord Himself has revealed to us in His Word.

In this day of the decline of the Western Church, what is going to happen to us? What is the Lord's intent for the remnant, the handful left who are still clinging to the Word by their fingernails? To find out, we need to examine God's long term plan for His redeemed: a plan He began to reveal to us through the patriarchs of ancient times.

# Chapter 2

# *Mount Moriah*

Four thousand years ago, an old man placed a load of wood on the back of his teenage son. Together they struggled up a rough rocky mountain.

"My father:" said the lad.

"Here am I, my son."

The boy asked, "I see the fire and the wood: but where is the lamb for a burnt offering?"

"My son," the old man said, "God will provide himself a lamb for a burnt offering." So they went on together.

When they reached the top, the weary old man built an altar, and laid the wood in order. He bound his son and laid him on the wood upon the altar. Then the old man stretched forth his hand, and took a knife to slay his son:

GEN 22:11-18 (excerpts) And the angel of the LORD called unto him out of heaven, and said, Abraham, Abraham: and he said, Here am I. And he said, Lay not thine hand upon the lad, neither do thou any thing unto him: for now I know that thou fearest God, seeing thou hast not withheld thy son, thine only son from me...And Abraham lifted up his eyes, and looked, and behold behind him a ram caught in a thicket by his horns: and Abraham went and took the ram, and offered him up for a burnt offering in the stead of his son. And the Lord called again unto Abraham out of heaven, By myself have I sworn, saith the LORD, for because thou hast done this thing, and hast not withheld thy son, thine only son...in thy seed shall all the nations of the earth be blessed; because thou hast obeyed my voice.

With this foreshadowing of the cross begins the recorded history of the mountains of Moriah. God provided a lamb for Abraham right there. Then two thousand years later, on that same hill, He provided another Lamb, "A lamb slain before the foundation of the world." With blood dripping from His hands and feet, God's own beloved Son died on the Cross, for you and me. "The Lamb of God which taketh away the sin of the world." In fact, throughout the ages, every event central to God's plan of salvation for fallen man has taken place on that mountain. Here is a quick history of God's mountain.

A thousand years after Abraham, Ornan built a threshing floor on that summit. David later bought that threshing floor for an altar, 1CH 21:22. In 966BC, his son Solomon built the 1st temple of the Lord on the same site, 1KI 6:1. 380 years later, in 586BC, that wonderful temple was destroyed by King Nebuchadnezzar of Babylon. That was during Daniel the prophet's time, when the Jews were in captivity in Babylon, 2CH 36:19. *(Chart No.1)*

Seventy years later, the Jews were restored to the Holy Land, and in 516BC, Ezra built the 2nd temple on that same site, EZR 3:11. In Jesus' lifetime that 2nd temple was refurbished by King Herod. Jesus Himself taught there many times.

Jesus died on that mountain, but like the Levitical sin offering which foreshadowed it, the Cross was "outside the camp," near where the ashes were poured out, LEV 4:12, HEB 13:11-13.

The Apostles taught in the 2nd temple after the Lord was glorified. God has sworn that those mountains would be Holy unto Him forever. Is it any wonder, considering what has taken place there? Abraham offered Isaac there. His Holy City Jerusalem is there, and His temple was in it. His Son died there. That is an awesome history:

> 2CH 7:16  For now have I chosen and sanctified this house, **that my name may be there for ever; and mine eyes and mine heart shall be there perpetually.**[5]

> EZE 43:5-7 (excerpts, NASB)  So the spirit took me up, and brought me into the inner court; and, behold, the glory of the LORD filled the house.   And he said to me, Son of man, the place of my throne, and **the place of the soles of my feet, where I will dwell in the midst of the children of Israel for ever...**

38 years after Jesus was crucified (in 70AD) the Romans so totally destroyed that magnificent 2nd temple, that not one stone was left standing upon another; and then nothing, right? God totally forgot about His mountain, right?

Of course not. Forever is a long time, and God said that His eyes would be there perpetually, and that mountain would be the footstool of His feet forever. Guess what: forever keeps on running, right on through the Christian Era! That is so important we need to say it one more time. The temple site is God's footstool forever, and forever includes the Christian Era. God's eyes have always been upon His Holy Mountain! That is a fact.

It is unbelievable that the Lord would not have given us a prophecy or two about what would take place in Jerusalem between the destruction of the temple and His return. Well maybe He has, and we have overlooked or misread those Scrip-

---

[5] In this and other Scripture quotes, verses and phrases central to the study are sometimes excerpted for brevity or clarification; or set in bold face to draw attention to a pivotal thought.  **No bold face exists in the original manuscripts,** the complete text of which may be found in your Bible. In no instance has this excerpting or boldfacing been used to unfairly weight a doctrinal view.

tures which tell us about it. So let's look at a brief history of that mountain, and see if anything of spiritual importance has taken place there since its destruction by the Romans.

After the 2nd temple was destroyed in 70AD, a few Jews remained in the city, and Jerusalem became a major center of the Coptic church. Except for a short lived temple of Jupiter, the temple mount itself remained in rubble until the latter half of the 7th Century. By then, the Coptic church had become very idolatrous, and the Lord allowed it to fall.

In 639AD, during their 1st Jihad, the Mohammedans took Jerusalem.[6] 46 years later, in 685AD, the Arab governor of Jerusalem, one Abd el Malik by name, began the construction of the Dome of the Rock and the Mosque of Omar. That Dome and mosque are memorials to Mohammed on God's Holy mountain.[7] They took 20 years to build, and those monuments to the false prophet trespass there to this day. The Dome is on the temple mount of God Most Holy, within 300 feet of the Holy of Holies which held the Ark of the Covenant before which the High Priest stood once a year to sprinkle the blood of the sin offering seven times on the mercy seat for the sins of the people. And the Lord forgot to tell us about it, right?

Not a chance! The Bible not only tells us about it, but also tells us to the year when The Dome of the Rock would be built. Scripture also tells us how long the Mohammedans would rule Jerusalem, and when new Israel would come into being. The Bible also tells us when Jerusalem itself would be free of Gentile domination. The church's belief in a restored Israel is not new. Throughout the Christian Era, men of God have been expecting it. Jonathan Edwards, a highly respected puritan pastor of the 17th Century, wrote the following:

> "Besides the prophecies of the calling of the Jew, we have
> a remarkable providential seal of the fulfillment of the great

---

[6] Jihad is a Moslem word meaning "holy war," but it is a holy war in name only. Historically, the jihad has been a convenient Mohammedan excuse to kill Christians and Jews. Islam is a religion with a history of violence and hatred. No one who makes a practice of killing God's people is on God's side.

[7] According to the Mohammedans it is their 3rd most holy place.

event, by a kind of continual miracle, viz. their being a distinct nation in such a dispersed condition for above sixteen hundred years. The world affords nothing like it...When they shall be called, that ancient people who were alone God's people for so long a time shall be his people again, never to be rejected more...Though we do not know the time in which the conversion of Israel will come to pass, **yet this much we may determine by Scripture, that it will be before the glory of the Gentile part of the church be fully accomplished, because it is said that their coming in shall be life to the Gentiles.**"[8]

The bold face is ours, but notice that our elder brother not only knew the Jews were to be restored, but also considered the Gentile believers to be only a part of the church. Jonathan Edwards was not alone in these beliefs. More than a century later, Theodore Spurgeon wrote:

"The day shall yet come when the Jews, who were the first apostles to the gentiles, the first missionaries to us who were afar off, shall be gathered in again. Until that shall be, the fullness of the church's glory can never be. Matchless benefits to the world are bound up with the restoration of Israel: their gathering in shall be as life from the dead."[9]

The problem is now this: When we really understand the verses which show the fulfillment of these things, our traditional end-times views can no longer be supported by Scripture. That could lead us to change our end time doctrines. Unthinkable for some, and admittedly a very hard thing to do. It was hard for the author, but he just had to face some new geography.

The New nation of Israel, and Jerusalem now under Jewish control, are THE two most monumental fulfillments of

---

[8] Quote by David Lurie in *The Covenant, The Holocaust, and The Seventieth Week*, Messianic Century Press, p108, from The Works of Jonathan Edwards, Vol. 1., The Banner of Truth Trust, p607.

[9] Quote by David Lurie in *The Covenant, The Holocaust, and The Seventieth Week*, Messianic Century Press, p108, from the writings of Iain H. Murray.

prophecy in the Christian Era! Some claim that the Lord is no longer dealing with physical Israel; that the church as spiritual Israel is all the Israel there is. That is not what the church has believed for centuries, and that view interprets away too many verses for comfort. Here are a few of them:

GEN 17:7 speaks of an unconditional everlasting covenant with the seed of Abraham.

LEV 26:44-45 shows that Israel's restoration was not to be conditional.

ISA 11:11 speaks of a second restoration of the Jews.

ISA 26:20-27:1 speaks of a final hiding of the children of Israel followed by Satan's complete judgment.

ISA 27:12-13 in context with the above, and speaks of a final regathering of Israel.

JER 30:4-8 speaks of the time of Jacob's trouble and future restoration.

JER 30:18-24 states that a restoration for the tents of Jacob will take place in the latter days, i.e. not the first restoration of 536BC.

JER 31:35-37 speaks of the permanent nation of Israel.

JER 33:24-26 is a definitive unconditional covenant with Jacob's descendants.

EZE 16:60-63 speaks of an unconditional everlasting covenant with the Jews.

EZE 37:1-28 speaks of an unconditional future restoration of Israel, followed closely by Armageddon in EZE 38-39.

HOS 11:9-10 speaks of a future restoration of Israel from the West.

JOE 3:1-3 predicts the restoration of Judah, followed by Armageddon.

AMO 9:11-15 speaks of an Israel restored to the land.

ZEC 8:7-8 speaks of a post-exilic unconditional restoration of the Jews to Jerusalem and the land.

ZEC 10 and 12 are more prophecies of a future restoration of the Jews.

ZEC 14 speaks of Armageddon, with the Jews in Jerusalem.

LUK 21:24 speaks of a dispersion, the time of the Gentiles, and a restoration following.

ROM 11:11 states that the Jews have not fallen.

ROM 11:17 states that only SOME of the branches were broken off.

ROM 11:17 further states that the church was grafted in AMONG the Jews.

ROM 11:28 states that the gospel age Jews are still elect.

ROM 11:29 states that God's calling of the Jews is irrevocable.

REV 7:4-9 speaks of the 12 tribes of Israel in the Christian Era.

REV 12:1-6 speaks of Israel in the Christian Era.

REV 7:4-9 speaks of the 12 tribes of Israel in the Christian Era.

REV 12:1-6 speaks of Israel in the Christian Era.

REV 15:3 in a passage primarily about the Christian Era, there are two songs, one for the Jews, one for the Gentile Church.

This is by no means all the biblical evidence, but these are verses which readily come to mind. A final restoration of Israel can be found in almost all of the Old Testament prophets. If we are to support a doctrine which holds that the Lord is done with physical Israel, we need positive statements from the Bible which negate, not just one or two, but all of the above Scriptures.

But how important is all this? Does the church have a different role because the Lord has restored the Jews to the Holy land? To find that out, we need to discover what time we are in. Or in biblical terms, when are we?

# Chapter 3

# *When Are We?*

The first few paragraphs in this chapter are doctrinal. They are here because later in our study, we will need these foundational concepts in place. Sometimes we get so bound up in our own little lives, or church, or denomination, that we lose sight of the big (spiritual) picture. God's overall plan. Bible prophecy doesn't focus on Main Street USA in the 90's, but looks at all creation, and the plan of salvation for fallen man from the Lord's eternal perspective. So let's stand in eternity for a minute and look at Earth's 6000 years of recorded history as one broad completed tapestry.

Without going into a lengthy "I" dotting and "T" crossing exegesis, the Lord has revealed three basic biblical epochs to us. Three different time frames. Within each time frame He has spoken to man in a different way:

(1)  4000BC to 1446BC  The years before Moses, called the Pre-flood Era, and the time of the patriarchs.

(2)  1446BC to 32AD  The years between Moses and the Cross, sometimes called the Era of the Law. During this time the Lord worked centrally through the nation of Israel.

(3)  32AD until NOW  The Christian Era, in which the Lord works through the church.

(1)  In the Pre-flood Era, man could be found pleasing to the Lord without knowing the Levitical code, or knowing who his Messiah would be. As far as we know, all they did back then was make an altar and burn a lamb on it. Witness Able, Enoch, and Noah. They had no Scripture and no doctrine that we know of, yet Enoch "walked with God, and God took him," GEN 5:22. He was taken up into heaven way back then, so he was found perfect in God's eyes 3000 years before the Cross. How?

(2) Under Moses and the Levitical code, but still without knowing who the Messiah to come would be, man could be found pleasing to God. Witness Moses himself, and Elijah. We saw them both covered with the glory of the Lord on the mount of transfiguration, MAR 9:2-8. Notice that this took place before the Cross, so they too were found perfect in God's eyes 1400 and 900 years before the Cross. How?

(3) In the Christian Era man can also be found pleasing to God. Witness the verses which declare that we have Christ's righteousness imputed unto us, right now; and that we are seated in the heavenlies with Christ, right now, EPH 2:6. Today, on the basis of the shed blood of the Lord Jesus, we too are found perfect in God's eyes; but we are after the Cross.

Here we have three different "doctrinal systems," two before the Cross, and one after; yet under each system it is equally possible to be found pleasing to God. How? Well, the blood of bulls and goats never saved anyone. The Levitical sacrifices were a only a symbol (for ancient man) of the sacrifice of the Messiah to come, HEB 10:1-10.

The Old Testament saints didn't know it, but they too were saved by the blood of Jesus, 1CO 10:1-4. No one can come to God except through the Cross of Calvary! Even though we see the Cross at a given point in history, God does not. God the Father sees His Son "As a Lamb slain before the foundation of the world," REV 13:8 KJV, 1PE 1:19-20. God has always seen creation through the Cross. If He had not, the moment Adam sinned, the world would have ended in a thunderclap. As an absolutely Holy God, He could not have looked at Adam's original sin, if He had not already seen the blood of His Son.

Once we grasp God's plan for fallen man from this perspective; when a man was born, and what God-ordained doctrinal system he was under, loses some of its importance. These different eras are different revelatory times, not special ages in which the method of salvation was changed! In the Father's eyes, the blood of Jesus transcends time, and has always been the only acceptable price for man's sin.

The Christian Era is just one segment of God's plan of salvation, a plan that has been running now for about 6000 years. We in the Christian Era naturally think that WE, and OUR era, are THE centerpiece of all creation, but in God's eternal eyes, no one, and no time, is of more importance than any other, PSA 145:8-9. The Lord loved those people in ancient Sumer, just as much as He loves you and me. Undoubtedly there were many people then who worshipped the Lord; we just have no record of it.

With that doctrinal background in place, just before Jesus went to the Cross, He told His disciples what they should expect to happen in this final major time frame of God's plan. Known to us as the Olivet Discourse, this talk is Jesus' chapter-long prophecy about the Christian Era. It is recorded in all three of the synoptic Gospels, in MAT 24, MAR 13, and LUK 21. Though they all agree, each Gospel records important information not contained in either of the others:

(1)  MAT 24:31 - Matthew tells us that the elect are gathered at the sound of a great trumpet.

(2)  MAR 13:14 - Mark says that the abomination of desolation is an "it" not a him.

(3)  Luk 21:24 - Luke defines the end of the time of the Gentiles.

Believe it or not , if we would accept as little children what the Lord has told us in those passages, much of our end-time doctrinal confusion would be over. Our contemporary Seven Year tribulation view, and others, would never be heard from again. There is a whole series of verses which will lead us to that conclusion. Let's begin with:

LUK 21:21-24 (excerpts) Then let them which are in Judaea flee... for there shall be great distress in the land, and wrath upon this people. And they (the Jews) shall fall by the edge of the sword, and shall be led away captive into all nations: **and Jerusalem shall be trodden down of the Gentiles, until the times of the Gentiles be fulfilled.**

What is "the time of the Gentiles?" When did it begin, and when will it end? If we look at the Holy Land when the Lord spoke these words, we find that Jerusalem was under the control of the Romans, a Gentile government. The city had already been under various foreign powers for 638 years.

In 70AD Titus destroyed Jerusalem, and in LUK 21:24 Jesus speaks of the dispersion to follow that destruction, and a time of Gentile domination of the city to continue past that. Note the tense of the verb "shall be led away captive." Shall be is future to when Jesus spoke. After Titus destroyed the city, the Jews were led away captive, were dispersed in the nations, and remained dispersed in the nations until this very century!

As a matter of historic record, Gentiles ruled Jerusalem through the 2nd Century, the 3rd, 4th, 5th, 6th, 7th, 8th, 9th, and 10th Century. Even the 11th and 12th Century crusaders were Gentiles. Gentiles continued to rule Jerusalem in the 13th, 14th, 15th, 16th, 17th, 18th, 19th, and on into the 20th Century, right up until 1967AD. Throughout the Christian Era, Gentiles always ruled in Jerusalem. "And Jerusalem shall be trodden down of the Gentiles UNTIL..." As a matter of historic reality, the city of Jerusalem did not again come under Jewish control UNTIL 1967AD! "...UNTIL the time of the Gentiles is fulfilled."

The only people that are not Gentiles are Jews, and Jews now govern Jerusalem for the first time in 2573 years! **Over there is a nation called Israel, filled with people called Jews who fit that Bible prophecy right to the letter!**

Before the 1967 Six Day War, we could argue about what the Lord meant by the time of the Gentiles, but not any more. From our vantage point in history we see the Jews now running Jerusalem. So we can conclude that the Lord was calling the total time of Gentile rule of the Holy City "the time of the Gentiles!" That Gentile rule began in 606BC and ended in 1967AD. Guess what? **The time of the Gentiles is over! Do we grasp the import of that? Gentiles will never again rule in Jerusalem. Their time is over!**

If the time of the Gentiles is over, WHEN are we now? If that epochal time is over, what kind of epochal time are we in? So far we have only seen three different eras, but we must be in some kind of time, because we are still here. The church is still on earth. Searching the Scripture from end to end, the author could only find one other epochal time which could fit after the time of the Gentiles:

DAN 12:4 But thou, O Daniel, shut up the words, and seal the book, **even to the time of the end:** many shall run to and fro, and knowledge shall be increased.

12:9 And he said, Go thy way, Daniel: for **the words are closed up and sealed till the time of the end.**

Since we are no longer in the time of the Gentiles (and we have to be in some kind of time), we are probably in Daniel's "time of the end," or "the end times" as the NASB translates it. *(Chart No.2)*

Now DAN 12:9 quoted above states that, in a sovereign act, God sealed the book of Daniel until the time of the end. That doesn't sound so earth shattering. How important can it be that a relatively obscure Old Testament prophet was sealed until the time of the end?

This important: If the time of the end began in 1967, and Daniel was sealed until 1967, then all views theorized out of Daniel before 1967 are at best incomplete, and at worst heretical!

Earlier we discussed how tradition bound the church has become. Well, here is a case in point. Most of the end time views now held by churches were theorized from studies made in Daniel long before 1967. If our understanding of when the end-times began is correct, then we have every reason to believe those traditional views are incorrect! Bible prophecy fulfilled in recent history eliminates any possibility that some of these positions are right; they can't be! God sealed Daniel until the time of the end.[10]

So, what is going to happen in these end-times? Since Daniel was sealed until the end-times, maybe Daniel has some answers. Surely it would be prudent to look again at Daniel, to see what new insights the Lord may have for us there.

---

[10] Many would use the Joel 2 quote in Acts 2:17-21 to support the view that the "time of the end" began at Pentecost, and continues through the whole church age. That argument cannot be well supported. "These last days," and "the time of the end" are two totally different concepts. "These last days" can indeed be the Christian epoch, but by definition the "Time of the End" is about the end of time. These are two different events. Peter himself stated that "these last days" of the Joel 2 quote were fulfilled at Pentecost, ACT 2:16. Daniel appears to be speaking of the end of creation as we know it.

# Chapter 4

# *What's An Abomination?*

When the author began this study of Bible prophecy eleven years ago, what he was really doing was searching Scripture to support a Seven Year Great Tribulation. Central pillars of that view are DAN 9:27 and DAN 12:11-12. A few other verses are tacked on, but these verses in Daniel are foundational! As he studied, a thought crossed his mind, "Is it possible that these verses could mean something entirely different than what we now believe; and if they do, what?" Out came the books....

In the third year of Cyrus the Persian (533BC), the Lord revealed a "matter of great importance" to His prophet Daniel, DAN 10:1. It was about the future of Daniel's people, the Jews then in captivity. The Babylonian empire had fallen some three years earlier and Daniel was now a very old man, probably in his late eighties. He had been held captive in Babylon for 73 years. The Jews had begun their trek, back from captivity to the Holy Land.

It was then that the Lord gave this dear old saint the final vision of his prophetic ministry, DAN 10:1-12:13. A major part of that prophecy is a detailed account of the Medo-Persian and Greek domination of the Jews in the Holy Land during the next 400 years, but in the final chapter there is a very curious passage which includes this verse:

> DAN 12:11 And from the time that the daily sacrifice shall be taken away, (is abolished, NASB) and **the abomination that maketh desolate set up,** there shall be a thousand two hundred and ninety days.

Curious indeed. What is an "abomination that maketh desolate?" Depends on who you are talking to, but from context, obviously temple sacrifices are involved. In this instance it would have to be something done to God's temple to defile it and make sacrifices impossible. Some abomination in the Lord's eyes which would keep His glory from dwelling there. An idol on the temple grounds, or an unclean sacrifice are examples of what would do that.

The Lord required the Jews to be quite uncompromising about the temple and its contents. In fact, anyone who desecrated it was to be stoned to death! Despite this, in 165BC a Greek king, Antiochus Epiphanies, sacrificed a pig on the altar of burnt offering! That was known then, and throughout the Christian Era, as an "abomination that made desolate." Afterwards the priests had to perform an extensive purification of the altar before they could again sacrifice to the Lord. As you remember from Old Testament history, the Israelites were not authorized to sacrifice anywhere else. So to the Jew, an abomination which makes desolate is anything which keeps the priests from offering sacrifices to the Lord on the temple site. It was true in Daniel's time, it is true now. God has not changed that definition for 2800+ years.

Which abolition of sacrifices is the Lord referring to in this prophecy to Daniel? Now please, let's not try to make a church doctrine from this Scripture. The addressees are clearly defined. This prophecy is in the Old Testament, in Hebrew, to the Jews, and about the Holy Land while Gentile powers would be ruling there. Context refers to "thy people," DAN 12:1. Daniel was a Jew, and the prophecy was given to him; so it is to and about the Jews during the time of the Gentiles.

If there is one thing the Lord is, He is timely. He addressed His prophets within a historic framework they understood. We have no reason to believe that the Lord was telling Daniel of some abolition of sacrifices to take place in the Christian Era. If the Lord had been speaking of the 70AD Roman destruction of the temple or some other event later on, He spoke to the wrong prophet. In that case, would He not have given this prophecy to a prophet after the exile? A prophet like Zechariah, or Malachi, or even to John, the prophet to the Christian Era?

Sacrifices were ended three times in the Old Testament. Before Daniel (under one of the kings of Judah), during Daniel's Babylonian captivity, and after Daniel by Antiochus Epiphanies. Which event is the Lord speaking of here, and what was the date? Well, when and to whom was this prophecy given? To Daniel in 533BC. Result: we have every reason to believe that the Lord was speaking of those sacrifices which were abolished during Daniel's own lifetime. An abolition to which Daniel could relate. Was it at the destruction of the temple? Nebuchadnezzar destroyed the temple in 586BC, but Jeremiah tells us that temple sacrifices continued after the temple was destroyed:

> JER 41:5 ...there came certain from Shechem, from Shiloh, and from Samaria, even fourscore men.... **with offerings and incense in their hand, to bring them to the house of the LORD.**

This journey to the temple from Shechem, Shiloh and Samaria took place during the governorship of Gedeliah. That was ten months AFTER the temple was destroyed. So there still had to be some purified priests in Jerusalem who were carrying on. Two more years pass, then in the very last chapter of Jeremiah we read:

> JER 52:30 **In the three and twentieth year of Nebuchadnezzar,** Nebuzaradan the captain of the guard carried away captive of the Jews seven hundred forty and five persons: all the persons were four thousand and six hundred.

**The year was 583BC. Remember 583BC, you will see it again.**[11]

Nebuchadnezzar ascended the throne of Babylon in 606BC. 23 years later is 583BC. The Babylonians took the nobles, the artisans, and the priests captive. From other scriptures, we know that before JER 52:30 was written, the total number of captives was 10,832. Who then is this 745 people and the new sub-total of 4,600 people? They have to be some unidentified sub-group. Probably the priests and Levites. That would have been a group of special interest to Jeremiah in his position as a prophet. So, this final captivity of 583BC is a scripturally supportable time for the sacrifices to have been abolished. There were apparently no purified priests left in the land who could offer sacrifices. What a devastating

---

[11] With only these Scriptures to go on, we can not positively prove that sacrifices were abolished in 583BC to the year. However we have NT prophecies which pin us to this date. They are fully discussed later.

experience this must have been for God's people in exile. *(Chart No.3)*

Oh, how the Jews repented. From the Babylonian captivity to this day, they have not departed from the Lord their God. As a conquered people in exile, they had 70 years of regret, and they never forgot it. Even today, with an annual feast, the Jews remember their restoration from captivity. Their repentance is best remembered by the unknown psalmist:

> PSA 137:1-4  By the rivers of Babylon, there we sat down, yea, we wept, when we remembered Zion. We hanged our harps upon the willows in the midst thereof. For there they that carried us away captive required of us a song; and they that wasted us required of us mirth, saying, Sing us one of the songs of Zion. How shall we sing the LORD'S song in a strange land?

Though he was hundreds of miles away from Jerusalem, Daniel knew all about these new hostages. Another group of captive Jews brought back to Babylon by the captain of the king's guard could not have escaped Daniel's notice. He was daily in King Nebuchadnezzar's court. How it must have hurt that saintly man to hear of the sacrifices being stopped, and of the Lord's temple in ruins. We can prove that it was abandoned during Daniel's lifetime from DAN 9:17, and EZR 3:2-3. Now that we have the historic background in place, let's look at DAN 12:11 again:

> DAN 12:11  And from the time that the daily sacrifice shall be taken away, (is abolished, NASB) and the abomination that maketh desolate set up, **there shall be a thousand two hundred and ninety days.**

The sacrifices had been abolished for 50 years when God gave this prophecy to Daniel. 1290 literal days are 3 1/2 years. Looking back, he could see that nothing of any special significance had taken place 3 1/2 years after the sacrifices had been abolished. Yet Daniel said "he understood the vision," DAN 10:1.

How could he have understood this vision if nothing had happened 46 1/2 years earlier? He understood because he was a very astute man who could put together when the sacrifices had been abolished with some other Scripture he already knew:

(1) The vision of 70 weeks had been given to Daniel three years earlier DAN 9:24-27. If those 70 sevens had been a literal 483 days, or 1 1/2 years, they should have been fulfilled already; but they were not. So from the 70 sevens Daniel knew that the Lord was not using literal days in prophecy.

(2) Daniel read his Bible, i.e., the Old Testament Scriptures. Daniel knew without question when the 1290 days began. He was a part of the Babylonian court, and was on the scene. But the Torah[12] and Ezekiel told him the 1290 days were not literal days. He knew they began in his lifetime but would not be fulfilled then. He knew that the 1290 days was a prophecy which would be fulfilled in the distant future.

Here's how it all fits together. Captive with Daniel, in the province of Babylon, was a priest named Ezekiel. He was the prophet who was inspired to write the Bible book of Ezekiel. That Daniel read Scripture in his devotions is provable from Dan 9:2. Besides Jeremiah, he no doubt read the Torah, which contains the book of Numbers, and he also must have read Ezekiel. Within those two books were the two little gems which gave him the necessary insight:

> NUM 14:34 After the number of the days in which ye searched the land, even forty days, **each day for a year,** shall ye bear your iniquities, even forty years, and ye shall know my breach of promise.

> EZE 4:5-6 **For I have laid upon thee the years... according to the number of the days,** three hundred and ninety days...so shalt thou bear the iniquity of the house of Israel. And when thou hast accomplished them...and thou shalt bear the iniquity of the house of Judah forty days: **I have appointed thee each day for a year.**

---

[12] The Torah is the Jewish name for the law of Moses. They are the first five books in our Bible: Genesis, Exodus, Leviticus, Numbers, and Deuteronomy. The church calls these same books the Pentateuch.

A day for a year. Here, in the only two places it appears in the Bible, the Lord tells Daniel that in His eyes one day is equal to one year. ONE DAY = ONE YEAR. Ezekiel was a prophet, so one prophetic day would also equal one year.[13] *(Chart No.4)*

With this new day=year unit of measure applied to his prophecy, Daniel could understand. *(Chart No.5)* He remembered when the regular evening and morning sacrifices were abolished in 583BC. He looked from 583BC down 1290 Hebrew years into the future. He saw that an unbelievable abomination was going to trespass on the temple mount. One that would make it desolate. An abomination that would defile it beyond belief, and prevent all future sacrifices. What could that terrible thing be? That Daniel could not know:

**1290 Hebrew years (1271.5 solar years) - 583BC = 688.5 AD**

688.5 AD is exactly 1290 Hebrew years after sacrifices were abolished. From 685AD to 705AD, Abd el Malik built The Dome Of the Rock, a memorial to Mohammed, on the temple mount! Thus, we now have a positive identification:

**The DOME OF THE ROCK Is The Abomination
Which Maketh Desolate![14]**

That is not a coincidence, or suppositional theology. The date of the construction of the Dome of the Rock is a provable historic fact that you can find for yourself in any good encyclo-

---

[13] The Lord has never changed "a day for a year" even in the New Testament. Consequently, neither should we. We are bound by Scripture to interpret days as years unless the Lord changes the definition later in His Word.

[14] Some will argue that sacrifices could have been abolished a year or two earlier, or a couple of years later than 583BC, as suggested by the author. But none argue that they were abolished earlier than the destruction of the temple, 586BC, nor more than ten years later. The Dome of the Rock was under construction for 20 years, from 685AD to 705AD. Leaving the widest latitude for scholarly argument, that 20 year window cannot be circumvented.

pedia or world history. This fits the exact words of DAN 12:11, and fits history to the year. How can the Jews offer sacrifices to the Lord, on His Holy Mountain, while a structure to the false prophet remains there? Today, over in Israel, the Hasidic Jews know they can't. That is why there is such an interest among the conservatives in Jerusalem about tearing it down. It is no secret to them that the Dome of the Rock is an abomination that makes desolate. *(Chart No.6)*

Remember that MAR 13:14 recognized the abomination as an "IT," not a him? Well, the Dome is an "IT," not a him! In the following chapters we will see how the New Testament fully supports this identity of the Dome of the Rock as the abomination of desolation.

**Now don't forget 688AD and the Dome of the Rock.** We're going to run into that date, and that building, again and again.

# Chapter 5

# 42 Months Is 1278.4 Days

From our position in the closing days of the 20th Century, we can just begin to see a little of God's exquisite plan. The Abomination of Desolation is not an antichrist in our future. Instead, it is a building which has been on Mount Moriah for almost 1300 years. Like the Lord said to Habakkuk, if He told us in advance we wouldn't have believed Him. Now that we can see it, we still can hardly believe it.

That the 1290 days of Daniel fits one incident in history is not enough to prove that we should use a day=year interpretation for all prophetic days. Not even when the 1290 days hits an event as remarkable as the construction of the Dome of the Rock on Mount Moriah right to the year. However, earlier in Daniel is the vision of 70 Sevens, DAN 9:24-27. We can show conclusively that 69 of those sevens are day-years which were fulfilled at the Cross.

If that is the yardstick the Lord used in one part of Daniel, where is our scriptural support to change yardsticks in a following passage of the same book? To leave a divinely ordained system which we can prove works, and try to interpret "days" in some other way would be poor theology indeed. In fact, it would go against God's declaration, "I give you a day for a year." So let's be consistent, and at least try for a day=year historic fit for the rest of the prophetic days in the Bible.

Revelation is a prophetic book much like Daniel. It is allegorical, too. It contains accounts of "beasts," and "heads," and "horns," and numbered days. As we discussed in the introduction, the official term for that type of writing is "apocalyptic language." This means it is written in a pictorial and visionary way. Now the Lord did not put Revelation in the Bible to keep it a secret. That would be no "revelation" at all, would it? The Lord titled the book "The Revelation of Jesus Christ," so there must be a way to understand it. How do we begin? Let's do as we suggested in the 1st chapter, and put ourselves in the sandals of the prophet the Lord revealed it to, the apostle John. Then let's do a little time travel, and jump back to the Isle of Patmos in the 1st Century.

In the 100 years following the crucifixion, the Jews were in a state of revolt against their Roman rulers. That wasn't anything new. They had been in rebellion ever since the Roman occupation began in 65 BC. Army after army had been sent to the Holy Land to quell the continual uprisings. Losing all patience, Rome, sending her best general, finally came against Jerusalem itself. In 70 AD, Titus and his legions sacked that city. An estimated 1,500,000 Jews fell to the sword, and the beautiful 2nd Temple was torn down to bedrock. It had taken 45 years to build, but stone by stone the Romans threw it into the valleys of Tyropoeon and Kidron. Finally, not one stone stood upon another, just as Jesus had foretold.

Jesus had warned His disciples of this coming devastation, 38 years earlier. A prophecy that is recorded in three places, MAT 24:2, MAR 13:2, and LUK 21:6. The Christians in the city were aware of Jesus' prophecy, and on the eve of its destruction, they all fled Jerusalem in haste. Early church records assert that no Christians were left in the city, and that not a single Christian life was lost in the massacre.

The demolition of the temple was so complete that even the memory of its exact location was lost. Then, except for that short lived temple of Jupiter, the Lord's temple site remained in rubble for over 600 years.

However, in 685AD to 705AD, the Mohammedan governor of Jerusalem, Abd el Malik, cleared the temple mount to bedrock. He used the local people to do it, including the Christians and Jews still living in the city. They found two solid rock promontories, one they named "as-Sakhra." Over as-Sakhra they built the Mohammedan memorial, the Dome of the Rock. You remember the numbers from the last chapter:

**1290 Hebrew days = 1271.5 Solar years - 583 = 688AD**

Over the other promontory (an unusually flat stone about 300ft North and slightly to the West of as-Sakhra) they constructed a little unimposing cupola they aptly named "The Dome of the Spirits," or "The Dome of the Tablets." Having no science of archeology in those days, guess what:

### They built the Dome of the Rock on the wrong rock![15]

The Mohammedans built their "holy place" on the wrong rock! I don't know how you feel while reading this, brethren, but as I write, it is all I can do not to laugh, and shout, and dance around the room. One almost has to laugh; as-Sakhra has no historic or spiritual significance whatsoever! The Dome of the Rock is in what was once the court of the Gentiles. Even ceremonially unwashed Canaanite slaves were allowed in the court of the gentiles. You didn't have to be a priest, or a Levite, or even a Jew to be there.

The House of the Lord, where only the sons of Aaron could enter, stood over that little flat rock some 300ft North of where the Dome now stands. We know exactly where the temple stood because of holes drilled in the bedrock which are spaced on the sacred cubit.[16] This sacred cubit could only be used in the temple itself, and these holes pinpoint the exact location of the House of the Lord.[17] The "Kodesh Ha-Kodeshim" (the Holy of Holies) was directly over that little flat rock. The ark of the covenant bathed in the Shekinah Glory stood there. "God's dwelling place, and the footstool of His feet, forever." It was exactly on an East to West line with the Golden Gate. The very gate through which Jesus walked on His way to teach

---

[15] How spiritually appropriate their building on the wrong rock has proved to be. There is only one rock on which to build, the rock Christ Jesus. Mohammed is not just a little false prophet, he is probably THE false prophet of REV 19:20! There are over 1,000,000,000 people in that false religion today. Mohammedans now outnumber the Christians 2 to 1. God help us when they gain the military power to be a serious threat.

[16] The Hebrews had two units of measure for the cubit. The ordinary cubit was about 18 inches long, while the sacred cubit was a cubit and a span, or about 21 1/2 inches.

[17] Temple Foundation Located, *Biblical Archeology Review*, Mar. 1983.

in the temple. Now, for the first time ever, we can discern the meaning of a baffling allegorical verse in Ezekiel:

> EZE 42:20 He measured it by the four sides: it had a wall round about, five hundred reeds long, and five hundred broad, **to make a separation between the sanctuary and the profane place.**

This spiritual wall of separation, probably guarded by holy angels, has stood on the temple mount for 1300 years, and we haven't seen it. The Dome of the Rock is 300ft to the South of the temple. That Dome is not now, and never has been over the old temple site! The Dome was, is, and as long as it stands, shall be right in the middle of the court of the Gentiles! *(Chart No.7)*

Isn't it wonderful to know that by permitting the temple's total destruction, the Lord protected His Holy of Holies from the profanity of having a memorial to the false prophet built over it. Of more importance, if the Mohammedans had not built on the wrong rock, it would be impossible for this next quote to be fulfilled. Now look carefully at the language, and see how perfectly it fits the situation on God's Holy Hill:

> REV 11:1-2 And there was given me a reed like unto a rod: and the angel stood, saying, Rise, and measure the temple of God, and the altar, and them that worship therein. But **the court which is without the temple leave out, and measure it not; for it is given unto the Gentiles:** and the holy city shall they tread under foot forty and two month.

"Leave out the court...it has been given to the Gentiles!" The Dome of the Rock is in the court, and it is a Gentile structure. So we have the location. Then we read that Jerusalem shall be under Gentile control for 42 months. Far fetched as it may seem, could this 42 months be turned into days and looked at as years? It was day=years in the Old Testament, and there is no Scripture anywhere that does away with that interpretation. So let's try for a historic fit using day=years.

A Solar year is 365.24 days. Since there are 12 months in a year, dividing by 12 gives us a month of 30.44 days. REV

11:2 speaks of 42 months, so 42 x 30.44 gives us 1278.5 days. If they are years, when do they begin and when do they end? We need the historical setting again.

On the 6th day of June 1967, at the end of the Six Day War, General Moshe Dayan and a tough, hard-bitten contingent of Israeli commandos stood before a wall of ancient stones. Their shoulders were shaking, and tears were streaming down their faces. They were at the Wailing Wall in East Jerusalem, that Holy Place from which they had been exiled so many centuries before. They were crying thanks unto God for restoring their ancient city to them. There they solemnly swore: "Never again will we be driven from this place." For the first time in 2573 years the Jews were in control of their Holy City. Could that touching moment be the historic end of, "and they (the Gentiles) will tread underfoot the Holy City for 42 months?"

### 1967AD - 1278.5 = 688AD, Construction of The Dome of the Rock!

So in the 1290 days of DAN 12, the Lord takes us from 583BC, and the cessation of sacrifices in Daniel's time, to 688AD and the Abomination which maketh Desolate, the Dome of the Rock. Then in the 42 months in Revelation 11, the Lord shows us the accuracy of that interpretation. He takes us from the restoration of Jerusalem in 1967 right back to 688AD, and the Dome of the Rock. We come to 688AD, right to the year, from both directions. As a result, it is apparent that, to the Lord, the central event in the time of the Gentiles is that abomination on His Mountain. *(Chart No.8)*

It is not just the numbers that work. Look at how this fits the very words of Scripture:

(1) "Sacrifices abolished."
(2) "Abomination set up."
(3) "Leave out the court."
(4) "Holy city tread underfoot 42 months."

There is no other interpretation known to the author which even comes close to fitting all these pieces together so well. This many factors coming together can't be just a numerical and verbal fluke, can it? That's pretty unlikely, and there are other fulfillments, using the same yardstick, still to come. When The Lord unlocks a book and opens our eyes, He does so in such a way that it cannot be ignored. He gives us proof upon proof:

> REV 12:1-5 And there appeared a great wonder in heaven; a woman clothed with the sun, and the moon under her feet, and upon her head a crown of twelve stars: And she being with child cried, travailing in birth, and pained to be delivered. And there appeared another wonder in heaven; and behold a great red dragon, having seven heads and ten horns, and seven crowns upon his heads. And his tail drew the third part of the stars of heaven, and did cast them to the earth: and the dragon stood before the woman which was ready to be delivered, for to devour her child as soon as it was born. And she brought forth a man child, who was to rule all nations with a rod of iron: and her child was caught up unto God, and to his throne.

> REV 12:6 **And the woman fled into the wilderness, where she hath a place prepared of God, that they should feed her there a thousand two hundred and threescore days.**

Who is this woman, and the man child? When we see His description, there is only one Person in all eternity who matches that portrait. Who will rule all nations with a rod of iron? Who ascended into heaven and descended? Who now sits at the right hand of the throne of God? None but Jesus Christ the Righteous. That makes the woman Israel, and the 12 stars the 12 tribes. The dragon is Satan, who tried to defeat the Lord at the Cross, and the fallen stars are the fallen angels.[18]

During the Christian Era the Jews were dispersed in the nations. The wilderness is the Gentile World, EZE 20:35. For centuries they have been hounded from country to country, made slaves of, been beaten and robbed and murdered wholesale, as in Nazi Germany, but never again. God has promised

---

[18] REV 1:20 tells us that the stars are the "aggelos" or messengers. That same Greek word is also used in REV 12:4. Aggelos is usually translated angels.

that never again would the Jews suffer anything like that holocaust in which 6,000,000 of the seed of Abraham were murdered:

> JER 30:3-8 For, lo, the days come, saith the LORD, that I will bring again the captivity of my people Israel and Judah, saith the LORD: and I will cause them to return to the land that I gave to their fathers, and they shall possess it.
>
> And these are the words that the LORD spake concerning Israel and concerning Judah. For thus saith the LORD; We have heard a voice of trembling, of fear, and not of peace. **Ask ye now, and see whether a man doth travail with child? wherefore do I see every man with his hands on his loins, as a woman in travail, and all faces are turned into paleness? Alas! for that day is great, so that none is like it: it is even the time of Jacob's trouble, but he shall be saved out of it.**
>
> **For it shall come to pass in that day, saith the LORD of hosts, that I will break his yoke from off thy neck, and will burst thy bonds, and strangers shall no more serve themselves** (make slaves, NASB) **of him:**

A more moving account of the terrors of the gas chambers is hard to imagine. There, in the snow, stood line after line of naked Jewish men. Their hands in front of them to cover their nudity. Shivering bodies, numb with cold, beatings, and starvation. Faces pale. They shuffled slowly into extinction. As your Son hung naked on the Cross so long ago, so now it has happened unto them, Oh God.

That is all in the past now. The time of Jacob's trouble is over. The Lord has broken Satan's yoke from off their neck, and the Jews will never be in bondage again. As of 1948 the Jews are no longer dispersed in the nations. On March 15th of that year, Israeli Prime Minister David Ben-Gurion stood on the floor of the Knesset. He declared the new nation of Israel to be a sovereign state. That is a historic fact which no one can deny. As of 1948AD the woman is no longer in the wilderness, and REV 12:6 should be fulfilled.

From the 6th verse we see that this woman Israel will be in the wilderness 1260 days. Could this be years again? In this instance the Lord gives us prophetic days straight out, no mathematics. Even a 3rd grader can figure this one out:

**1948 - 1260 = 688AD!! Construction of The Dome of the Rock!**

It was exactly 1260 years from the construction of the Dome of the Rock to the establishment of the New nation of Israel. This is "so great a cloud of witnesses," it would take a closed mind indeed to deny that these days are fulfilled as years in the Christian Era. *(Chart No.9)*

How come we couldn't see it sooner? God planned it that way, and even told us so. Remember in Daniel 12:9 when He said that this book was sealed until the time of the end? Until the new nation of Israel and a free Jerusalem became historic realities (which began the time of the end), there was no way to decipher these days. We did not have the end-time pins to show that Revelation affirmed the 1290 days which took us to 688AD, and the Dome of the Rock.

You may realize by now that, in the Seven Year tribulation view, all these days are believed to represent either the first or the last half of the great tribulation. They are considered by many folks to be pillars of that view. Obviously, that is not what they mean at all. But pillars of tradition are like that. The Lord takes them down, if we have an open heart, and ask Him to. We will see other pillars topple shortly.

# Chapter 6

# *Lacunza*

Believe it or not, you have now seen all of the verses used to support the Seven Year tribulation view, except one. All have been fulfilled in the last 40 years by new Israel. The only verse we have not considered, DAN 9:27, will be discussed in the next chapter.

But first, we should see how the Seven Year tribulation view got its start, and then got its almost universal hold on evangelical thinking. You are either going to love this chapter or hate it; but every word is true, and can be proven from existing records kept at Oxford University Library, in Oxford, England.

There was a Spanish family living in Chili named the de Lacunzas. In the year of our Lord, 1731, they had a baby boy. Fifteen years later, the lad was sent to Spain to become a Jesuit priest. Twenty-two years after that, in 1767, the Jesuits were expelled from Spain because of their brutality. The now "Father" Manuel de Lacunza y Diaz had to move. He went to Imola, Italy, where he remained for the rest of his life.

In Imola, he claimed to be a converted Jew. Under the alias of "Rabbi Ben Ezra" he wrote a book. The title: "The Coming of Messiah in Glory and Majesty." In that book he theorized that the church would be "raptured" (taken up to be with the Lord) some 45 days before the real return of Jesus to the Earth. During that 45 days (while the church was in heaven with the Lord) God would judge the wicked still on earth.

This Jesuit cum "Rabbi" theorized the earliest mini-tribulation, pre-trib rapture view on record! He derived this view from a faulty interpretation of the 1290 and the 1335 day=years of DAN 12:11-12. We know his view is faulty because we now understand what those days mean.[19] Manuel de Lacunza died in Imola in 1801, and that should have been the end of that.

---

[19] The 1335 days are explained in a later chapter.

But after his death, de Lacunza's views were taught in Spain. In 1821 his book was published in Spanish. Six years later it was translated into English by the Scottish radical Edward Ervin. It could also have died right there, for most in England thought Ervin to be heretical.

But then, like a cancer, it begins to spread. In that same year, J.N. Darby, founder of the Plymouth Brethren, "came to an understanding of this new truth." Later, in his letters, he admitted that he had been influenced by de Lacunza's teaching. Not satisfied with that Jesuit's rather simplistic 45 day tribulation (not long enough for God's wrath to do a proper job on the unsaved, I suppose), Darby added a new wrinkle: That the 70th week of DAN 9:26-27 was a Seven Year Great Tribulation period which would take place at the end of the Christian Era! Then by various leaps of logic: the temple would be rebuilt, and animal sacrifices would be reinstituted. An antichrist would appear who would rule the world, turn against the Jews, and stop the sacrifices. It goes on and on in a dizzying profusion of unsupported conjectures. All built on a shaky foundation, the dubious validity of the Seven Year Great Tribulation view, itself!

If J.N. Darby had not visited the United States, the Seven Year view could have died right there, too. After all, the Plymouth Brethren weren't a very large denomination. But while in the States, Darby met C. I. Scofield. C.I. was so taken with this new creed, that he included it in the Bible notes upon which he was working. Sound Bible scholars of the day such as A.J. Gordon, W.G. Moorhead, C.R. Eerdman and others refuted these concepts. Three noted members of Scofield's revision committee even resigned because of this view, but their voices were not heard. The view remained, and the Lacunza-Darby ideas were incorporated into the notes in the Scofield Bible.

In the following decades, the Scofield Bible became the most widely read Bible in the English language. That annotated Bible was one of the primary vehicles by which the Seven Year Great Tribulation view was spread throughout the whole English speaking church. By many, Scofield's notes were presumed to be all but inspired. Even today, some folks think that commentator's notes below the line are as valid as the Scripture above it.

It is almost impossible to believe that a major end time doctrine of the Protestant world began in the mind of a Jesuit priest, who claimed to be a Jew, and wrote under an assumed name. But the historic record of the origin of this creed is unassailable. John Bray, who did the research, has even offered a large cash reward to anyone who can find a different or earlier source.[20]

Some have questioned the importance of knowing the origin of this doctrine; but in any court of law, the jury is entitled to know the credibility of the witness. So the church has every right to ask, "Would a priest of an organization known for its brutality, masquerading as a Jewish Rabbi, be a credible witness on spiritual matters?"

Unfortunately, Ironside of Moody Bible Institute thought the view sound. Dallas Theological Seminary and other centers of dispensational thinking also promoted it. Since that time, there have been some weighty rebuttals (read only by theologians), but few clear headed scholars have bothered to scripturally refute the de Lacunza-Darby view in a language the every day saint can understand.[21]

Many a Seminary student has tried to reconcile the plain assertions of Scripture with the great tribulation position, but

---

[20] The whole church is indebted to evangelist John L. Bray who was led of the Lord to dig to the very roots of the pre-tribulation rapture position. His little book, "The Origin of the Pre-Tribulation Rapture Teaching" was one of the author's best sources for this information. It may be purchased from the John Bray Ministry at P.O. Box 90129, Lakeland, FL 33804.

[21] When these doctrines were first taught, the Jews were not home, nor was Jerusalem free, so there was less data available then than there is now. As a result, one must be careful not to speak ill of the brethren who taught this error unwittingly. But an error is an error regardless of who teaches it, and false doctrines will remain if no one is willing to stand against them. Some things can't be whitewashed, and God holds a teacher responsible for what he teaches, JAS 3:1. Among 20th century evangelicals, the pre-trib rapture and the Seven Year Tribulation are the most widely believed myths there are.

Today's Christian schools have perpetuated these counter scriptural dogmas. How? To be considered authorities, professors have spent their lives studying what past men had to say about the Bible. De Lacunza et al is only one glaring example. Despite the unprecedented prophetic fulfillments which have taken place in our lifetime, little original work is now undertaken within the Bible itself. As a result, our end time views do not address today's realities, and do not meet the needs of the church.

to no avail. Eventually the student just accepts it; and after he becomes ordained, goes out to teach it in his church. Not once does he seriously question the quivering foundation upon which he is trying to build: the questionable opinions of the Jesuit "Rabbi" who started it all.

As a result, evangelicals of many denominations have hugged this view to their bosoms in a glow of zealous but misguided fervor. Believing it to be orthodox, this monumental folly has been allowed to remain in the church even until now. The view is so counter to the plain statements of the Bible itself, particularly the last trumpet, that one wonders how it has managed to command so many adherents. Believe it or not, the following uncomplicated little quotes are the death knell to the Seven Year Tribulation and pre-trib rapture theories. They are quoted here to get you thinking about them:

> 1CO 15:51-52 Behold, I shew you a mystery; We shall not all sleep, but we shall all be changed, In a moment, in the twinkling of an eye, **at the last trump: for the trumpet shall sound, and the dead shall be raised incorruptible, and we shall be changed.**

> REV 10:6-7 ...there shall be no more time, But **in the days of the voice of the seventh angel, when he shall begin to sound, the mystery of God should be finished**, as he hath declared to his servants the prophets.

These verses about the "last trumpet" will be fully discussed in a later chapter, but now, back to the story. Different Scriptures were later seen to disagree with de Lacunza's and Darby's original interpretations. End time doctrines had to get more and more complicated to reconcile these problem verses. Dispensationalism became really complex.

In some of the more radical views, there are as many as seven different "raptures." Which one you go up in supposedly depending on how sanctified you are, or which "kingdom" you are in. That is a basic misunderstanding of the plan of salvation. What ever happened to the "simplicity that is in Christ Jesus" to which we are supposed to cling? We do not get to heaven earlier or later on the basis of our works, good or ill. Works accomplish nothing in relation to salvation. We are either totally cleansed by Jesus' blood and are going to heaven, or we are not and going to hell.  If God counts even one sin against us, we are in an eternal world of hurt.  We go to heaven on the strength of the imputed righteousness of Jesus Christ, and in the power of His shed blood only!  To Him be all the glory.

In other end time views, the lunar calendar, or fanciful slide rule interpretations of Noah in the Ark, or astrological star conjunctions have to be taken into consideration.  God help us, the church is exactly where the Lord predicted it would be at the end:

> 2TI 4:3-4  For the time will come when they will not endure sound doctrine; but after their own lusts shall they heap to themselves teachers, having itching ears;  **And they shall turn away their ears from the truth, and shall be turned unto fables.**

Now it has been almost 200 years since de Lacunza's adventure into theoretical theology, and new evidence has come to light.  In 1948 the new nation of Israel was born.  In 1967 Jerusalem was freed from Gentile governmental control for the first time in 2573 years.  The Jews are home as the Lord told us they would be in numberless Old and New Testament scriptures.[22]

We can now show conclusively that all the scriptures used to formulate the de Lacunza-Darby view, including the 70th week of DAN 9:27, have been fulfilled in those almost unbelievable current events.  That is so important that it needs to be said again:

**All Scriptures used to formulate the Seven Year Great Tribulation view have been fulfilled in the new nation of Israel!**

---

[22] In 165BC, when Antiochus Epiphanies offered a pig on the Altar of Burnt Offering, the Jews revolted against Syria. This led to a short period of self rule by the Maccabees. However, the monarchy was not restored, and the Holy Land was never totally free of Greek control. War continued with Syria until the Romans conquered the Holy Land in 65BC.

# Chapter 7

# *The Seventy Weeks*

So far, we have stood with Daniel in the third year of Cyrus, with John at the beginning of the Christian Era, and with the de Lacunzas in Chile. Now, let's go back to Daniel, but to a time three years earlier, to the fall of the Babylonian Empire in 536BC, DAN 9:1-27.

It had been some night. Earlier, Daniel had interpreted the handwriting on the wall, and Belshazzar promoted him to third ruler of the empire. The walls of Babylon were impregnable, and the Babylonians were so confident in them that they never even considered the possibility of invasion. They were feasting and drinking, and having an enormous jamboree. But Darius the Mede diverted the Euphrates River and sent his army into the city on the dry river bed. The Babylonians weren't even watching. It was an easy victory, and King Belshazzar was slain.

In this new Medo-Persian Empire, Daniel was again just an ordinary citizen. What would happen to his people under this new government? Darius promoting him to the post of chief satrap of the province, and his being thrown into the lion's den were still in the future.

Daniel went home to read the Scripture, and pray. He has now been a captive in Babylon for 70 years. From Jeremiah 25:11-12 and 29:10, and the fall of Babylonian Empire itself, he knew that the 70 years of captivity should be over. That prayer of his wasn't some little "Thank you for our food, in Jesus name...Amen," kind of prayer. He fasted, and sat in sackcloth and ashes, probably for days, DAN 9:3. Before he went before the Lord he may have thought a long time about what he was going to say, and then written down his prayer; for surely, this is one of the most eloquent and touching prayers in all Scripture. Here is part of what Daniel prays:

> DAN 9:16-19 ...O Lord, according to all thy righteousness, I beseech thee, let thine anger and thy fury be turned away from thy city Jerusalem, thy holy mountain: because for our sins, and for the iniquities of our fathers, Jerusalem and thy people are become a reproach to all that are about us. Now therefore, O our God, hear the prayer of thy servant, and his supplications, and cause thy face to shine upon thy sanctuary that is desolate, for the Lord's sake. O my God, incline thine ear, and hear; open thine eyes, and behold our desolations, and the city which is called by thy name: for we do not present our supplications before thee for our righteousnesses, but for thy great mercies. O Lord, hear; O Lord, forgive; O Lord, hearken and do; defer not, for thine own sake, O my God: for thy city and thy people are called by thy name.

Daniel confesses his sins, and the sins of his people. This wonderful man of God knew that he, and the rest of the Jews, deserved nothing from the Lord. But because of God's great mercy, and because of His prophecies through Jeremiah: weren't the 70 years of captivity over yet? While Daniel was praying, the Lord sent the angel Gabriel to comfort him, and because the 70 years of captivity were indeed over, to tell him of a new and different 70, of a seventy of sevens:

> DAN 9:24 Seventy weeks are determined upon thy people and upon thy holy city, to finish the transgression, and to make an end of sins, and to make reconciliation for iniquity, and to bring in everlasting righteousness, and to seal up the vision and prophecy, and to anoint the most Holy.

> DAN 9:25 Know therefore and understand, that from the going forth of the commandment to restore and to build Jerusalem unto the Messiah the Prince shall be seven weeks, and threescore and two weeks: the street shall be built again, and the wall, even in troublous times.

> DAN 9:26 And after threescore and two weeks shall Messiah be cut off, but not for himself...

There are a lot of things to consider in understanding this prophecy. Who is it to and about? It is to the Jews, and about Jerusalem. What does v24 tell us will be accomplished in these 70 sevens.

1. "Finish transgression."
2. "Make an end of sin."
3. "Make reconciliation for iniquity."
4. "Bring in everlasting righteousness."
5. "Seal up vision and prophecy."
6. "To anoint the Most Holy."

When will it take place, and what is the time frame? We are told to start counting time after a decree is sent out to restore Jerusalem, and that it will be a time of trouble. The time frame is 7 weeks and 62 weeks. Now that is peculiar, why not simply say 69 weeks? Next, Messiah will be killed at the far end of the 69 weeks, but not for his own sake. To help us interpret this prophecy, there are some things we already know right up front.

First: There were four decrees granted by the Medo-Persian Empire. But almost 100 years after Gabriel spoke to Daniel, a special decree was granted to Nehemiah by Artaxerxes III. This was the only decree recorded in Scripture which gave the Jews permission to restore Jerusalem, and rebuild its walls.[23] Just as Daniel predicted, Nehemiah had lots of trouble doing so. The people then living around Jerusalem tried to stop him every way they could. Just like the ungodly who surround Christians today, they even tried to get the government down on him, NEH 4:1-23.

Second: the Messiah is Jesus, and He was crucified in 32 or 33AD. He did not die for Himself, but for the sins of the

---

[23] Records show four decrees issued to the Jews by Medo-Persian kings. Which is the correct one to use? Since Scripture relates to Scripture, it is theologically sound to count from the decree which the Lord considered the most important. The whole book of Nehemiah is about the events which followed the Artaxerxes III decree. Furthermore, the events recorded in Nehemiah perfectly match Daniel's prophecy of them. The dating of the Nehemiahan decree is firm at 444-445BC.

world, 2JO 2:2. We already know about the day=years. If these 69 are sevens of years, we have 69 x 7 = 483 years.

Third: The Lord always spoke to His prophets in a language they could understand. Daniel was a Jew, probably of the royal family, 2KI 20:18, and the Jews had their own 360 day Levitical year. Since our history is recorded in solar years of 365.24 days, we need to convert 483 Hebrew years to solar years: 483 x .9857 = 476 solar years.

### 476 - 444BC, Artaxerxes Decree = 32AD and the Cross!

The Cross, right to the year. *(Chart No.10)* But what about those six points which were supposed to be fulfilled during these weeks. Aha, every one of them was fulfilled on the Cross. Did not Jesus finish transgression eternally, make an end of sin, make reconciliation for iniquity, bring in everlasting righteousness, and anoint the Most Holy with His own precious blood?

Of course, praise the Lord; but point 5 was left out: "Seal up vision and prophecy." True, and this is where that peculiar 7 weeks and 62 weeks comes in.

### 7 x 7 Hebrew = 48.3 Solar Years - 444BC = 396BC, Book of Malachi written.

Malachi was inspired to write the last book of the Old Testament in about 396BC. The Scripture to the Jews was complete, and no more was written until after the Cross! Vision and prophecy were sealed up. As one dear old Rabbi lamented about a hundred years after Old Testament canon was closed, "The Holy Spirit has departed from Israel." Look at *Chart No.10* again, and you will see how this all fits together.

### SHAVUIM

So far, every prophecy in Daniel has either related to the Jews, or the Messiah, or Jerusalem in the time of the Gentiles. If the Lord is consistent, DAN 9:26-27 should also relate to the Jews and Jerusalem, particularly when the Scripture says so:

DAN 9:24 Seventy weeks are determined upon **thy people and upon thy holy city**...

DAN 9:26-27 (NIV) ...and its end will come with a flood; even to the end there will be war; desolations are determined. But he will confirm a covenant with many for one seven, but in the middle of the seven, he will put an end to sacrifice and offering, **and one who causes desolations will place abominations on a wing of the temple**...

But without any Scriptural or historic support whatever, Darby theorized that DAN 9:27 was a Seven Year Tribulation at the end of the Christian Era. He added an imaginary 2000 year gap between the 69th and 70th weeks to make it fit his theory. DAN 9:26-27 is the very foundation of the Seven Year Tribulation view. Revelation shows no seven year period at the end of time. In fact, there is no other verse in Scripture which even suggests a seven year period at the end of the Christian Era; and once we understand DAN 9:27, neither does this one. Previously, we interpreted the "days" in Daniel and Revelation as time divisions in the Seven Year Tribulation; but now we know that the day=years are fulfilled in 1948 and 1967AD. Does the same hold true for the 70th Week? Can it also relate to New Israel and a freed Jerusalem?

To find out, let's go back to basics. Who is this prophecy to, and what is the geographic location? This prophecy is in the Old Testament, in Hebrew, and v24 plainly states it is to the Jews, and about Jerusalem! John is the prophet to the church in the Christian Era; but Daniel is to the Jews, and the prophet of the time of the Gentiles. Since this prophecy is in Daniel (and the time of the Gentiles is over, LUK 21:24), it is reasonable to conclude that the 70th Week is also over!

To prove it, we'll need to know exactly what that verse says in the original. A little word study in Hebrew, and a look at a couple of different translations might help. Baker's Interlinear Bible, makes no concessions to conform to English grammar, so let's begin with Baker's bare bones, absolutely literal translation; then let's look at the NIV translation:

DAN 9:26-27 (BAKER) And it's end with the flood, and until end war are determined desolations. And he shall confirm a covenant with the many week one. And in the half of the week he shall make cease sacrifice and offering **and upon a wing abominations a desolator** even until end. And that which was decreed shall pour out on the desolator.

DAN 9:26-27 (NIV) ...And its end will come with a flood; even to the end there will be war; desolations are determined. But He will confirm a covenant with many for one seven, but in the middle of that seven, he will put an end to sacrifice and offering, **and one who causes desolations will place abominations on a wing of the temple**, until the end that is decreed is poured out on him.

If your Bible is a king James, you will read, "for the overspreading of abominations he will make it desolate;" or if in the NASB, "on the wing of abominations one will come who makes desolate." Now what in the world is a "wing of" or "overspreading of" abominations? Doesn't make sense, does it?

Abominations, and desolations are two very important words in both translations above. We have already positively identified the Dome of the Rock as the Abomination which maketh Desolate, DAN 12:11. The NIV translates this passage to say: abomination will be "on a wing ot the temple." From Baker's Interlinear, we see that the NIV translation is quite plausible. We can relate to an abomination that makes desolate on a wing of the temple. That's where the Dome of the Rock is, on a wing of the temple![24] It is in the court of the Gentiles! The dome is not over the old temple site itself, but 300ft South of it:

**So the Dome of the Rock is what the 70th week is all about.**

Now that abomination was placed on a wing of the temple in the middle of the week. So the 70th week stretches back in

---

[24] If, as many archaeologists believe, the straight joint on the East wall marks the South East corner of the Solomonic wall, then the Dome of the Rock is indeed on the South "wing" of the temple. If the Dome had been placed much further South, it would have missed the Solomonic temple platform.

time, and forward in time. The question is, for how long? When did this week begin; and when does it end?

Here is how it works. Hebrew students suggest that "Shavuim," is an unusual plural form of "shavuot," or seven. Daniel is the only book in the whole Bible in which "Shavuim" is used. It can mean a week of days, or **weeks of years**, or any multiple of sevens.[25] Exodus and Leviticus state that the Lord gave the Israelites two different kinds of weeks. A week of days, and a week of years, EXE 32:21 and LEV 25:3-4. Weeks of days, **and weeks of years**, were equally familiar to Daniel. The 69 sevens in Daniel 9:24-25 we now recognize as days, which EZE 4:6 lead us to interpret as years. But, the 70th Week may be different. **It could be a week of years!**

In Leviticus 25:4-11 there is an unusual series of weeks. One week of years, added to six more weeks of years, followed by one individual year, the unique year of the Jubilee. A total of fifty years:

> LEV 25:4-11 (excerpts) But in the seventh year shall be a sabbath of rest unto the land, a sabbath for the LORD: thou shalt neither sow thy field, nor prune thy vineyard...And thou shalt number seven sabbaths of years unto thee, seven times seven years; and the space of the seven sabbaths of years shall be unto thee forty and nine years...And ye shall hallow the fiftieth year...it shall be a jubilee unto you...ye shall not sow, neither reap that which groweth of itself in it, nor gather the grapes in it of thy vine undressed.

The year of the Jubilee was the last year of a 50 year series, and very special. In Jubilee, all debts were paid, and no one could work nor harvest his fields. In essence, Jubilee was 360 days of Sabbaths, all compressed into one year.

Daniel was given a new series of 70 Sevens. 7 sevens, 62 sevens, and one seven at the end. Same principle, different numbers. Daniel would have known that last seven was also special. The question is, special in what way?

Since the year of the Jubilee is unique with 360 Sabbaths, is this final 70th Week a seven of Jubilees (a week of years),

---

[25] David Lurie, *The Covenant, The Holocaust, & The Seventieth Week*, Messianic Century, pp83-86.

each with 360 days?  The language in both Leviticus and Daniel suggests that possibility, and Daniel would have understood the week of years concept.  If it is, by using the same day=year procedure we have everywhere else, 360 x 7, that final week would represent 2520 Hebrew, or 2484 solar years.  Running that up and down the fabric of history, look at what it fits:

**2484 - 536BC = 1948AD  The End of Babylonian Captivity to New nation of Israel!**

536BC is the exact year that Daniel had the vision of the 70 Weeks, and New Israel was exactly 2484 Hebrew years into the future!  So it appears that God is showing Daniel how long the time of the Gentiles still had to run.  This is either the correct interpretation, or one has to admit it is an incredible coincidence.  Coincidences happen, but the day=year method of interpretation gives us too many historic fulfillments to disregard.

In the 70 Weeks, the Lord shows that He is sending His Son to die on the Cross.  He also shows us the total time Gentiles still had to rule in the Holy land.  He saw that in the middle of their rule an absolute horror would stand on His hill, but South of His temple.  In due season God wanted us to know that He is sovereign, and knew all along what would happen, but He wanted it hidden during the Christian Era, so He hid it in a week, in Daniel's Hebrew calendar.

Isn't God's preservation of His Word amazing, the tiny little details which He has hidden away in it.  If only a word or two had been altered over the centuries, we could have never found what the Lord has now uncovered for us.  But what about the Middle of the week, and sacrifices ended:

**2484 divided by 2 = 1242 - 536BC = 706AD.**

Construction of the Dome and the Mosque of Omar began in 685AD, and ended in 705AD.  From that time, until this very day, neither Jews nor Christians could worship on that temple mount. *(Chart No.11)*

It shouldn't disappoint anyone that this calculation of the middle of the week doesn't hit 688AD to the year.  We're not dealing with day=years here. What words did the Lord use? A rather inexplicit "in the middle of the week." 688AD is in the middle of the week, but so is 706AD! Here is a little illustration of that point. Someone makes an appointment for the middle of the week. If he meets you on Wednesday, that's the middle of the week. He could see you anytime Wednesday and still be on time. 706AD is like a few minutes past noon on Wednesday. God didn't say exactly high noon Wednesday, only "in the middle of the week." It is futile to seek for a more precise solution than is called for by the language the Lord used.[26]

But who is this "he?" Satan himself, or one of his minions. Daniel goes to great lengths to show that we are in a spiritual battle; that satanic princes are behind the human rulers of this world. One angel tells Daniel:

> DAN 10:20 Then said he, Knowest thou wherefore I come unto thee? and now will I return to fight with the prince of Persia: and when I am gone forth, lo, the prince of Grecia shall come.

The princes this angel is facing are no ordinary mortals. They are princes of darkness, fallen angels. These same dark princes of Medo-Persia, Greece, and other countries, are mentioned in DAN 7:25, DAN 8:24, REV 9:14-15 and REV 16:13. Later in the book, we will see these grim enemies again.

---

[26] If we use the solar calendar in this calculation, we arrive at the dates of 589BC, 688AD, and 1967AD. This hits the Dome of the Rock and free Jerusalem right to the year, and some authorities believe that the temple was destroyed as early as 589BC. Indeed, that is when the siege of Jerusalem began; and most Jewish authorities believe the captivity began at the destruction of the temple. However, Daniel was taken captive in 606-605BC, and the author believes that the Lord would use the events the prophet was involved in. Consequently, the author does not believe this to be the correct explanation.

# Chapter 8

# *Will The Real Antichrist Please Stand Up!*

Out of the Seven Year tribulation position came a lot of other doctrines. Some contrived whole cloth, and some as add-ons from prior beliefs. Among those ideas is the doctrine of an end-time antichrist who is supposed to do a lot of evil things at the end of the Christian Era. We are looking for a mythical end-time ruler who has been the subject of fanciful conjecture for centuries.

Mythical? Impossible. Everyone "knows" that antichrist is coming, don't we? No, we don't know! Most of what we hear about him is one theologian's theory built upon another's supposition. This goes all the way back to the 1st Century. Who and where is he? Is this how we'll know the second coming of Jesus is near, when some monster of evil in human form is revealed? What does Scripture state, and what is mere speculation? To find out, let's think about all we have heard. All the things antichrist is supposed to be and do; those things that we supposedly know about the antichrist. Among other assumptions, antichrist is supposed to:

1. Appear at the end of the age.
2. Rule the world for:
   3 1/2 years as a good leader.
   3 1/2 years as an evil leader.
3. Have the temple rebuilt.
4. Reinstitute temple sacrifices (first 3 1/2 years)
5. Turn against the Jews (second 3 1/2 years).
6. Stop temple sacrifices (middle of the 7 years)
7. Cause all to worship him.
8. Start the battle of Armageddon.
9. Persecute the "Seven Year Great Tribulation" saints (and anyone else he can get his hands on).
10. Misc. other legends (depending on school of thought) including that as 666, he is Satan incarnate.

If you can believe it, not one of those ideas can be directly supported from Scripture. Not a single one! Some are total fabrications. Most of them came from interpreting the 70th Week as a Seven Year tribulation. Antichrist does appear in the Bible; so really, who and when is he? Let's look at every verse in the Bible which mentions antichrist by name. Don't worry, it is a very short list. If you think there are others, get your concordance out and find them. Though he has searched the Scripture diligently, the author has not been able to find another single verse!

> 1JO 2:18, NASB   Children, it is the last hour; and just as **you have heard that antichrist is coming,** even now many antichrists have arisen; from this we know that it is the last time.

> 1JO 2:22, NASB   Who is a liar but the one that denies that Jesus is the Christ? **This is the antichrist, the one who denies the Father and the Son.**

> 1JO 4:3, NASB   And every spirit that does not confess Jesus is not from God; and **this is the spirit of the antichrist, of which you have heard that it is coming; and now it is already in the world.**

2JO 1:7, NASB  For many deceivers have gone out into the
world, those who do not acknowledge that Jesus Christ is
come in the flesh. **This is the deceiver and the antichrist.**[27]

Hard as it may be to believe, that's all of them. There are
only four verses in the whole Bible which mention the antichrist by name. That doesn't fit what we have heard about
THE antichrist at all, does it? Sorry, that is still all the direct
references there are. Everything else we have heard is
interpretive guesswork. Read those verses again. Do they say
that a special personage, "the antichrist," is going to appear?
If they do, the author fails to find it.

Who do the above four verses in 1st and 2nd John tell us
the antichrist is? They tell us that the antichrist is anyone
who denies that Jesus Christ has come in the flesh, and is the
Christ. 1JO 2:18 and 4:3 state, "you have heard; you have
heard." The Holy Spirit through the apostle John does not
state that a specific antichrist is coming. He only said that
you "have heard" that one is coming.

To put that in today's language, you have heard that the
moon is made of green cheese. That does not make it so, nor
does saying that you have heard it mean that you believe it.
You are not declaring, "the moon is made of green cheese," as
a fact. Only that you have heard people say that it is.

Neither is the Lord declaring in 1st and 2nd John that
"the antichrist" is coming sometime in the future. Instead, it
appears that He is using the same figure of speech to deny it:
to straighten out a false 1st Century church belief. The Holy
Spirit seems to be saying, Look here church, you are sitting
there with a false doctrine. You have heard that antichrist is
coming. I am telling you that he that denies that Jesus is the
Christ, or that denies that Jesus Christ has come in the flesh
is "the antichrist," and he is already in the world!

Brethren, since that is what the Bible says, we can believe
it as an article of faith. Everyone who denies the basic truths

---

[27] The NASB translation appears to be a little clearer in these verses
than the KJV. The definite article is translated. All of those who deny
Jesus are identified not just as "an" antichrist, but as "THE" antichrist.

about the Lord Jesus is "the antichrist," and the Christian Era has been full of them.

But for centuries, one pseudo-prophet after another (using the numerology of the Greek or Roman calendar), has "decoded" the 666 of Rev. 13:14 and announced which special conqueror, potentate, pope, or guru was the one and only genuine antichrist:

> REV 13:18 Here is wisdom. Let him that hath understanding count the number of the beast: for it is the number of a man; and his number is **Six hundred threescore and six.**

On the basis of slide rule dexterity applied to that verse, and that verse alone: Nero, Domitian, Charlemagne, Constantine, Napoleon, Kaiser Wilhelm, Adolf Hitler, Anwar Sadat, Kennedy, Nixon, Reagan, various popes; and oh yes, let's not forget Khadaffy, and (would you believe) Henry Kissinger, have all been positively, and I mean POSITIVELY, identified as THE antichrist! Because of the scar on his head, now it is Gorbachev. Next it will be Bush, the psychopathic Abu Nidal, Ali Akbar Mohtashemi, or Saddam Hussein. Throughout the centuries, Christians not grounded in the Bible have followed the false prophets, disguised as mathematical wizards, who have made these predictions. Thousands have donned their white robes and, with hands upraised, have stood on some mountain peak or other, knowing the end was near. God help us, we are really slow learners. Instead of seeing the error of our way, we wait around for some new soothsayer to pin a new tail on a different donkey.[28]

We have forgotten where the Christian's battle is. It is spiritual. One more time: our battle is spiritual! Satan's generals are not stomping around in shiny boots at the head of some army. Nor do they wander about in staff cars, or direct battles from front line bunkers. The real war is for men's

---

[28] Not understanding the intent of prophecy, some attempt to predict to the day when Jesus shall return. They lead many astray. Many families have sold businesses and homes, and their faith has been disturbed. When the predicted day passes, the unsaved can't help but mock with, "Where is the day of His coming," 2PE 3:4. Thus, the way of truth is held opened to ridicule.

minds and hearts, not for some fancy bit of real estate. Satan is a spirit, and he is fighting for the souls of men, REV 18:8-13.

His real generals and high priests are in our high schools and on our college campuses, even on so-called Christian ones. Since we are not tuned in to the kind of battle we are supposed to be fighting, we don't even know who Satan's real generals are: Kant, Spinose, Freud, Jung, Spengler, Hume, Voltaire, Sagan, Moon, Hari Krishna, and the New Age. It is a long roll call. Included are the names of everyone who teaches a doctrine which rejects Jesus as the Savior of the world, 1JO 2:2. Sad to say, they are temporarily winning the war.

If there are so many antichrists, why does the Bible say "the antichrist?" Because, our God sees each person as an individual. His Son died for each of us, individually. He sees the terrible rebellion of each fallen man's heart. Every single person who turns from His Son is "the" person who rejected Jesus. That is hard for humans to understand, but it is God's way of looking at things.

Now one of the major passages in Scripture interpreted to mean the antichrist, is "the man of sin" of 2TH 2. Let's look at that next.

# Chapter 9

# *The Man Of Sin*

In his second letter to the Thessalonian church, Paul addresses several doctrinal issues of importance to the believers of that city. From context, it appears that they too were just sitting around on the top of some mountain, waiting for Jesus to appear at any moment. Paul affirmed their doctrinal view of the imminent return[29] of the Lord (doing away with the pre-millennial view in the process[30]), but he also warns the saints that a few things had to take place before the second coming.

For openers, have we not all heard that before Jesus returns there will be a great revival? That is exactly the opposite of what the Bible teaches! In 2TH 2:3 quoted below, we find that a great falling away precedes the Lord's return. This may not be the only doctrine we have that is opposed to Scripture. The following verses were usually thought to be about the antichrist. Now that we can't biblically support a future antichrist any more, maybe we better look at the verses about the man of sin again, to see if we can find out what they really mean:

---

[29] The "imminent return" is a term used in theological circles which means that Jesus could return at any moment. The Lord so wrote His Word that every generation believed that Jesus could return for the church in their lifetime. This view has been misused by some to predict the Lord's return to a given moment. This has lead pastors to fear new evidence which pins world history to Bible prophecy. Wanting to remain orthodox, pastors cling to counter-scriptural positions brought into question by this new evidence.

[30] The pre-millenialists believe that Jesus comes for the saints at one time, and 1000 years later the wicked are judged at the great White Throne. 2TH 1:9-10 shows that Jesus comes for the saints and judges the wicked on the same day!

2TH 2:2  Now we beseech you, brethren, by the coming of our Lord Jesus Christ, and by our gathering together unto him,

3  Let no man deceive you by any means: **for that day shall not come, except there come a falling away first,** and that man of sin be revealed, the son of perdition;

4  Who opposeth and exalteth himself above all that is called God, or that is worshipped; **so that he as God sitteth in the temple of God, shewing himself that he is God.**

5  Remember ye not, that, when I was yet with you, I told you these things?

6  And now ye know what withholdeth that he might be revealed in his time.

7  For the mystery of iniquity doth already work: only he who now letteth will let (restrains will restrain, NASB & NIV), until he be taken out of the way.

8  And then shall that Wicked be revealed, whom the Lord shall consume with the spirit of his mouth, and shall destroy with the brightness of his coming:

9  **Even him, whose coming is after the working of Satan with all power and signs and lying wonders,**

10  **And with all deceivableness of unrighteousness in them that perish; because they received not the love of the truth, that they might be saved.**

11  **And for this cause God shall send them strong delusion, that they should believe a lie:**

12  That they all might be damned who believed not the truth, but had pleasure in unrighteousness.

What temple do you suppose the Lord is speaking of in v.4?  In the Old Testament, God's temple was in Jerusalem. But this epistle to the Thessalonians is in the New Testament, and where is the temple of God in the New Testament? "Our bodies are the temple of the Holy Spirit." Think that through. Because of the location of 2TH in the Bible, it is sound theology to conclude that the temple spoken of here is the human heart.  Matter of fact, it is poor theology to conclude otherwise. The same Paul who wrote 2TH wrote the following:

1CO 3:16  Know ye not that **ye are the temple of God,** and that the Spirit of God dwelleth in you?

2CO 6:16 And what agreement hath the temple of God with idols? **for ye are the temple of the living God;** as God hath said, I will dwell in them, and walk in them; and I will be their God, and they shall be my people.

EPH 2:22 In whom all the building fitly framed together **groweth unto an holy temple in the Lord: In whom ye also are builded together for an habitation of God** through the Spirit.

A physical temple in Jerusalem may be applicable for the unenlightened Jew, but it is heresy for the church to think of its temple as a building on Mount Moriah, and Paul was no heretic. Furthermore, 1TH 2:16 implies that the books to this church were written after the Temple was destroyed in 70AD, and Paul makes no mention of building a new one. If Paul in 2TH is speaking of a physical temple in Jerusalem, he departed from the Holy Spirit's revelation to him of where God's temple is now located. That is most unlikely.

Remember in 1st and 2nd John how the Lord used the singular term, the antichrist, to refer to all who did not confess Jesus? If singular referred to all in 1JO, why not use the same guideline to refer to all in 2TH? If we do, and all who reject Jesus are "the antichrist," then all who are totally lawless are "the man of sin." When we look at the whole 2TH 2 passage in this light, a different interpretation fits perfectly:

v.3: **"the apostasy must come first."** It is almost impossible to believe how different the church is today from what it was only 40 years ago. In that short a time, there has been world wide a falling away from the Lord unprecedented in all church history. Europe was the cradle of the reformation, yet less than 3% of today's Europeans still cling to the faith. For instance, in most church congregations in Holland, not one single born again believer remains. Many churches are even being turned over to the Mohammedans[31] In our own land, it is estimated that at best, the true followers of the Lord do not exceed 10% of the total population, some conservative

---

[31] Franz Zegers of Den Helder, Holland, in a July 1990 letter to the author.

groups claim that no more than 5% of Americans are true Christians.

Some of our "Evangelicals" deny the whole purpose of the Cross. They preach that it is "negative" to inform the sinner of his lost condition. Forgetting the balance of Scripture, they only want to preach a positive gospel, which is no gospel at all. "For all have sinned and come short of the glory of God," and "the wages of sin is death." The word Gospel means good news, and the good news is that Jesus died to save us from our sins. The blood of Jesus is the very essence of the gospel. Promised persecution is forgotten, and we have adopted a materialistic, "Claim a Cadillac" theology.[32]

Despite a population explosion in the third world, there are fewer missionaries in foreign lands than there were just a generation ago. Thousands of retiring missionaries are returning home with only a handful being sent out to replace them. Access to foreign fields is becoming more restricted by local leaders. Whole continents are turning away from the Lord.

In many New Testament churches here at home, the Bible is treated with a carelessness that would have horrified our forefathers. Scripture is ignored or culturally interpreted to fit the lifestyle of the congregation. TV ministries, many of them openly heretical, have corrupted the Word of God with false doctrine, but they are still looked up to by all as trustworthy servants of the Lord.

> 1TI 4:1-2  Now the Spirit speaketh expressly, that in the latter times some shall depart from the faith, giving heed to seducing spirits, and doctrines of devils; Speaking lies in hypocrisy; having their conscience seared with a hot iron...

---

[32] Here are two of many verses which invalidate today's prosperity doctrines:

JOH 16:2,33 " ...the time cometh, that whosoever killeth you will think that he doeth God service...In the world ye shall have tribulation: but be of good cheer; I have overcome the world."

2TI 3:12 "Yea, and all that will live godly in Christ Jesus shall suffer persecution."

As was true in the dark ages, the established churches have again taken the Bible away from the people, but this time the theft is more subtle. The individual believer has been strongly advised that he isn't qualified to understand the Word without extensive formal training (translate that as boning up on our traditions and commentaries, and lots of secular studies). This puts to nought the Scripture which states: "the Holy Spirit will lead you into all truth," JOH 16:13. Then the every day Christian is programmed to accept denominational dogma, regardless of whether or not that dogma is compatible with Scripture.

As a result, modernistic seminaries now have a death grip on the local evangelical churches. Churches can not last long if their leaders do not believe in the very Bible they have been commissioned to defend. Our crucified Jesus is the life of the church. If His life is not in it, all we have is a pile of bricks. Current events are showing this to be true. Major denominations are on the verge of collapse.

Some churches are growing. In the fastest growing denominations, witchcraft disguised as Pentecostalism is trapping the unwary.[33] Few are in enough obedience to the Scripture to recognize the demonic origin of these doctrines. As a sad addendum: It is estimated that up to 60% of unmarried Christian teenagers are sexually active. Along with the great apostasy, from the above we can see that the man of lawlessness is right in the church today: No waiting! Please come quickly Lord Jesus, or just as you asked, will the faith be on the earth when You return, LUK 18:18?

v.3 **"...the man of lawlessness is revealed, the son of destruction,"** Since the second world war, out in the world, there are an ever increasing number of atheists, agnostics, and other cultists who are in the lawless state of total defiance against God. 1JO 3:4 tells us that sin is lawlessness. The rebellious unredeemed, still in their sins, are men of lawlessness, and doomed to destruction. At no other time in The Christian Era has there been such an open disregard for God's revealed Truth.

---

[33] E. Skolfield, *Sunset of the Western Church*, Fish House, 1987.

v.4 **"...who opposes and exalts himself above every so-called god or object of worship,"** I hate to even write this, but secular humanists say that man is a god, their manifesto declaring: "Man made God in His own image." By these declarations they exalt themselves above every god. They replace God in their hearts with scientific formula, trading a knowledge of the giver of life for a limited understanding of what He has made.

v.4 (cont.) **"...so that he takes his seat in the temple of God, displaying himself as being God."** In some of the charismatic churches, demons are invading humans, giving false gifts and claiming to be the Holy Spirit speaking.[34] Guru or pentecostal, the doctrine is the same, only the wrappings have been changed to trap the unwary. Leaders of numberless cults declare, "Look to the god within yourself," or, "Get in touch with your inner self." How about "Channel with a master." This is supposed to be your inner god-like voice communicating with an ascended spirit (translate that, demon!). All these suggest that the power of a god is within man himself. This places man's ego in the temple of the Holy Ghost, claiming an authority there, which by sovereign right, is God's alone.

v.7 **"...only He who now restrains will do so until He is taken out of the way."** Throughout the whole Christian Era, the Holy Spirit has quickened the heart of man to his need for a personal relationship with God. However, in GEN 6:3 the Lord tells us that some time in the future He would restrain His Spirit from doing so. Though the Holy Spirit will never leave the heart of the believer, the Lord makes no such promise to those who remain in rebellion to Him. A few months ago one godly old pastor told the author, "I don't see the Holy Spirit working in the hearts of the unsaved like I used to." That is truly frightening. If the Holy Spirit stops

---

[34] The enemy's intellect should not be underestimated. This satanic attack is brilliant. Satan has brought false doctrine and false spiritual manifestations into the church under the guise of being the Holy Spirit. Many are afraid to speak against these sins for fear of blasphemy against the Holy Spirit. If we don't know our Bibles, we get caught in this trap. This is the subject of *Sunset of the Western Church*, E. Skolfield, Fish House, 1987.

restraining the evil in man's heart, we Christians face a terrifying future.

v.9 **"...with all power and signs and false wonders,"** Now we have guided missiles and hydrogen bombs bringing fire down out of heaven, nuclear submarines and Venus probes, movie special effects and TV wizards. TV is a wonder indeed. It shows an "image" of the world system, and people worship it several hours a day, REV 13:15. It shows little but lies. If these are not false wonders, what does it take to qualify?

Our medical science keeps empty bodies alive long after the Lord has taken the soul. Paleontologists deny even the existence of God with their billion year calendars. Psychologists, with their conscience soothing techniques, try to deal with our guilt, without leading us to Jesus; ignoring the truth that Jesus' blood is the only thing in heaven or on earth which can wash away our sins. Psychology is a "rational" interaction with the occult, which keeps man's eyes averted from the Cross.

So now we see the man of sin all around us. The worldly, the disbelieving, the liberal scholar who tries to disprove the Bible. All the other enemies of God. Hateful, unrepentant, sometimes even "disguising themselves as servants of righteousness..." 2CO 11:14. The man of sin isn't some superhuman potentate just waiting for the right time to take over the world. He's the unmerciful landlord, the drug pusher, the dishonest business man, the Satan worshipper with his hidden rites, the occultist, and the crooked judge who steals from widows for a price. Today, he's all around us. He's everyone's neighbor, from our own home town, to the blackest hole in Calcutta.

## *Chart No.1*

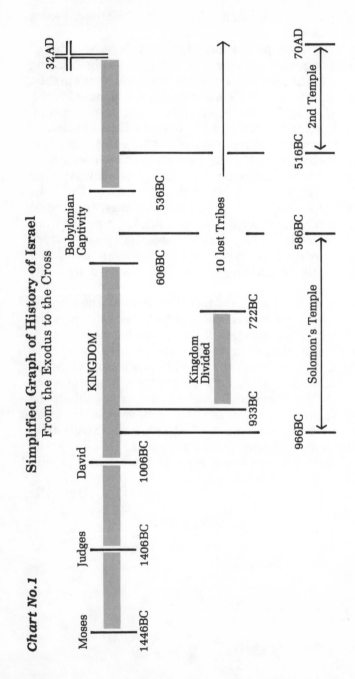

**Simplified Graph of History of Israel**
From the Exodus to the Cross

| | | | |
|---|---|---|---|
| Moses | Judges | David | |
| 1446BC | 1406BC | 1006BC | |

KINGDOM

933BC

Kingdom Divided

722BC

606BC

Babylonian Captivity

536BC

10 lost Tribes

32 AD

966BC    Solomon's Temple    586BC    516BC    2nd Temple    70AD

NOTE: This graph presents the conservative historic    reference work such as Halley's Bible Handbook or
position. The dating may be verified in any conservative    Zondervan's Pictorial Bible Encyclopedia.

*Chart No.2*

The Time of the Gentiles
LUK 21:24

LUK 21:24 And they shall fall by the edge of the sword, and shall be led away captive into all nations: and Jerusalem shall be trodden down of the Gentiles, until the times of the Gentiles be fulfilled.

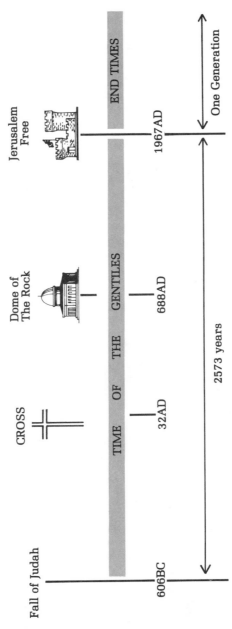

NOTE: When Jesus defined "The Time of the Gentiles" in 32AD, Jerusalem was then under Roman authority, and had been under various foreign governments for some 638 years, back to the fall of Judah in 606BC. Looking through time in both directions as only He could, He saw that His Holy City would remain under Gentile control another 1935 years, a total of 2573 years. This Gentile domination of Jerusalem ended at the Six Day War of June 1967. That ends "The Time of the Gentiles!"

## Chart No.3

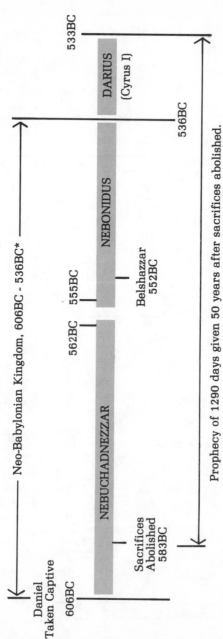

**Daniel's Captivity**
Daniel 1 through Daniel 12

Neo-Babylonian Kingdom, 606BC - 536BC*

533BC

DARIUS
(Cyrus I)

NEBONIDUS

536BC

Belshazzar
552BC

562BC    555BC

NEBUCHADNEZZAR

Daniel
Taken Captive
606BC

Sacrifices
Abolished
583BC

Prophecy of 1290 days given 50 years after sacrifices abolished.

* The chronology used in this and other charts in this book reflects the conservative position. Dating may be verified in Zondervan's Pictorial Bible Encyclopedia, 1975. Vol 1, pp.836-845; in Halley's Bible Handbook, 24th edition, 1965, or in almost any other conservative work on Bible history. The dates used are common knowledge, and are not subject to a disagreement of more than one to three years.

## *Chart No.4*

## "I Give You A Day For A Year"
### EZE 4:6

EZE 4:6  And when thou hast accomplished them, lie again on thy right side, and thou shalt bear the iniquity of the house of Judah forty days: **I have appointed thee each day for a year.**

a day    is equal to . . . .

a year

O.T. 360 DAYS

N.T. 365.24 DAYS

In other words, after this Word to Ezekiel, when "days" are spoken of in a prophetic sense, they should be interpreted as either Hebrew years or Solar years, unless context clearly dictates otherwise.

Hebrew Year = 360 days, or .9857 Solar years.
Used ONLY for interpreting Old Testament prophecy.

Solar Year = 365.24 days.
Used for interpreting New Testament prophecy.

## *Chart No.5*

# How Daniel Understood

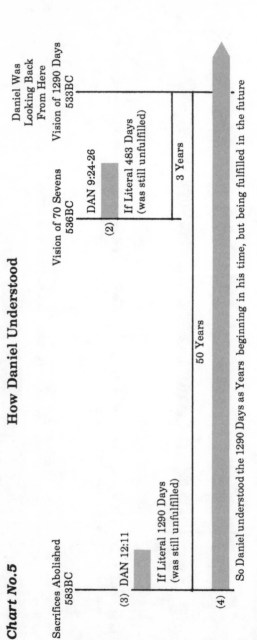

**Sacrifices Abolished**
583BC

(3) DAN 12:11

If Literal 1290 Days
(was still unfulfilled)

**Vision of 70 Sevens**
536BC

DAN 9:24-26

(2)

If Literal 483 Days
(was still unfulfilled)

**Vision of 1290 Days**
533BC

Daniel Was
Looking Back
From Here

50 Years

3 Years

(4)

So Daniel understood the 1290 Days as Years beginning in his time, but being fulfilled in the future

1. "I give you a day for a year," EZE 4:6

2. The vision of 70 weeks (483 days), given three years earlier, was still unfulfilled. If the 483 days were literal days, they would have been over for 1 1/2 years when Daniel said "he understood the vision." Instead, they were still in the future.

3. Since the Sacrifices had been abolished 50 years earlier, if the 1290 days had been literal days, they

would have been fulfilled 46 1/2 years before God gave the prophecy. Daniel could see that nothing had taken place back then.

4. Putting that all together, Daniel saw that both visions were using the same measure of prophetic time: 1 DAY = 1 YEAR.

5. Daniel could look back at two visions that should have been fulfilled if they were in literal days.

*Chart No.6*          The Abomination of Desolation
DAN 12:11

DAN 12:11 and from the time that the daily sacrifice shall be taken away, and the **abomination that maketh desolate** set up, there shall be a thousand two hundred and ninety days.

MAT 24:15 When ye therefore shall see the **abomination of desolation**, spoken of by Daniel the prophet, stand in the holy place, (whoso readeth, let him understand:)

MAR 13:14 But when ye shall see the **abomination of desolation**, spoken of by Daniel the prophet, standing where it ought not, (let him that readeth understand,) then let them that be in Judaea flee to the mountains:

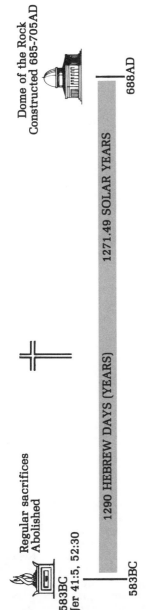

Dome of the Rock
Constructed 685-705AD

Regular sacrifices
Abolished

583BC
Jer 41:5, 52:30

1290 HEBREW DAYS (YEARS)

1271.49 SOLAR YEARS

583BC

688AD

NOTE: In MAR 13:14 the abomination is referred to as "IT" rather than him. Central to understanding the end times is the recognition that Mohammed is the "false prophet" of Rev.19:20, and that the fundamentalist Moslems are the most malignant enemy of the church of Jesus Christ in the Christian Era! They have a bloody history of destroying the brethren and the Jews. A key phrase in both Gospel quotes above is "...let the reader understand..." It is in this generation that the Rev.11:2 and 12:6 historic pins were fulfilled in the new nation of Israel. As a result, the prophecies which surround these disclosures are to us. We are the ONLY generation which can understand...

## Simplified Illustration of the Temple Mount

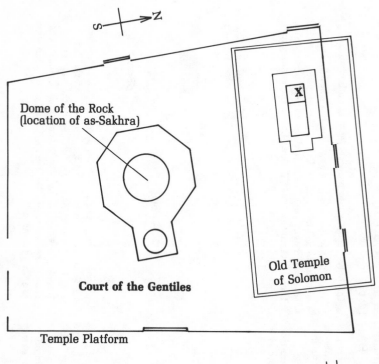

Dome of the Rock
(location of as-Sakhra)

**Court of the Gentiles**

Old Temple
of Solomon

Temple Platform

X location of flat bedrock.

Old City Wall

Golden
Gate

This sketch of the Temple mount shows the Mohammedan Memorial
"The Dome of the Rock" to be some 330 feet south of the sites for
both the first and the second temples. The double line shows the
position of the Temple of Solomon. Notice that it faces directly
toward the Golden Gate. The temple of Nehemiah (not shown) oc-
cupied about the same area. For reasons unknown it was turned
some 6° more easterly. In both temples, the flat bedrock which is
now under the little "Dome of the Tablets" was part of the floor of
the Kodesh Ha-Kodashim, or Holy of Holies.

## *Chart No.8*

## The 42 Months
### REV 11:2

REV 11:2 But the court which is without the temple leave out, and measure it not; for it is given unto the Gentiles: and the holy city shall they tread under foot forty and two months.

1. A month is 365.24 days divided by 12 or 30.437 days.
2. 42 months × 30.437 days = 1278.34 days.
3. "I give you a day for a year.",
4. Dan. 12:11 (the 1290 days) takes us to 688.5AD.
5. June 6, 1967, Jerusalem free of gentile domination!

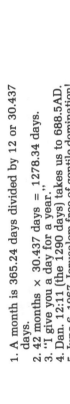

Dome of the Rock
Construction 685-705AD

**688AD**

42 MONTHS

1278.34 DAYS (YEARS)

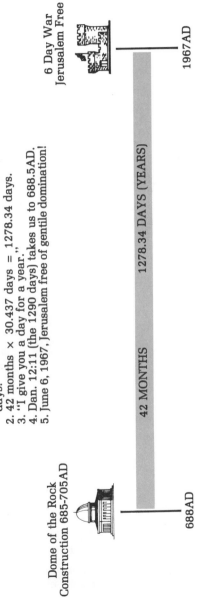

6 Day War
Jerusalem Free

1967AD

NOTE: Study REV 11:2. This fits history too well to be interpreted in any other way. "Leave out the court.." The Dome of the Rock is built 300 feet South of the Solomonic temple.

# Chart No.9

# Woman In the Wilderness
## REV 12:1-6

REV 12:5 And she brought forth a man child, who was to rule all nations with a rod of iron: and her child was caught up unto God, and to his throne.

REV 12:6 And the woman fled into the wilderness, where she hath a place prepared of God, that they should feed her there a thousand two hundred and threescore days.

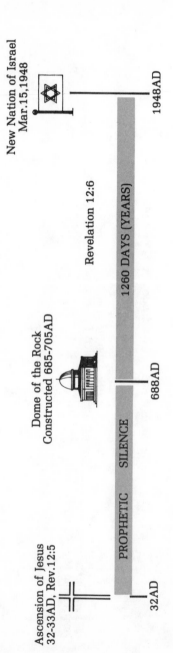

New Nation of Israel
Mar.15,1948

Dome of the Rock
Constructed 685-705AD

Revelation 12:6

Ascension of Jesus
32-33AD, Rev.12:5

32AD

PROPHETIC    SILENCE

688AD

1260 DAYS (YEARS)

1948AD

NOTE: Before 688AD, both the Jews and the Gentile church could worship freely in Jerusalem. They were not thrust into the wilderness until the Mohammedans made it unsafe for them to worship the Lord in that city. That is why the 1260 days started in 688AD. The Lord relates all prophecy in some way to that city. It is still His footstool.

## The 69 Sevens
### DAN 9:24:26

DAN 9:24-26  Seventy weeks are determined upon thy people and upon thy holy city...from the **going forth of the commandment to restore and to build Jerusalem unto the Messiah the Prince shall be seven weeks,** **and threescore and two weeks...And after threescore and two weeks shall Messiah be cut off, but not for himself...**

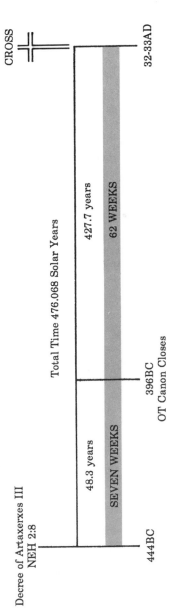

Decree of Artaxerxes III
NEH 2:8

444BC

48.3 years

SEVEN WEEKS

396BC
OT Canon Closes

Total Time 476.068 Solar Years

427.7 years

62 WEEKS

CROSS

32-33AD

69 weeks (sevens) = 483 Hebrew day years = 476 solar years. 476 - 444 = 32AD. The date of the Crucifixion!

7 Hebrew sevens = 48.3 solar years - 444 = 396BC. Close of the Old Testament.

62 Hebrew sevens = 427.7 solar years - 396 = 32AD. Date of the Cross.

Note: Our history is written in solar years of 365.24 days. Hebrew prophetic years had 360 days. To convert to our calendar what the Lord revealed to Daniel the Hebrew, use the following formula:

360 divided by 365.24 = .98565
Or: 69 x 7 = 483 x .98565 = 476.068

This conversion is for the Old Testament ONLY! The New Testament was written in Greek, and the apostles used a Roman calendar very similar to the one we use today.

## Chart No.11

## The 70th Seven

DAN 9:27 (NIV) ...but in the middle of that seven, he will **desolations will place abominations on a wing of the** put an end to sacrifice and offering, **and one who causes** **temple,** until the end that is decreed is poured out on him.

1. The Dome of the Rock on a wing of the temple.
2. The Dome is abomination which maketh desolate, DAN 12:11.
3. Abomination set up in the middle of the week.
4. Jews and Christians kept from "sacrifice" since Dome built.
5. 706AD acceptable. "Middle of the week" not a precise time.

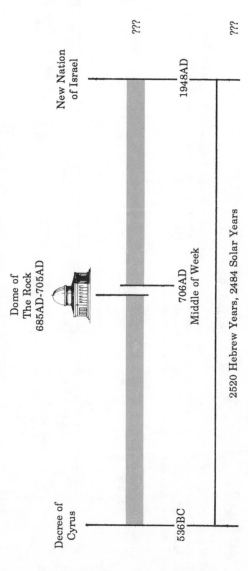

Decree of
Cyrus

536BC

Dome of
The Rock
685AD-705AD

706AD
Middle of Week

New Nation
of Israel

1948AD

???

???

2520 Hebrew Years, 2484 Solar Years

BOOK 2

# The Dual Church

Photo courtesy Biblical Archeology Review

We are filled with reverence and awe when we realize that under this little cupola, upon the now exposed bedrock, stood the Holy of Holies of the Temple. On this rock stood the Ark of the Covenant. When Solomon dedicated the Temple in 966BC, this very space was filled with the Glory of the Lord.

The Ark of the Covenant was lost during one of Nebuchadnezzar's sieges of Jerusalem. Jewish tradition states that the prophet Jeremiah took the Ark, and the original Tabernacle through a secret tunnel under Jerusalem and buried them on Mount Nebo. There is no record of the Ark having ever been in the temple of Nehemiah, still standing when Jesus was on earth. This second temple was totally destroyed by Titus, the Roman General, in 70AD...and, as the Bible states, not one stone was left upon another.

# Chapter 10

# *Mystery's End*

In Book 2, we will center on who the Lord's servants are in the Christian Era, on the dual nature of the total church, and on the structure of the prophetic books.

Since we can't find a Seven Year Great Tribulation anywhere, what should we look for next? Well, one thing for sure, at the end of the Christian Era the Lord is returning to Earth to take the church unto Himself. That is agreed upon by all who believe the Bible to be the Word of God. It has been estimated that one out of every 25 verses in the New Testament either states directly, or refers to, the return of the Lord. The differences among believers about the second coming stem from differing views of the chain of events before Jesus returns. But, now that the Seven Year theory is out, we need a new end-time chronology.

There is a Great Tribulation sometime, just as MAT 24:21 tells us. So the next questions are: When is it? How long will it last? Will the church be taken to be with the Lord before, during, or after it?

There are so many conflicting ideas being tossed about these days, that we need a revolutionary approach. Let's make a little agreement between the Lord, you, and me. Let's take all our commentaries and set them aside for a while. Then let's take the Bible, and only the Bible, and see what it has to tell us about this sequence of events. Please be patient with the author for making this a very nit-picking chapter. All the "I's" are dotted and all the "T's" are crossed because, if this position is correct, most of our current end times ideas will need rethinking. Let's start with a quote that is familiar to almost every Christian:

1TH 4:16-17 For the Lord himself shall descend from heaven with a shout, with the voice of the archangel, and **with the trump of God:** and the dead in Christ shall rise first: Then **WE** which are alive and remain shall be caught up together with them in the clouds, to meet the Lord in the air: and so shall we ever be with the Lord.

All agree that these verses refer to the so-called "rapture"[35] of the church. In fact, this is one of the central passages in Scripture which supports the physical return of Jesus to this Earth. Note the "we." Paul was speaking of the church of which he was part. We have every scriptural reason to believe that "we" includes us. Every other time "we" is used to refer to the church, we say it's us. So to be consistent, let's do so now. WE is us. That's relatively simple, isn't it?

Another thing to note is that Jesus is returning with the trump of God. A-ha! "The trumpet of God" will be blown when He returns. Now the Bible is full of trumpets, including the seven in Revelation. So the next logical question is: which trumpet is this? Of all the trumpets in the Bible, at which one of them is the Lord returning?

1CO 15:51-52 Behold, I shew you a mystery; **WE** shall not all sleep,but **WE** shall all be changed, In a moment, in the twinkling of an eye, **at the last trump:** for the trumpet shall sound, and the dead shall be raised incorruptible, and **WE** shall be changed.

We found it. The LAST trumpet! Compare this 1CO passage with 1TH quote above it. In both, the dead in Christ are raised; plus, in 1CO 15:51-52 there is also a trumpet, and three more "we's"! Here is the point: If the "we" Paul was

---

[35] "Rapture" is in quotes, because the author does not find the return of the Lord for the saints so characterized anywhere in Scripture. It is believed to have come from the Latin Vulgate's use of the word "raptao" in reference to this event. By definition, the word "rapture" seems more suitable for the mystery religions, than it does for sober Christians looking forward to the most awesome event in all history, the return of Jesus as our God and King. Rapture was probably brought into common usage by Margaret MacDonald, a 15 year old Scottish visionary of the 19th century. John Bray, *The Origin of the Pre-Tribulation Rapture Teaching*, John Bray Ministry, 1981.

speaking of in 1TH 4:17 refers to us, so do the "we's" in 1CO 15:51-52. We can't just arbitrarily pick through the "we's," and choose which "we" is for us on the basis of some doctrine we like. That is pretty funny sounding, I know; but believe it or not, there are those who say that 1TH 4:16-17 is about us, but 1CO 15:52 isn't. All these "we's" are us, or none are. So isn't this just a different description of the same happening?   Of course, and there is that trumpet again, only this time we know which trumpet it is. We are taken to be with the Lord at the LAST trumpet!

Look at that trumpet very carefully. Trumpet is singular, so no other trumpets are blown with it. That last trumpet is blown by itself. Also there are no modifiers like, except the trumpets of judgment, or except the trumpets in Revelation. That needs to be emphasized:

**There are no "excepts!"   No trumpets in the Bible are left out!**

So we will be taken to be with the Lord at the last trumpet there is. The last trumpet of all time! There are some denominational theologians who declare that this last trumpet does not include the seven trumpets in Revelation. Unbelievable as it may sound, they theorize that Revelation's seven trumpets are "special" trumpets of judgment excluded from the mandate of 1CO 15:52.

There is absolutely NO scripture for their view, and it is counter to the plain testimony of the Bible! The declaration that we are taken to be with the Lord at the LAST trumpet. Our trumpet is either the very last trumpet of all time, or 1CO 15:52 is a lie. The Bible is infallible truth, so one more time: We will be taken to be with the Lord at the one and only last trumpet!   That is just believing what the Word of God says straight out, and it simplifies a doctrinal point that the church has been arguing about for 70 years.

MAT 24:21 For then shall be **great tribulation,** such as was not since the beginning of the world to this time....

MAT 24:29 Immediately **after the tribulation** of those days...the powers of the heavens shall be shaken:

MAT 24:31   And he shall send his angels with a great **sound of a trumpet** (Great Trumpet, NASB), **and they shall gather together his elect** from the four winds, from one end of heaven to the other.

Note the sequence of events:

(1) Tribulation.
(2) After the tribulation.
(3) Great trumpet.[36]  *(Chart No.12)*

Since our trumpet is the last trumpet, this great trumpet either has to be our trumpet or our trumpet would have to come after it!  If we are going to support a pre-tribulation rapture position, we would have to rewrite the Scripture! We would have to put MAT 24:31 before MAT 24:21!  Think that through.  First, great tribulation.  Second, after the tribulation. Third, the great trumpet.  It is obvious from MAT 24 that our trumpet (the last trumpet) comes after the tribulation.  *(Chart No.13)*

That's not all.  Some believe that the church is "raptured" out at the end of REV 3.  Why?  Because the word "church" is not mentioned after that.  Guess what...trumpets are.  Trumpets are recorded all the way through REV 11.  The last trumpet in Revelation (the 7th trumpet) is not blown until REV 11:15.  The 7th trumpet of REV 11:15 has to be our trumpet, or our trumpet would  have to come after that one, too.  Our's is still the last trumpet.

What does that tell us?  Well, we now have Scriptural proof that the church will be on earth through six of the seven trumpets of Revelation.  This is not just another end time theory.  If we have ears to hear it, this is what the Word of God declares.

This 7th trumpet in Revelation is obviously a pretty important trumpet. We need to know if it is indeed our trumpet, or can our's come later?  The 7th trumpet itself is

---

[36] The NASB translates this trumpet as the "Great Trumpet" rather than "the great sound of a trumpet" as does the KJV. Is this not the greatest trumpet of all time, the culmination of the ages? So the author uses "Great Trumpet" throughout the text because he just likes it better.

blown in REV 11:15, but what takes place around that trumpet blast is described in REV 10:

> REV 10:6-7   And He sware by Him who lives for ever and ever... that **there should be time no longer:  But in the days of the voice of the seventh angel, when he shall begin to sound, the mystery of God should be finished,** as he hath declared to his servants the prophets.

What a tremendous verse that is.  If there is a central Scripture about the second coming of the Lord, this is it!  First, there is no more time after the 7th trumpet, so our trumpet can't come after this trumpet.[37]  **If there is no more time, there surely isn't enough time for any more trumpets, or a tribulation, or a millennium or anything else for that matter, except the eternal kingdom of God.**

Since ours is the one and only last trumpet of all time, our trumpet can't come before this 7th trumpet either, or our's wouldn't be the last.  So the 7th trumpet of Revelation is our last trumpet.  It is the very trumpet at which we, the church, are taken to be with the Lord!

That trumpet sound is not going to stretch over several years.  The phrase, "When he shall **begin to sound**," tells us so.  At the very first note of that trumpet, there is no more time!  Time as a natural phenomenon will cease to exist, and we will be in the eternal Kingdom of God.

---

[37] The definition of the Greek word "chronos" is time,  It is so translated in the KJV.  The more modern translation of "chronos" as "delay" is probably invalid.  Greek has a definite word for delay from the same root. That word is "chronizo."  If delay had been intended, why did the Lord not use the right word?  Our reasons for translating "chronos" delay, rather than time, are not linguistic but doctrinal. The argument for this conclusion is contained in the verse following, "But in the days of the voice of the seventh angel, when he shall begin to sound, the mystery of God should be finished, as he hath declared to his servants the prophets."  If the mystery of God is brought to a final end at this trumpet (as that verse declares in any language) we are then in the eternal kingdom of God.  We are in timeless eternity, and time as a natural phenomenon is over.  As is true of other places in Scripture, context has helped to determine the translation. REV 11:15 reinforces this contention by showing that the eternal kingdom of God begins as the last trumpet blows.  But even if we insist on delay for "chronos" in REV 10:6, there is no way to dodge the declarations of REV 10:7, and 11:15.

The "mystery of God" is the church in Christ Jesus. There are lots of verses on the subject; here are two, EPH 1:9, COL 2:2. So the church as a betrothed body of believers on Earth will be concluded at this trumpet.

"As He hath declared to His servants the prophets." Which prophets? We don't see any excluded, so these prophets are all the prophets in the Bible, both Old Testament and New. All prophecy will be fulfilled at this trumpet. Of course, this cannot include those few verses which refer to the Eternal Kingdom of God. That timeless State continues into infinity. *(Chart No.14)*

Now let's look at the verse where that trumpet blast sounds. The 7th trumpet is blown right in the middle of Revelation, after the Seven Churches, after the Seven Seals, after six other trumpets, and after the Two Witnesses:

> REV 11:15  **And the seventh angel sounded;** and there were great voices in heaven, saying, The kingdoms of this world are become the kingdoms of our Lord, and of his Christ; **and he shall reign for ever and ever.**[38]

The 7th angel sounds, and the Lord reigns forever. Right then, forever! That verse declares that when the 7th angel sounds the Lord will reign for eternity! This verse does not allow any time for a tribulation after it blows, or time for a 1000 year millennium either. Why? Because we go straight into the eternal Kingdom of God when that last trumpet sounds. There is the whole chronological story. We will show later how REV 20 (the so-called millennium) is an allegory of the Christian Era.

So when is the great tribulation? Matthew 24:21 tells us there was going to be one. First of all, who gets tribulation? The Greek word for tribulation is "thlipsis." Thlipsis, also translated affliction and trouble, is used 37 times in the New Testament. In almost every instance, thlipsis is used to refer to the suffering of whom? The saints! Here are a couple of familiar verses:

---

[38] Salpizo is the Greek word which is translated "sounded" in this verse. By definition, salpizo is a trumpet blast. This is not a shout or some other kind of sound.

JOH 16:33 These things I have spoken unto you, that in me ye might have peace. **In the world ye shall have** (thlipsis) **tribulation:** but be of good cheer; I have overcome the world.

ROM 12:12 Rejoicing in hope; **patient in** (thlipsis) **tribulation;** continuing instant in prayer;

2TH 1:4 So that we ourselves glory in you in the churches of God for your patience and faith **in all your persecutions and** (thlipsis) **tribulations** that ye endure:

There are 30 more. If you need more evidence, look them up in your concordance. Generally speaking, the unsaved don't go through thlipsis, they are destined for "orgy" or "thumos," God's wrath, ROM 9:22, EPH 5:6, 1TH 1:10, REV 16:19. Orgy and thumos are the two Greek words for wrath. So it is we the saints who are troubled, but we are not destined unto wrath, exactly as 1TH 5:9 tells us. So when is the tribulation? John tells us:

REV 1:9 **I John, who also am your brother, and companion in** (the thlipsis) **tribulation,** and in the kingdom and patience of Jesus Christ, was in the isle that is called Patmos, for the word of God, and for the testimony of Jesus Christ.

In both the NASB and the NIV, the above verse is translated, "I John, your brother, and partaker in **THE** tribulation..." Greek has a definite article "te," which means the. That definite article is in the Greek text! Now John did not say he was in "a" tribulation, "one of the" tribulations, or "an" tribulation. John said he was in "THE" tribulation! John was declaring that he was in the only tribulation there would ever be. But how long did it last?

Oh brethren, God forgive us for forgetting what suffering the saints of the past have gone through. Between 2,000,000 and 20,000,000 Christians were killed by the Roman Empire in tortures unimaginable. In the middle ages, the Catholic church killed many millions more. Estimates vary from a low of 6,000,000 to an unbelievable high of 64,000,000. The truth probably lies somewhere between. In our own generation alone, the Nazis murdered 6,000,000 Jews and countless Christians. We don't read The Pilgrim Church, Fox's Book of Martyrs, or Martyr's Mirror anymore, so we aren't aware anymore, thus fulfilling the Scripture:

> MAT 25:29-30 For unto every one that hath shall be given, and he shall have abundance: **but from him that hath not shall be taken away even that which he hath**...

The Lord has taken away our spiritual insight. We are so into our own little lives that we have lost sight of the Lord's big spiritual picture. The Great Tribulation of the Church began with the stoning of Stephen, and continued until the time of the Gentiles ended. There are scriptural reasons for believing that.

MAT 24:21 tells us of a great tribulation. MAT 24:29 tells us of a time after the tribulation, closely followed by the gathering of the saints, v31. Now according to a parallel passage, LUK 21:24-31, there will be only one generation after the time of the Gentiles. Daniel also leads us to believe that we are in the end-times. So, when can this time "after the tribulation" be? Now! In the time of the end, because that is all the time we have left. Brethren, the great tribulation is over!

From the Scriptures quoted above, it appears that the Great Tribulation is an epochal time, running within the Christian Era. In fact, since the saints have suffered ever since the Cross, it is possible that the Great Tribulation is the Lord's own name for the Christian Era. Look again at *Chart No.12*. Makes more sense now, doesn't it? Nevertheless, there will be a final short period of suffering for the church. REV 3:10 speaks of an hour of trial which is to come upon the whole inhabited earth. That is in our future.

That's it brethren. Our end time chronology is now in place. The Seven Year Tribulation view is mistaken, and so is the pre-tribulation rapture. When we understand the last trumpet, it is obvious that both go directly against the Word of God! But no sense crying over past miscalculations, let's just ask the Lord to show us what Revelation is really all about.

REV 1:19  Write the things which thou **hast seen,** and the **things which are,** and the **things which shall be hereafter;**

This is a key verse in the book.  As we discussed in Chapter 1, Revelation is not all futuristic.  Instead, it contains the past, present, and future from the Apostle John's own time.  If we are going to have any idea of the Lord's message to us in that book, we need to separate what is past, from what is still to be fulfilled.

Though the Lord designed Revelation to summarize His dealings with fallen man throughout the ages, the book centers on the people and nations involved in the great spiritual battle of the Christian Era.  By understanding who the Two Witnesses are, we can identify the earthly armies of the Lord who are involved in this struggle.

# Chapter 11

# *Two Witnesses*

We can't go to Revelation with our doctrine in place and expect the Holy Spirit to teach us anything from that book. The Two Witnesses of REV 11:3-7, are good examples of why. When we understand who these Two Witnesses are, and when their ministry is, it may change our basic belief about who might be included in the elect of the Christian Era.

In our present end time views, there are a lot of loose ends, among which are:

(1) The influence of the Jews on the New Testament church. As an example: Without the Jews, we would not have all the Scripture we have today. Every English Old Testament now in use is a translation of a Jewish 10th Century manuscript called the Massoretic Text.

(2) His eternal concern for that old temple site which (despite the crusades) has been all but forgotten by Christians for 1900 years. We found that the Lord remembered when we understood the day-years.

(3) The Lord's unfailing love for the Jewish people. The nation of Israel could not have maintained its identity over nineteen centuries of dispersion, under continual persecution, unless the hand of God protected them. The Lord affirms this in the Bible. Listen to what He says:

> JER 31:35 Thus saith the LORD, which giveth the sun for a light by day, and the ordinances of the moon and of the stars for a light by night, which divideth the sea when the waves thereof roar; The LORD of hosts is his name: **If those ordinances depart from before me, saith the LORD, then the seed of Israel also shall cease from being a nation before me for ever.** Thus saith the LORD; If heaven above can be measured, and the foundations of the earth searched out beneath, I will also cast off all the seed of Israel for all that they have done, saith the LORD.

Our dear loving Heavenly Father has not forgotten these words. He stated right there that the children of Israel would be a nation before Him FOREVER. So He remembered the plight of His chosen people all along. He proved it back in 606BC, at the beginning of the time of the Gentiles, when He sent the prophet Daniel to tell the Jews what their future would be. They couldn't understand most of what was prophesied then, because to fulfill His eternal purpose, the Lord sealed Daniel until the time of the end. But now, with Daniel open, new light has been shed on Revelation.

So far we have seen that prophetic days have fit history as years. If we stay consistent, we would also use the day=year method to explain the Two Witnesses. They too witnessed for 1260 days. But if we use day=years here, that makes it look like these witnesses lived for 1260 years. What kind of people can live for 1260 years? Maybe the text itself will enlighten us:

> REV 11:3 And I will give power unto my two witnesses, and **they shall prophesy a thousand two hundred and threescore days,** clothed in sackcloth.

> REV 11:4 **These are the two olive trees, and the two candlesticks** standing before the God of the earth.

As we have seen, Revelation is full of allegorical language. Obviously REV 11:4 is also allegorical. The Lord would not be speaking of a couple of wooden olive trees, and two brass candlesticks as witnesses, would He? Not likely, so candlesticks and olive trees must describe some people who witnessed for God. We need to look for a biblical definition of these allegories. Some other verses in Scripture which would tell us what these olive trees and candlesticks might represent.

> REV 1:20 The mystery of the seven stars which thou sawest in my right hand, and the seven golden candlesticks. The seven stars are the angels of the seven churches: and **the seven candlesticks which thou sawest are the seven churches.**

A-ha! Right in REV 1:20 the Lord defines candlesticks for us. Since seven candlesticks are seven churches, two candlesticks would be two churches. So, the Two Witnesses are two churches. Wait a second, aren't they supposed to be Enoch and Elijah, with Moses standing in the wings as an optional extra?

That is what some traditions teach us sure enough, but that is creative theology. Someone's guess. The Bible is its own best dictionary, and right in Revelation, candlesticks are defined as churches. If candlesticks are churches in REV 1, they are also churches in REV 11, unless the Lord Himself changes the definition. Churches is the Scripture's own definition.

So which churches? There are all kinds these days. Is it the Baptists and the Presbyterians, and are the Catholics included? The answer is far broader than that; and the Lord gave us another clue to show us so. Maybe the answer can be found in the meaning of the two olive trees:

> ROM 11:24-25  For **if thou wert cut out of the olive tree which is wild by nature, and wert graffed contrary to nature into a good olive tree:** how much more shall these, which be the natural branches, be graffed into their own olive tree?  For I would not, brethren, that ye should be ignorant of this mystery, lest ye should be wise in your own conceits; **that blindness in part is happened to Israel, until the fulness of the Gentiles be come in.**

So the Bible defines: wild olive tree = the Gentile Church, cultivated olive tree = the Jews.[39]    **One more time: the church is one olive tree, and the Jews are the other!** That is not creative theology. That is just believing the Bible's own definition of who those Two Witnesses are. In God's eyes the Two Witnesses are the Jewish people and Gentile Church. The author has taught this truth for 10 years, and has yet to hear a single sound biblical refutation of that point. If you know of one, he would be glad to hear it.

Prophetic days have fit history as years in every example we have seen so far. To change the yardstick for the 1260 days of the Two Witnesses, REV 11:2-3, would be very poor theology indeed.

---

[39] To use the ZEC 4:2-6 interpretation of olive trees and candlesticks to define a NT prophecy is hermeneutically unsound. We do not use OT allegories to define NT prophecies, when there are NT definitions which fit perfectly.

Now these Two Witnesses can not be after the time of the Gentiles. Why? Because Jesus told us there would not be 1260 years left after that time. "This generation (after the end of the time of the Gentiles) will not pass away until all things are fulfilled," LUK 21:24 and 32. A generation can not be over 70 years, PSA 91:10, and is usually considered to be 40 years. So we need to go back in history. Let's run that 1260 years up and down the church's past to see where they plug in. The author could find only one exact 1260 year period of spiritual significance in the whole Christian Era:

### 1948 - 1260 = 688 AD! The Construction of the Dome of the Rock!

And this fits history perfectly! As of 1948 the Jews are no longer witnessing in the nations. The abomination that maketh desolate was set up in 688AD, and the Jews were driven into the wilderness of the nations at that time, EZE 20:35. 1260 years later they are back home in Israel. *(Chart No.15)*

We can see 688AD to 1948AD as the time of Jewish witness, but what about the church? How can that apply to us, we are still here?[40] Yes, but look at what has happened to the church since 1948. In that very year, The National Council of Churches (to which your own church probably belongs) joined the World Council of Churches. Many believe that organization to be a communist front. Their declared goal is to cause social change rather than teach the gospel of Jesus Christ. The ungodly activities of that association have been catalogued by others many times over. It is said that through this group, millions of dollars from main line denominational churches (your tithes included) have gone to buy guns to

---

[40] Since there have been Jewish believers all the way back to Abraham's time, and the church has existed since the Pentecost, why do the 1260 days start in 688 AD? Because, before that date both Jew and Christian were free to worship in Jerusalem, even on the temple mount itself. After 688 the Mohammedans persecuted the Christians and Jews and drove them out of the land. That is when the most final of all the dispersions of the Jews took place. By now we should begin to get the picture. God's Word is eternal, and regardless of what nation ruled in the Holy Land, that old temple site was always of inestimable importance to the Lord.

support various insurgent "liberation fronts" in the third world. May God have mercy on us for the bloodshed and anguish caused by those church dollars.

Because of our careless disobedience of the Word, and the sin and apathy which has followed, the Gentile Church has now fallen into apostasy.[41] The fall into satanism and immorality within the Christian nations quickened in 1948, and the Western Church has done little to slow the decay. This will eventually lead to a worldwide rejection of the Lord, and of the Scripture. Now, for the first time since the invention of the printing press, books on astrology, satanism, and the occult are outselling the Bible.

Our initial reaction is that things can't really be that bad, and the author is just another doomsday alarmist. But our daily rubbing elbows with the iniquity around us, has led us to develop a tolerance to sin. Now it is just an everyday, ho-hum, happening that Bill does a little marijuana, or Joe leaves his wife and runs off with Martha, or little 14 year old Sally down the street gets pregnant. Sin is like appendicitis. It gets a little worse every day. We fool ourselves into believing that it isn't too bad, or that it will go away. Sometimes we don't even notice it, but in the back of our minds we always know it's there. When it is almost killing us, we might admit that it hurts a little. We figure we'll get around to fixing it some day. Then we wait too long, the appendix bursts, and we die. Most of the churches in this country are in that condition, terminally ill. Many have already fallen away, they are beyond reach, "the sin unto (spiritual) death."[42]

"We wrestle not against flesh and blood"; our battle is primarily spiritual. So one is inclined to wonder if the coming

---

[41] Apostasy, as usually defined, means a departure from the truth to such a degree that the lost can no longer hear the Gospel of Jesus Christ, and cannot come to the Lord through the message that is preached.

[42] 1JO 5:16 "If any man see his brother sin a sin which is not unto death, he shall ask, and he shall give him life for them that sin not unto death. There is a sin unto death: I do not say that he shall pray for it."

destruction of the church may not be more spiritual than physical. If so, we are frighteningly close to that hour:

> EPH 6:12 For we wrestle not against flesh and blood, but against principalities, against powers, against the rulers of the darkness of this world, against spiritual wickedness in high places.

> REV 11:7 And when they (the Two Witnesses) shall have finished their testimony, **the beast that ascendeth out of the bottomless pit shall make war against them, and shall overcome them, and kill them.**

One way or another, in the final hours of this age the Two Witnesses are going to be destroyed. That is not a guess. Read REV 11:7 in any translation you want. They all predict the violent end of the church. From context it appears that it is spiritual power we are losing, the power of the Holy Spirit which enables us to witness effectively. When the individual Christian no longer stands, a ruthless and devastating evil will be unleashed upon this planet with an intensity unknown since the flood. It has already begun. How true God's words to Noah ring today:

> GEN 6:5-7 And GOD saw that the wickedness of man was great in the earth, and that every imagination of the thoughts of his heart was only evil continually. And the LORD said, **I will destroy man whom I have created from the face of the earth; both man, and beast, and the creeping thing, and the fowls of the air; for it repenteth me that I have made them.**

> LUK 17:26-27 **And as it was in the days of Noe (Noah), so shall it be also in the days of the Son of man.** They did eat, they drank, they married wives, they were given in marriage, until the day that Noe (Noah) entered into the ark, and the flood came, and destroyed them all.

> 1PE 4:17-18 **For the time is come that judgment must begin at the house of God: and if it first begin at us, what shall the end be of them that obey not the gospel of God?** And if the righteous scarcely be saved, where shall the ungodly and the sinner appear?

2PE 3:7  But the heavens and the earth...are...reserved unto
fire against the day of judgment and perdition of ungodly
men.

The church is one of the Two Witnesses, and the Jews the
other.  Since the 1260 days of the Two Witnesses were over in
1948, what will our two roles be until Jesus returns?  We know
a lot about the church, but precious little about the Jews.  It
is now time to learn something about the position of the
Israelite in the Christian Era.  The Bible indicates that, before
the Lord returns, they will be partners with the church.

We have now finished our study of all the Biblical
day=years.  *Chart No.16* shows a summary of those years.

# Chapter 12

# *The Sons Of Judah*

Just before the Lord describes the battle of Armageddon in the 38th and 39th chapters of Ezekiel, He tells us of the restoration of Israel to the Holy Land. He concludes this allegorical prophecy of the "dry bones" with:

> EZE 37:11 ...Son of man, these bones are the whole house of Israel: behold, they say, Our bones are dried, and our hope is lost: we are cut off for our parts...Therefore prophesy and say unto them, Thus saith the Lord GOD; **Behold, O my people, I will open your graves, and cause you to come up out of your graves, and bring you into the land of Israel.**

Noting the context, these dry bones are speaking of 1948AD and the new nation of Israel. Armageddon follows closely at the heels of this prophecy. How soon will that battle be? End time slide rule prophets notwithstanding, Scripture doesn't tell us. However, we can now cross reference these bones with one of the final prophecies of Daniel:

> DAN 12:1-2 And at that time shall Michael stand up, the great prince which standeth for the children of thy people: and there shall be a time of trouble, such as never was since there was a nation even to that same time: and at that time thy people shall be delivered, every one that shall be found written in the book. **And many of them that sleep in the dust of the earth shall awake, some to everlasting life, and some to shame and everlasting contempt.**

If this verse was speaking about the final resurrection of the dead, all would have been brought back to life, not just "many." So here is another figurative description of the persecution of the Jews, and their ensuing restoration to the Holy land. As the Lord put flesh on dry bones laying in their graves, EZE 37; so those who slept in the dust awoke, to be restored to Israel, DAN 12. Same event, different allegorical language. As an interesting side note, God tells us that all who came to life (returned to Israel) would not be believers. However, despite their spiritual condition, the Lord is assembling the forces which are going to take a stand for Him in the final battle:

> EZE 37:16,19  Moreover, thou son of man, take thee one stick, and write upon it, For Judah, and for the children of Israel his companions: then take another stick, and write upon it, For Joseph, the stick of Ephraim and for all the house of Israel his companions:  Say unto them, Thus saith the Lord GOD; **Behold, I will take the stick of Joseph, which is in the hand of Ephraim, and the tribes of Israel his fellows, and will put them with him, even with the stick of Judah, and make them one stick, and they shall be one in mine hand.**

Note there are two sticks. Keeping it simple, Ephraim and the 10 northern tribes are one stick; Judah is the other; and God plans to make one stick of them.

Now, historic Israel had 12 tribes. The covenants the Lord made with Israel were with all 12 tribes. Those we know as Jews today, were primarily the inhabitants of the southern kingdom of Judah. That little country was populated by only two tribes, Judah and Benjamin and a few refugees from the northern kingdom. In fact, Judah is the tribe from which we get the name Jew. As Hosea tells us, when Sennacherib of Assyria destroyed Israel in 724-722 BC, the ten northern tribes were "mixed in the nations," HOS 7:8. Over a two year period, they were deported into Assyria, and we have no historic record of them ever returning. To date, they have been mixed in the nations for over 2600 years. So that must be it! It's all over for Ephraim, right? God has totally forgotten the ten northern tribes, right?

As we have read in Jeremiah, the heavens would have to pass away first. Instead, the Lord tells us that He is going to put Israel back together with Judah just before Armageddon. Impossible! They are gone. 2600 years gone. We don't even know who they are, or where to look. Ahhh...but God does. Our eternal Father knows where every single descendant of those lost tribes is. From the Scripture we read above, in the final hours, He is going to make Ephraim an ally of the new nation of Israel. Since "all Israel will be saved," ROM 11:25, it would have to include those 10 lost tribes.[43]

Where the Lord has hidden them and how they will be saved is the subject for a later chapter. But for now, let's see how the Lord has preserved the Israel we know, the Jewish people.

Whether or not Israel is one of the Two Witnesses of the Christian Era can no longer be biblically questioned. That was determined in the last chapter. Our question is only one of mechanics. A witness how? Can the Jews be witnesses without being Christians? Can Israel be a witness without being saved? Or if she is saved, how can she be, since the Jews do not know that Jesus is their Messiah. Sometimes they have even been the enemies of the church, as ROM 11:28 declares. Is there any way for a Jew to be saved without becoming a New Testament Christian? Believe it or not, Scripture is clear on the subject, and the Jew being one of the Two Witnesses affirms it.

Earlier we quoted JER 31:35-37 in which the Lord declares that Israel would be a nation before Him forever. There are literally hundreds of verses in the Old Testament which maintain this truth. But it might be wise to quote this Jeremiah passage again. The author likes this one best, because the Lord ties this promise to the Jews with the existence of sun, moon, and every star in the heavens. If they have not continued to be a nation in God's eyes, it would be pretty dark out:

---

[43] Israel was redefined in the New Testament and the church is spiritual Israel indeed. We have been grafted in. However, this does not nullify God's eternal promises to physical Israel.

JER 31:35-37 Thus saith the LORD, which giveth the sun
for a light by day, and the ordinances of the moon and of
the stars for a light by night, which divideth the sea when
the waves thereof roar; The LORD of hosts is his name: **If
those ordinances depart from before me, saith the
LORD, then the seed of Israel also shall cease from being
a nation before me for ever.** Thus saith the LORD; If
heaven above can be measured, and the foundations of the
earth searched out beneath, I will also cast off all the seed
of Israel for all that they have done, saith the LORD.

The sun, moon, and stars were shining when the Lord
spoke to Jeremiah. Look outdoors. Are they still shining? If
they are, Israel is still a nation before Him. And unless we are
big enough to knock the sun out of the sky, Israel will remain
a nation before God until the New Heaven and the New Earth!
How beautiful. When our Eternal Father makes an everlasting covenant, it's unbreakable. Does this include the Christian
Era? Of course.

There are some who would like to spiritualize this
passage. They would suggest that the Lord doesn't mean
physical Israel; that He really means spiritual Israel, the
church. Unless those ingenious theologians can demolish the
sun, moon, and stars, their view cannot be supported by the
Bible. Tiresome isn't it: people giving you their opinion of
what God means, when they don't want to believe what He
says.

However, in this instance "nation" can not reasonably be
understood to be anyone but the physical nation of Israel.
Jeremiah was written at the fall of the nation of Judah, in
Hebrew, in the Old Testament. The addressees were clearly
the people in Jerusalem about to go into captivity. The Lord
declared, to them, that Israel would be a nation before Him
forever. So, physical Israel remains a nation before the Lord
in the Christian Era. How can that be if they don't know
Jesus? "There is no other name under heaven, given among
men, whereby ye must be saved."

Well, first we have to ask: Were the Jews ever saved at
all? Were the Old Testament saints ever born again in the
New Testament sense? There are some dispensational and

covenant positions which argue the point, so let's see what Scripture has to say.

In His discussion with Nicodemus, Jesus puts a name to what happens in the human heart when we turn to the Lord. He called it being "born again." JOH 3:3, 3:7, and 1PE 1:23 are the only places in the Bible where this experience is so named. When Jesus talked with this ruler of Israel, the Cross was still in His future; and yet He makes a doctrinal statement which many think applies only to the church. From JOH 3:3 and 10 that position is questionable:

> JOH 3:3,10   Jesus answered and said unto him, Verily, verily, I say unto thee, **Except a man be born again, he cannot see the kingdom of God...Art thou a master of Israel, and knowest not these things?**

Jesus has not yet gone to the Cross, and Nicodemus is still under the Levitical code. The church is still in the future, and yet the Lord expects Nicodemus to know what being born again is all about! How could Nicodemus possibly be expected to understand the born again principle before the Cross? The answer must be, Jesus could only expect Nicodemus to understand being born again before the Cross, if an Old Testament believer could be born again before the Cross. Nicodemus should have known, as did a scribe of his time, that God required a changed heart:

> MAR 12:32-33   And the scribe said unto him, Well, Master, thou hast said the truth: for there is one God; and there is none other but he:  And to love him with all the heart, and with all the understanding, and with all the soul, and with all the strength, to love his neighbour as himself, is more than all whole burnt offerings and sacrifices.

So, Old Testament believers were born again before the Cross, just like we are after the Cross!  Since Jesus said, "Except a man be born again he cannot see the kingdom of heaven;" Noah, Abraham, Moses, David, Elijah, Job, Daniel, and the rest of the great Old Testament saints had to be born again, or we will not see them in heaven.  We saw Moses and Elijah in their glorified bodies on the Mount of Transfiguration with Jesus, so we can prove they were born again, unless we wish to suggest that God's glory would shine forth from the unregenerate. This is a major issue in some quarters, so make an effort to understand the argument. It will prove to be important to your spiritual well being, and will aid you in your future comprehension of the Bible.

The Old Testament is full of verses which declare that faith rather than sacrifice is the central aspect of salvation.[44] The whole 11th chapter of Hebrews teaches that Old Testament saints were saved by faith. They were not justified by the Levitical code, nor by the works of the law. So a changed heart was also the requirement for the Old Testament saint. That changed heart is what being born again is all about.

In JOH 3:3 quoted above, the Lord declares "except a man be born again he cannot see the Kingdom of God." When He said that, Jesus did not say "Only New Testament church members may apply." So the need to be born again includes every man who ever lived, from Adam on down to you and me. Jew or Gentile, everyone who is going to be in the eternal kingdom of God, must by faith, be born again, and that through Jesus Christ:

> 1CO 10:1-4 Moreover, brethren, I would not that ye should be ignorant, how that all our fathers were under the cloud, and all passed through the sea. And were all baptized unto Moses in the cloud and in the sea; And did all eat the same spiritual meat; And did all drink the same spiritual drink: **for they drank of that spiritual Rock that followed them: and that Rock was Christ.**

---

[44] Here are four of many Old Testament verses which stress faith unto obedience above ritualistic observance:

GEN 15:6 And he believed in the LORD; and he counted it to him for righteousness.

HAB 2:4 Behold, his soul which is lifted up is not upright in him: but the just shall live by his faith.

PSA 51:16-17 For thou desirest not sacrifice; else would I give it: thou delightest not in burnt offering. The sacrifices of God are a broken spirit: a broken and a contrite heart, O God, thou wilt not despise.

MIC 6:8 ...what doth the LORD require of thee, but to do justly, and to love mercy, and to walk humbly with thy God?

Old Testament or New, there is no difference in how we are saved. The only difference between us is in how the Lord willed to reveal Himself to us. That translates into our doctrinal positions. One more time: Old Testament or New, the method is faith. The difference between us is doctrine, not method.

We said all that to get to this: When Jesus went to the Cross, there were Old Testament believing Jews spread throughout the whole known world. They were in Africa, Spain, and England, and even as far away as India. If they were true believers, then they must have been born again. Elect, just like we are, ROM 11:28. It is reasonable to believe that many of them were unaware of Jesus' ministry, death, and resurrection.

Now we ask: Did they lose their salvation the moment Jesus went to the Cross, and they suddenly and unknowingly came into the Christian Era? Not a chance, if we believe in the security of the believer, or ROM 11:28. That verse states, **"...as touching the election,** they are beloved for the sake of the fathers."** Numerous times in the Old Testament the Lord speaks of His everlasting covenant with the children of Israel, including:

GEN 17:7  And I will establish my covenant between me and thee and thy seed after thee in their generations for an **everlasting covenant,** to be a God unto thee, and to thy seed after thee.

PSA 105:8  **He hath remembered his covenant for ever,** the word which he commanded to a thousand generations.

PSA 105:10  And confirmed the same unto Jacob for a law, and **to Israel for an everlasting covenant:**

JER 32:40  And I will make an **everlasting covenant** with them, that I will not turn away from them, to do them good...

EZE 16:60  ...I will remember my covenant with thee in the days of thy youth, and I will establish unto thee an **everlasting covenant.**

Here is the point: If a Jew, under God's covenants given to him through Abraham, Moses, and the prophets, can be saved by faith in His coming Messiah for one millisecond into the Christian Era; then a Jew in that same spiritual condition can be saved under those same covenants 100, 1000 or even 1900 years later![45] The only way that would not be true is if our salvation is based upon where we are positioned in history, and the exactness of our doctrine. Every verse in the Bible about the method of salvation shows us a different picture. Salvation is by faith, and faith alone.[46] Since faith in God's Old Testament covenant was good enough to save Moses and Elijah, then it is good enough to save a Jew today IF (and it is a big IF), the Holy Spirit has not revealed to that Jew that Jesus is his Messiah. That he now needs to recognize Him as his Messiah and personal Savior.[47]

So the next question becomes: Is it possible for a Jew in this age of mass media to be unaware that Jesus is his Messiah. Well, there are a lot of Jews spread all over this

---

[45] Some have suggested that it is impossible for a Jew in this age not to know about Jesus. If we were dealing in the natural realm, the author would agree, but we are not. God blinded their spiritual eyes, ROM 11:8, and only He can cause them to see again! If the Lord blinded their eyes in the Christian Era so that they would be lost, then He broke faith with the Patriarchs and His many covenants to Israel are null and void. NUM 23:19 states "God is not a man, that he should lie; neither the son of man, that he should repent: hath he said, and shall he not do it? or hath he spoken, and shall he not make it good?"

[46] Not for a second is the author suggesting some sort of Jewish universalism. It was only a remnant who had not bowed the knee to Baal in Elijah's time, and there is no reason to believe it is more than a remnant today. Not all those who claim to be Jews have the circumcision of the heart any more than all those who go to church are Christians.

[47] There is no easier way to tell if a Jew is saved than there is to tell the spiritual condition of a gentile. But, if the Holy Spirit reveals to a Jew that Jesus is his Messiah, he is no longer blind. If he then rejects the Lord, he is as lost as any gentile who does. So our witness to the Jew is as necessary as it is for any Gentile. If he already has that circumcision of the heart, ROM 2:28-29, and the Holy Spirit takes the veil away, the believing Jew WILL turn to Jesus. Why? Because, the same Spirit that takes the veil away will point him straight to God's Son. Only the Lord knows what his true heart condition is. "Man looketh upon the outward appearance, but the Lord looketh upon the heart," 1SA 16:7.

planet. Many of them in third world countries can't even read or write. They know nothing but what their fathers have taught them from the Torah (the Old Testament), and the Bible says:

ROM 4:15  ...**where no law is, there is no transgression.**

That Scripture states, if you are unaware of a law, you are not responsible for it. In God's eyes, you have not broken the law. Does that also apply to the Jew in his blindness to Jesus being his Messiah?  Jesus gave us a marvelous parable in Luke which gives us a clue:

LUK 5:33-39 (excerpts)  And they said unto him, Why do the disciples of John fast often, and make prayers, and likewise the disciples of the Pharisees; but thine eat and drink?  And he said unto them, Can ye make the children of the bridechamber fast, while the bridegroom is with them?...And he spake also a parable unto them; No man putteth a piece of a new garment upon an old; if otherwise, then both the new maketh a rent, and the piece that was taken out of the new agreeth not with the old...No man putteth new wine into old bottles; else the new wine will burst the bottles, and be spilled, and the bottles shall perish. **But new wine must be put into new bottles; and both are preserved.**

The Pharisees were questioning why the disciples did not keep the Jewish traditions.  Jesus replied that the children of the bridegroom did not fast while the bridegroom was present, speaking of Himself and the disciples.  Then He likened the gospel to new wine, and the Jews to old wineskins.  He went on to say that He would not put this new wine of the gospel into the old wineskins of the Jewish people, lest He destroy them.  Jesus concludes with the categorical statement that He did not will for the old bottles to perish, so new wine is put in new wineskins, **and both are preserved!** That is a mystery indeed.  How can a Jew be preserved if he does not understand the gospel?  Let's see if God accomplished it.  He promised Moses He would:

LEV 26:33-45 (excerpts)   I will scatter you among the heathen, and will draw out a sword after you...And they that are left of you shall pine away in their iniquity in your enemies' lands...And yet for all that, when they be in the land of their enemies, I will not cast them away, neither will I abhor them, to destroy them utterly, and to break my covenant with them: for I am the LORD their God...**But I will for their sakes remember the covenant of their ancestors, whom I brought forth out of the land of Egypt in the sight of the heathen, that I might be their God: I am the LORD.**

# Chapter 13

# A Beloved Enemy

Let's imagine that just before Moses died, God in His sovereign power took him up from Mount Nebo in 1406BC, traveled him 3500 years forward in time, and dropped him back on Mount Nebo in 1990AD. Moses then dies in 1990AD, without seeing anyone, or talking to anyone. Would this mighty man of God be lost because he died in the Christian Era and hadn't heard about Jesus? If Moses could be lost under those conditions, the following verse is meaningless, "Man looketh on the outward appearance, the Lord looketh on the heart." The heart of Moses would be no different on Mount Nebo in 1990, than it had been on Mount Nebo in 1406BC. Our God exists outside of time. To Him, the first day of creation is the same as the last. 1406BC and 1990AD are the same to Him. The Lord looketh on the heart regardless of when we are.

Throughout the centuries, the Holy Spirit has kept the Jew under the law, GAL 5:2-3. As stated before, for the Jew the Old Testament is all the Bible there is. His Messiah is still to come, and Oh, how he longs for His appearance, just as we do. He believes in Him, and trusts in Him, because of the promises of God given to him in the Old Testament. Can his faith be in vain? The Bible spells it out for us, just read it and believe it:

ROM 11:2-25 (excerpts)  **God hath not cast away his people which he foreknew**...there is a remnant according to the election of grace...and the rest were blinded. (According as it is written, **God hath given them the spirit of slumber, eyes that they should not see, and ears that they should not hear;**) unto this day.  I say then, **Have they stumbled that they should fall?  God forbid:** but rather through their fall salvation is come unto the Gentiles, for to provoke them to jealousy...And if **some of the branches be broken off,** and thou, being a wild olive tree, wert **graffed in among them, and with them** partakest of the root and fatness of the olive tree...Boast not against the branches. But if thou boast, thou bearest not the root, but the root thee...For if thou wert cut out of the olive tree which is wild by nature, and wert graffed contrary to nature into a good olive tree: how much more shall these, which be the natural branches, be graffed into their own olive tree?  **For I would not, brethren, that ye should be ignorant of this mystery, lest ye should be wise in your own conceits; that blindness in part is happened to Israel, until the fulness of the Gentiles be come in.**

ROM 11:26  And so **all Israel** shall be saved...

ROM 11:28-29  As concerning the gospel, they are enemies for your sakes: but **as touching the election, they are beloved for the fathers' sakes.  For the gifts and calling of God are without repentance.(are irrevocable, NASB)**

First of all, we are going to re-quote ROM 11:28-29 again. Please spend some time on these verses.  See what they say in plain American English.  Then ask yourself, "Why not believe exactly what the Lord inspired Paul to say here?"

ROM 11:28-29  As concerning the gospel, **they** (the Jews) **are enemies for your sakes: but as touching the election, they are beloved for the fathers' sakes.**  For the gifts and calling of God are without repentance. (**ARE IRREVOCABLE,** NASB)

Do we have ears to hear those verses?  The gifts and callings of God are irrevocable!  Do we comprehend what that means?  If the Israelites were ever called, they still are!  Now ROM 24-28 cannot be talking about the Jewish Christians.

Jewish Christians are not enemies of the gospel. So it must be the blind Jews of the Christian Era who are the enemies of the gospel. They are enemies of the gospel, but still elect! God's elected them; and ROM 11:28 declares that their election is irrevocable!

Some Protestant denominations put a lot of emphasis on their own election. We can't claim other Scriptures to prove the election of the church, and deny election for the Jews in these verses. Let's have a level playing field, please. It is the same Greek word! "Eklektos" used in ROM 11:28 is the identical word used throughout the New Testament to describe the eternal predetermined salvation of the saints, MAR 13:20, EPH 1:4, COL 3:12, TIT 1:1, and 1PE 1:4.

It was God Himself who placed a spirit of blindness on Israel, ROM 11:8. If God did not then also provide a way for them to be saved, He damned them by sovereign decree. If He did, that's not much of an everlasting covenant is it? The overall passage declares: **Israel was not hardened so as to fall**, but that salvation might come unto the Gentiles. So the Jews are not going to fall. Israel was not grafted into the church, but the church into Israel. Israel is an enemy of the gospel for the church's sake, but elect for the sake of the fathers!

Now, this is where those Scriptures lead us: If the church is "elect," and Israel is "elect," wherein lies the difference between us? Only in our historic position, and the accuracy of our doctrine (neither of which saves us). The Old Testament saints knew their Messiah was coming, even though they did not know who He was. They were born again, even though they did not know His identity. They were saved by faith in that coming Messiah, not by their doctrine, just like we are. Praise God we are saved because Jesus is perfect, not because we are; and He was even perfect for the Jew who did not know His name.

The Jew throughout the Christian Era has still been looking for his Messiah. If we say that the faith which was enough to save the Jew before the Cross is not enough to save him now; we are saying that salvation is based on doctrine and historic position, rather than by faith. That goes against every verse in the Bible which declares we are saved by faith!

Brethren, in ROM 11:26 above, we have been commanded not to become "wise in our own conceits" toward the Jews, because we have been permitted to understand the gospel while they have not. We went ahead and did it anyway; and it has resulted in our blindness too. We just knew we had it all, and the Jews were without hope.

Many will still not be able to see these truths. But until the Holy Spirit takes the scales from our eyes, we too will remain blinded to God's plan. If any of us were saved by the depths of our spiritual knowledge, and the accuracy of our doctrine, we would all be lost. In speaking of this spiritual blindness upon the Jew, the Bible goes on to say:

2CO 3:14-16 But their minds were blinded: for until this day remaineth the same vail untaken away in the reading of the old testament; which vail is done away in Christ. **But even unto this day, when Moses is read, the vail is upon their heart.** Nevertheless when it shall turn to the Lord, the vail shall be taken away.

So when a Jew reads the Old Testament his blindness to Jesus as his Messiah is reinforced. Note also (in the last sentence) that sometime in the future God will take that vail away. In Hebrews the Lord gives us more on the Jewish position in this era:

HEB 10:26 For **if we sin wilfully after that we have received the knowledge of the truth,** there remaineth no more sacrifice for sins,

That verse from Hebrews is little understood these days, and is usually quoted out of context to scare people to death. Frightening folks into heaven is not the intent of that verse at all. We just need to remember its Scriptural setting. What is the name of the book? Hebrews. So who is it to? Hebrews was written to Jewish Christians to update their doctrine. Many of them were still looking to Moses and the prophets, and they needed to know that the Levitical priesthood had been done away with in Christ. That the blood of bulls and goats had been replaced, once and for all, by the shed blood of the Lord Jesus. If the knowledge of that truth was willfully ignored, then the Old Testament observances were no longer in effect for them. This is where the blindness comes in. Since God has blinded the Jew to the identity of his Messiah, it would take a sovereign act of God to take that blindness away. Until God does, The Jew is not responsible for his blindness, and he can not sin willfully against that knowledge of the truth. So for those who are still blind, the Old Testament covenants are still in effect.

That is so important it must be stated again: **For those Jews who are still blind, the Old Testament covenants are still in effect!**

Knowing all this changes the way we witness. Rather than grabbing a Jew by the throat and telling him he is lost, we need to tell him that we too are looking for his Messiah. The difference between us being that we know who he is. Watch and see how he responds to that. My experience has been, that this opens a door through which you may both talk about the Lord.

Sad as it sounds, most Jews believe that Christians hate them. They may not show it right up front, but down inside the Jew believes it. It is a deplorable fact that this belief is based on centuries of persecution by the church. Terrible things have been done to Jews in the name of Jesus. As a glaring example: SS extermination efforts were based on the pretext that the Jews had killed Christ. Result: The church has reinforced the Jew's blindness. Think it through. We mistreat the Jew until he doesn't want to accept the Lord. Then we blame him because he doesn't. Talk about being between a rock and a hard place. We are partly responsible for his plight. Unless we show the Jew that we love and understand him, we have little hope of leading him to God's Son.

Oh, my brethren, you and I killed Jesus. Jesus died because you and I sinned. When Jesus hung on the Cross, he looked down through time and saw your sins, and mine. When He said, "Father forgive them, they know not what they do," He was also speaking of our own sin, which caused His death.

Now why can't a Jew see this? Why did the Lord decree this blindness upon them? Standing back and looking at the Lord's overall plan for the Christian Era, it becomes transparent as glass. If the Jew as a nation had known that Jesus was his Messiah, he would have been absorbed into the church, and the nation of Israel would have disappeared from the face of the earth. That doesn't sound so bad does it, so how significant can that be?

It is of such monumental importance that it needs amplification. If the Jewish people as a nation had accepted Christianity, Israel as a nation would be no more. Our faith in the Bible would then be seriously shaken, because half the prophecies in the Old Testament could never be fulfilled. The fulfillment of every one of the prophecies we have quoted so far, and hundreds more, depended on the Jews not knowing who their Messiah is!

Like the Lord said to Habakkuk, if God had told us what He was going to do in advance, we still wouldn't have believed it. In spite of their not recognizing God's dying Son as their Messiah, the Lord put His loving hand over the eyes of His people Israel, and saved them. Do we even begin to grasp the caring and forgiving nature of our Heavenly Father? All He had to do for them to be lost was nothing, just nothing. Instead, He blinded them so they could not sin against a knowledge of the truth. Oh, what it has cost those dear, precious people. What sufferings they have endured through the centuries because of their inability to see the Savior who went to the Cross for them.[48]    Spiritually they suffer still, looking dimly ahead, through darkened Old Testament eyes, for the coming of their beloved Messiah.

> ROM 11:31-32 **...For God hath concluded them all in unbelief, that he might have mercy upon all.**

> ROM 11:33 O the depth of the riches both of the wisdom and knowledge of God! how unsearchable are his judgments, and his ways past finding out! For who hath known the mind of the Lord? or who hath been his counsellor? Or who hath first given to him, and it shall be recompensed unto him again? For of him, and through him, and to him, are all things: to whom be glory for ever. Amen.

---

[48] Certainly many of the Pharisees rejected the Lord so as to be lost, but not all. Nicodemus and Joseph of Arimathea are notable exceptions. Nor would it surprise the author to see Gamaliel in heaven. He defended the brethren in Acts 5:37-39, and that he feared the Lord is unquestionable.

The God of the universe had a plan in eternity. It is a good plan, because God is good. It is a loving plan, because God is love. It is a just plan, because God is just. It is a holy plan, because God is holy. It is a merciful plan, because the Lord delights in unending mercy. These attributes of God are not suppositional. They are spelled out for us all over Scripture. No doctrine of man's, no matter how well thought out, can be correct if it goes contrary to the Bible or any of God's attributes. A Holy God cannot make a plan that is contrary to Himself, or He would cease to be Holy. If we don't understand the eternal immutability of God's attributes, we have little hope of comprehending His plan.

In eternity God saw all history. The Christian Era is part of His eternal plan. If we say that the Jew in the New Testament age is lost, then we say that our God, in His sovereign foreknowledge, went against His own nature. We further say that He predetermined that millions of His chosen people would be lost, before He gave His everlasting covenant to Abraham! If we as sinful men would not tell a bold face lie like that, how dare we attribute such duplicity to a Holy God? He gave Israel an everlasting covenant. That makes them His chosen people still; and He did not chose them to lose them.

Before we contend that all the Jews of the Christian Era are lost as part of God's eternal plan, we better have solid proof texts. Verses that say so straight out. Their damnation better not be based on some outlandish doctrine of man's, because such a doctrine would fly in the face of every one of God's Old Testament promises to the Israelites. **And remember, the Old Testament is ALL the Holy Spirit has permitted the Jews to recognize as scripture, 2CO 3:15.**

The Lord desires a more open heart in the church than we have yet displayed. He wants us to understand all this so we can be careful and loving to our Jewish brethren, moving them to jealousy so they will accept His Son. Instead of moving them to jealousy, the Christian nations have ostracized them, put them in ghettos, persecuted them, and slaughtered then en masse.

As the Lord foretold, no one would ever again gather figs of Israel, MAR 11:12-14; and so it has come to pass. The Old Testament faith has not grown beyond the Jewish synagogues. Has God forgotten His people? Allegorically, Israel is the fig tree. In our own generation, that fig tree has again put forth leaves, MAT 24:32, and summer is near. Blindness is upon Israel until the fullness of the Gentiles is come in, ROM 11:25. Maybe that day is at hand, for thousands of Jews are now turning to the Lord.

But the Lord has yet to take the scales from the eyes of all, and many Jews still look to Moses and the prophets. In HEB 7:1-9, we read that when Abraham gave tithes to Melchizedek (the Lord Jesus), he did so for those who would proceed from his loins. So Father Abraham paid tithes for the future generations of the children of Israel. Now what was Melchizedek's response to Abraham? He set a table before him, and on it bread and wine, GEN 14:17-20. Bread and wine. Oh, the richness of the foreknowledge of God. Do we have eyes to see what the Lord Jesus did there? As Abraham gave tithes for the children of Israel yet to be born, so in like manner, Melchizedek had communion with the children of Israel yet to be born; and our God is a covenant keeping God.[49]

---

[49] The foregoing chapters are highly controversial, and the author knows he will be considered in grave error by many. He just points you to the Bible and says, "That is what it states." The Scriptural case for the spiritual condition of the Jew in the Christian Era is so strong that the author wonders how the church has been able to maintain any other.

# Chapter 14

# *Iddan & Moadah*

So far, all prophetic days have been shown to be years. But these are not the only kind of prophetic times in the Bible. Twice in Daniel and once in Revelation, we are given time, times, and half a time:

> DAN 7:25 And he shall speak great words against the most High, and shall wear out the saints of the most High, and think to change times and laws: **and they shall be given into his hand until a time and times and the dividing of time.**

> DAN 12:7 And I heard the man clothed in linen, which was upon the waters of the river, when he held up his right hand and his left hand unto heaven, and sware by him that liveth for ever **that it shall be for a time, times, and an half**; and when he shall have accomplished to scatter the power of the holy people, all these things shall be finished.

> REV 12:14 And to the woman were given two wings of a great eagle, that she might fly into the wilderness, into her place, **where she is nourished for a time, and times, and half a time**, from the face of the serpent.

What can "time" mean? Is a "time" a year like the day=years are? One thing for sure, "times" are not years. Here is how we know. God gave us "a day for a year," not a "time" for a year. The Hebrew word for day is "yom." "Iddan" and "moadah." are the High Syriac and Hebrew words for time. Those are the words translated "time" in Daniel. God knows the difference between "iddan, moadah," and "yom," and God gave us a "yom" for a year, not an "iddan" or "moadah" for a year. So "iddan" (time) and "moadah" (time) must mean something else. What about the cryptic way these words are used, "time, times, and the dividing of a time?" How many "times" are we dealing with here?

As is true of English, Hebrew is full of idiomatic language. For instance, the Hebrew idiom "cut off" means to kill. "Ate the pieces of" means to bring malicious accusations against, and so on. Can "time, times, and the dividing of a time" also be an idiom? Let's see if we can find Scriptural support:

> 2KI 6:10 And the king of Israel sent to the place which the man of God told him and warned him of, and saved himself there, not **once nor twice.**

> **JOB 33:14 For God speaketh once, yea twice,** yet man perceiveth it not.

> JOB 40:5 **Once have I spoken; but I will not answer: yea, twice;** but I will proceed no further.

> PSA 62:11 **God hath spoken once; twice have I heard this**; that power belongeth unto God.

Here we see the same idiomatic form. The words are different, but the style is the same. "Once" is one, and "twice" is only one more, for a total of two, $1 + 1 = 2$. That's a Hebrew idiom. A singular "one" followed by a plural "twice" is only two. In the same way a singular "time" followed by a plural "times" is only two. If God had said, "time, yea times" we would have seen it right away. Let's employ the same idiomatic language to interpret time, times, and half a time. "Time" = one, "times" = one more, for a total of two times. Add a half a "time" and we have two and a half "times," or $1 + 1 + 1/2 = 2.5$. That is pretty simple isn't it. So why have people been saying "time, times, and half a time" is three and a half years? Who knows, probably because it fits the great tribulation scheme. Hebrew students have told me that the Hebrew grammar does not support it.

If a time isn't a year, how long is it? Daniel understood day=years alright, but he didn't understand "times." Why? Because, day=years were defined for him in the Old Testament Scriptures. Time was not. In fact "time" was not defined until late in the New Testament epistles:

> 2PE 3:8 But, beloved, be not ignorant of this one thing, that **one day** (Greek word, hemera) **is with the Lord as a thousand years,** and a thousand years as one day.

On the surface that doesn't look like much of a definition
for time does it? It sure doesn't work in English. But something is wrong here. God has already given us a definition for
"day." He has already told us a day = a year. Is the Lord
changing His definition for prophetic "days?" No, we can prove
that days are still years in the 42 months and 1260 days of
Revelation 11 and 12. So what we have here in 1PE 3:8 is: An
"X" with the Lord is as a 1000 years. How do we solve for "X"?
Let's start by doing a word study in Greek. That is the
language the New Testament was written in. The Greek word
in 2PE 3:8 translated day is "hemera." It is an ambiguous
word. How that word is translated usually depends upon
context. Elsewhere it has been translated as period, moment,
season, year, and, guess what: TIME!

In the 2PE 3:8 verse quoted above, the translation is
arbitrary. Context does not suggest the correct word. So the
translators have gone with "day" which is the most common
usage. However, "hemera" is translated as "time" in twelve
different places in the NASB. So "Time" is a very acceptable
translation. Maybe then "time" is 1000 years.

If "time" is a thousand years, and we have two and a half
of them, "time, times, and half times" could be 2500 years.
Thus far we only have a supposition. But that is all we had
for the day=years, until we started plugging them into history.
So let's see if we can find a historic 2500 years which agree
with the Bible's description of these "times."

After Nebuchadnezzar of Babylon died, three of his sons
ruled for a couple of years each. The kingdom was unstable.
Daniel must have been walking on eggs to avoid the plots and
political intrigue in the Babylonian court. Though the archives
don't tell us about it, reading about those middle eastern
empires gives us a picture of what was going on. Heads must
have been rolling all over the place. The Lord protected our
brother in that dangerous environment. Many of his fellow
rulers in Babylon hated him, DAN 6:4-13.

Then in 555BC, a nephew of Nebuchadnezzar seized
control. His name was Nabonidus and he proved to be an able
ruler. However, he couldn't stomach the Babylonian court life,
so three years later, in 552BC, he chose a close relative,

Belshazzar, to rule the city for him. Nabonidus then wandered around Arabia making war and writing poetry.[50]

It was during these turbulent times that the Lord gave Daniel the vision of four great beasts coming up out of the sea.[51] Scripture tells us when this was to the year, "In the 1st year of Belshazzar," DAN 7:1. In pictorial language, the vision then describes the four great kingdoms that were to rule in the Holy Land during the time of the Gentiles. At the end of that prophecy, the Lord tells Daniel about "times:"

> DAN 7:25 (NASB) And he will speak out against the Most High and wear down the saints of the Highest one, and he will intend to make alterations in times and in law, **and they shall be given into his hand for a time, times and half a time**.

Sometimes our doctrine gets messed up because we don't think about who the Lord is speaking to, and when. In this instance to Daniel in 552BC. In Daniel's day, who spoke out against God? Then as now, Satan speaks out against God. Who were the saints in Daniel's time? The Jews. So from the time that prophecy was given, the Lord is telling Daniel that the Jews would be under satanically controlled Gentile powers for two and a half times, or possibly 2500 years. That from Daniel's time, the Holy land would be ruled by strangers far into the future. Let's run that up and down the framework of history and find what it fits:

**2500 - 552BC = 1948...The New Nation of Israel!!!**

If that is not the correct interpretation, then it has to be one of the most remarkable coincidences in history. It fits

---

[50] To date there is no direct archeological evidence for the 552BC dating of the 1st year of Belshazzar. However, that date can be deduced by correlating supporting evidence about the reign of Nabonidus, and many authorities accept that date.

[51] The sea is the peoples of the Earth. REV 17:15, "And he saith unto me, The waters which thou sawest, where the whore sitteth, are peoples, and multitudes, and nations, and tongues."

Scripture and history exactly. But remarkable as it may be, we would still have only a theory if this were the only time these 2500 years fit antiquity. The Lord is so kind to us. When He takes the blinders off, He gives us plenty of proof that we are on the right course.

At the end of Daniel's prophetic ministry the Lord gave him another vision. The full story of that vision is in the 10th through the 12th chapters of Daniel. That prophecy includes the 1290 days which took us to the Dome of the Rock. From the Bible itself, this last vision may be dated at the third year of Cyrus the Persian, 533BC.

> DAN 10:1 **In the third year of Cyrus king of Persia** a thing was revealed unto Daniel, whose name was called Belteshazzar...

Daniel is a very old man. He knows he is going to die. He has seen the temple abandoned, and sacrifices abolished. He knows that an abomination of desolation is going to be on the temple mount in less than 1300 years. Will the Jews ever rule Jerusalem again? Of course. Many Old Testament scriptures have told him so. But when? The Lord tells him, but then hides it so no one can understand it until the time of the Gentiles ends:

> DAN 12:7-8 and 13. And I heard the man clothed in linen, which was upon the waters of the river, when he held up his right hand and his left hand unto heaven, and sware by him that liveth for ever that **it shall be for a time, times, and half;** and when he shall have accomplished to scatter (shatter, NASB) the power of the holy people, all these things shall be finished. And I heard, but I understood not: then said I, O my Lord, what shall be the end of these things...But go thou thy way till the end be: for thou shalt rest, and stand in thy lot at the end of the days.

Cyrus has given a decree that will let the Jews return to the Holy Land. They have started back, and soon they will begin building the 2nd temple. By this decree a satanically controlled empire has made an agreement with the Jews that they can sacrifice again. That agreement was broken 1290 days-years later by another satanic prince, Abd el Malik at the

Dome of the Rock. But God knew the end of that time, too. When was the vision given? In 533BC, the third year of Cyrus. So this "time times, and half a time" should begin in the third year of Cyrus:

**2500 - 533BC = 1967. Jerusalem free of Gentile domination!!!**

Brethren, I'll accept a 2500 year fit as a coincidence once, but not twice. This solution for "X" matches two different incidents in our time right to the year. They are not fulfilled from events that just happened last week, either. They are tied to two remote incidents in ancient history. That is a statistical impossibility! So we no longer have a theory. We have a historically supportable doctrine. *(Chart No.17)*

In the next chapter we will look at the history of Ephraim, and some associated scriptures which support an unusual rationale. What we have been building all through this book is an empirical argument. A jigsaw puzzle with one piece fitting into another. Each concept is just one piece. We can argue about the placement, color, or shape of each piece; but when the whole puzzle is finished, we stand back and view a complete picture. A completed picture, in which all the pieces fit, is not easy to dispute. If it is not of God, it will crumble back into its original pieces on its own, but if it is of God, it will remain, no matter who comes against it, ACT 5:35-39.

# Chapter 15

# A People Lost

The Old Testament tells us a lot about Ephraim.  He was the youngest son of Joseph, Jacob's son.  To begin Ephraim's record, our first historic setting is the Egypt of 3800 years ago.  The seven year famine is long past.  Joseph is still a ruler in the land second only to Pharaoh.  The rest of Jacob's sons are living in a part of the Nile delta known as the land of Goshen.  Jacob, also called Israel, was Abraham's grandson.  He is old and full of years, and almost blind.  Now he is about to die.

Israel calls his twelve children around him to give them his final blessing.  Joseph and his two sons, Manasseh and Ephraim, are ushered in first.  Joseph came in herding his boys before him, just as all parents do when they want you to notice their children:

> GEN 48:13  And Joseph took them both, Ephraim in his right hand toward Israel's left hand, and Manasseh in his left hand toward Israel's right hand, and brought them near unto him.
> 14  **And Israel stretched out his right hand, and laid it upon Ephraim's head, who was the younger,** and his left hand upon Manasseh's head, guiding his hands wittingly; for Manasseh was the firstborn.
> 15  And he blessed Joseph, and said, God, before whom my fathers Abraham and Isaac did walk, the God which fed me all my life long unto this day,
> 16  The Angel which redeemed me from all evil, bless the lads; and let my name be named on them, and the name of my fathers Abraham and Isaac; and let them grow into a multitude in the midst of the earth.
> 17  And **when Joseph saw that his father laid his right hand upon the head of Ephraim, it displeased him: and he held up his father's hand, to remove it from Ephraim's head unto Manasseh's head.**
> 18  And Joseph said unto his father, Not so, my father: for this is the firstborn; put thy right hand upon his head.
> 19  **And his father refused, and said, I know it, my son, I know it: he also shall become a people, and he also shall be great: but truly his younger brother shall be greater than he, and his seed shall become a multitude of nations.**

So Manasseh would be a great tribe but, sometime in the future, the descendants of the half tribe of Ephraim would become a multitude of nations.  Remember that, Ephraim is to become a multitude of nations!

The twelve tribes of Israel remained in Egypt for 430 years, and they were in the wilderness for another 40 years.  Then they were in the promised land for 300 more years under the judges.  During the judgeship of Samuel, they demanded a king.  God gave them Saul, and then David.  With David began the Davidic line of kings through which Jesus would be born.  The kingdom remained unified for only two generations.  If you read the account carefully, it appears that Solomon, the wisest man who ever lived, had a son who was one of the most inept. Rehoboam's decision to raise taxes caused a revolt. So, during Rehoboam's reign the Lord divided the kingdom. God separated Judah and Benjamin from the ten northern tribes. The twelve tribes then became two separate nations known as Israel and Judah. Jerusalem remained the capitol of Judah. Samaria became the capitol of Israel. *(Chart No.18)*

During the kingdom age, Israel was in continual rebellion to the Lord, resulting in constant conflict with the nations around them. In 748BC, Tiglath-pileser of Assyria made them a vassal state and took some captives off to Assyria. Then in 725BC, Shalmaneser began the deportation of the rest of the Israelites, and put Samaria under siege. Samaria fell in 722BC. The inhabitants of the city were taken away, never to be heard from again.

But...but...can the Bible be wrong? During all that time Ephraim was only a tribe in Israel. Big as she got, she never became a multitude of nations as Jacob prophesied. Does Ephraim never get to be that multitude of nations that God promised? Of course she does! The Word of God stands forever. If Ephraim did not become a multitude of nations before she disappeared, then she must have become a multitude AFTER she disappeared!

Now that's exciting. Where are these nations? What are they called? Obviously they are not out there trumpeting that they're Israel. They must not even know who they are themselves. Where has the Lord hidden them, and can we prove it biblically?

Just before Samaria fell, the Lord sent a prophet named Hosea to Israel. He was to the ten northern tribes what Daniel was to Judah. He foretold what would take place AFTER the northern kingdom's captivity. Read the prophet carefully and you will notice that the destruction of Israel and Samaria is fixed. It's going to happen, no matter what. The book of Hosea is not a call to repentance to save the northern kingdom. Instead, the prophet describes the Lord's plans for the ten northern tribes AFTER they disappear. Here we begin to see the everlasting love of our heavenly Father for His wayward Israelites. While they were busy conniving ways to go it on their own, God already had a design in place to save them. A plan spanning thousands of years. All the following verses are in that setting. Israel is just about to go into captivity when God tells them:

> HOS 1:10 Yet **the number of the children of Israel shall be as the sand of the sea, which cannot be measured nor numbered;** and it shall come to pass, that **in the place where it was said unto them, Ye are not my people, there it shall be said unto them, Ye are the sons of the living God.**

> HOS 11:8-10 (excerpts)    **How shall I give thee up, Ephraim? how shall I deliver thee, Israel...**mine heart is turned within me, my repentings are kindled together...I will not execute the fierceness of mine anger, **I will not return to destroy Ephraim: for I am God, and not man; the Holy One in the midst of thee...then the children shall tremble from the west.**

Now HOS 1:10 is a paradoxical scripture. Note the tense of the verb, "shall be." That is future. Israel is going into captivity never to be heard from again. Then the Lord tells them that they are going to be numerous beyond count. Furthermore, He tells them that no one will know that they are His Israelites. Nonetheless they will be called the sons of God. Isn't that mystifying?

HOS 11:8-10 is no easier. God is not going to give Ephraim up, period! Notice that the Lord's heart is set on delivering them. When He asks how, it is a rhetorical question. He knows exactly how He is going to do it. He knows that he will not again let them be destroyed as a people, and they will return to Him from the West!

Return from the West? Now that is peculiar. Ephraim's lands bordered the Mediterranean Sea on the West. Wherever they are coming from then, it has to be by sea!

> HOS 2:14 Therefore, behold, **I will allure her, and bring her into the wilderness,** and speak comfortably unto her.

This is interesting, too. We already know from EZE 20:35, and REV 11:6, that the wilderness is the nations. So the Lord tells us here that He will hide the ten tribes in the nations.

HOS 2:15-17 **And I will give her vineyards from thence,** and the valley of Achor for a door of hope: and she shall sing there, as in the days of her youth, and as in the day when she came up out of the land of Egypt. And it shall be at that day, saith the LORD, **that thou shalt call me Ishi; and shalt call me no more Baali.**

Though the Lord is going to give Israel a very pleasant land out in the nations, "Achor" is Hebrew for trouble. So trouble will lead to blessing for Ephraim. Here again the Hebrew is handy. "Ishi" means my husband, and "Baali" means my master. So Israel in the future will not be in the servant role, but the bride role. Jesus told His disciples, "Henceforth I call you not servants; for the servant knoweth not what his Lord doeth: but I have called you friends..." Who is the bridegroom, who is the bride? In this New Testament era, our relationship with the Lord is no longer just master to servant, but bridegroom to bride, and friend. Can you imagine the Lord calling sinners like us friends; no, but He does. Suddenly some flash bulbs start to go off over the author's head, because in speaking of Israel the Lord goes on to say:

HOS 2:19-20 **And I will betroth thee unto me for ever...I will even betroth thee unto me...**and thou shalt know the LORD.

HOS 2:23 And I will sow her unto me in the earth; and I will have mercy upon her that had not obtained mercy; **and I will say to them which were not my people, Thou art my people; and they shall say, Thou art my God.**

If we have a picture in our mind of how seed was sown in the old days, we can understand this. With a bag of seed under one arm, the farmer cast seed with the other hand to scatter it evenly over the earth. That is what the Lord did with Israel. He scattered the Israelites from South Africa to China. That needs repeating, too. God scattered Ephraim over the whole known world. Then the Lord declares that this lost and scattered people will be a bride. A bride whether they know it or not. Impossible from man's standpoint , but an accomplished fact from God's.

Again, there are many who would like to spiritualize this. They would say that this is not literal Israel here, but spiritual Israel, the church. That's the way you handle it these days, when for some doctrinal reason or other you don't want to believe what God says.

> HOS 7:8 **Ephraim, he hath mixed himself among the people; Ephraim is a cake not turned.**

This is one of the author's favorite verses. Ephraim is mixed among the nations, as the NASB puts it. She is bread not turned. What does that mean? The Israelites made a pan bread which they baked one side at a time. Some of today's cookbooks call that same primitive bread, Arab Bread. It takes time to bake one side, and more time to bake the other. The Lord in figurative language tells us that at the time of the prophet Hosea, Ephraim's past is only half the story, one side of the bread. For the future, the cake will need to be turned over. That's after the captivity! The Lord's pictorial language is truly a marvel.

> HOS 9:13-17 (excerpts) Ephraim...is planted in a pleasant place: but **Ephraim shall bring forth his children to the murderer**...Oh LORD: what wilt thou give? give them a miscarrying womb and dry breasts...yea, though they bring forth, **yet will I slay even the beloved fruit of their womb...and they shall be wanderers among the nations.**

After Israel is dispersed, she will be in a pleasant land. In these terrible texts, we see that Ephraim's future would not always be a pleasant one. A warrior tribe still, they will be involved in foreign wars. Many of their children will die unborn. That is either abortion or miscarriages. Then, they will be wanderers. Now how can Israel be wanderers and also planted in a pleasant land? One plausible solution is that they are the Gypsies. The Gypsies claim they are Ephraim. But a more likely explanation is that the Lord is referring to different episodes in their future. To date, that has been thousands of years. Even the author has wandered and been settled at times in his short life.

Actually, Ephraim's dispersion has been 2800 years long, and in our generation all things will be fulfilled, LUK 21:24-32. As of 1967, all the day=years have been fulfilled. Except for the battle of Armageddon, there is very little prophecy left to go before Jesus returns. So, within this generation, Ephraim, for the first time in that 2800 years, will again be united with Judah, or that Scripture will not have time be fulfilled. They better hurry up and find out who each other are, don't you think?

To help us in our identification, let's look at a prophet who came after the Babylonian captivity. Zechariah prophesied in 518BC, while the 2nd temple was being built. Zechariah is truly mysterious, and few claim to understand him very well. Much of that book relates to the Lord's birth and earthly ministry, but part of it is about the time of the end. When it was written, the ten tribes had been lost for over 200 years:

> ZEC 9:13-14 **When I have bent Judah for me, filled the bow with Ephraim, and raised up thy sons, O Zion, against thy sons, O Greece**, and made thee as the sword of a mighty man. And the LORD shall be seen over them, and his arrow shall go forth as the lightning: and **the Lord GOD shall blow the trumpet,** and shall go with whirlwinds of the south.

Unbelievable! The tribe of Ephraim has been lost for 200 years, and the Lord is still talking about it. But this time He tells us that when they are united with Judah there will be a war. Here is more pictorial language. Judah is seen as a bow of war, and Ephraim as the arrows.[52] So Judah and Ephraim will be allies. Knowing what we now know about trumpets, any time one is sounded next to a Scripture about regathering Israel and a war, we need to sit up and take notice. This trumpet of ZEC 13:14 is probably the sixth trumpet of REV 9:13 through REV 11:15. That's Armageddon! Note that Israel and Judah are fighting the "sons" of Greece. The Greek empire

---

[52] Though ZEC 9:13 was written in 518BC, it cannot be referring to the Maccabean wars of 165BC. Ephraim and Judah were not united during those conflicts. Only the Jews were involved. James recognized that the twelve tribes were scattered abroad during apostolic times, JAS 1:1.

spread over the whole known world from 332BC to 65BC. Lebanon, Iraq, Iran, and Syria are those "sons" in a very real sense. That is the home of the Shiite Moslems. So this is a different view of those radical Moslem powers, and the Bible points to that historic arch enemy of Israel and the church. Now let's tie it all together...

# Chapter 16

# *A People Found*

There is a third "time, times and half a time" in the Bible. It is recorded in REV 12:14, and this one is probably the most remarkable prophecy of the three. REV 12 is about the woman with 12 stars. That prophecy of the woman in the wilderness took us from 688AD, to the new Israel in 1948AD. Then in v.9, Satan is cast to the Earth, and his angels with him. In v.12, he knows his time is short and he goes forth with great fury to destroy. Indeed, when did the major spiritual troubles start within the church and out in the world? 1948! So that all fits. But suddenly there is a abrupt change of pace, and a change of subject:

> REV 12:14  And to the woman (Israel) were given two wings of a great eagle, **that she might fly into the wilderness, into her place, where she is nourished for a time, and times, and half a time,** from the face of the serpent.

We know that this woman is Israel from REV 12:1-5. But now we are in Revelation, and in Revelation the Lord speaks of Israel as all 12 tribes. That is clear from REV 7:4-8. We know where Judah and Benjamin are. They are the Jews, but where are the rest? Where are the ten tribes who were lost during the invasion of the Assyrian king, Shalmaneser in 725-722BC. The Bible records that incident in 2KI 17:3-6.

The two "time, times and half a time" in Daniel were 2500 years. So unless we find a solid scriptural reason to deny it, this time, times, and half a time should be 2500 years, too. This 2500 years cannot be in the future, either. LUK 21:24-32 tells us that there isn't that much time left. So again we have to run this time slot up and down history to see where it fits.

Now, the last we heard of the ten tribes was when they were taken captive into Assyria. Samaria, the capital of Israel, did not fall until 722BC. But the major captivity took place about two years earlier in 724BC. Hosea tells us "Ephraim is mixed with the nations," and his book was written before the fall of Samaria. Could this be when this "time, times and half a time" began?

### 2500 - 724BC = 1776AD...The United States becomes a nation!!!

For years people have been looking for the United States in prophecy. Now that we have found some solid evidence that this nation contains the ten lost tribes of Israel, do you suppose anyone will believe it? Probably not. We would rather hang in there with the Seven Year tribulation view for which there is NO evidence at all. But, unless we can think of some other incident of major significance that took place on or near 1776, the United States becoming a nation is probably it. That makes America and the United States the fruitful land where the Lord hid Ephraim.[53] *(Chart No.19)*

Read Hosea carefully and hear what the Lord is saying. The author paraphrases: "My people Israel have turned away from Me, but I won't give up on them. My Son will die on the Cross in 700 years. Through My Spirit, I will lead them unto Him. They won't know they are My people. But I will save them anyway for My great Name's sake, and because of My covenants with Abraham, Isaac, and Jacob." Here is the New Testament verse to prove it:

---

[53] The author does not believe that all Americans are the descendants of Israel. They were mixed in with gentile immigrants. However, they probably represented a major portion of the original settlers. The author further realizes that the evidence for the identification of Ephraim is not as strong as that for the day=years and last trumpet. He might even be thought to be out on a limb here. Because of the contents of some of the preceding chapters, there will be many eager to saw that limb off. Nevertheless, the evidence for identifying Ephraim with the US is strong enough to warrant presenting to the church. As stated earlier, this whole book is an empirical argument. One brick of the wall might be questioned for its soundness, but the whole wall is not so easy to tear down.

ROM 11:25-27 (excerpts) ...blindness in part is happened to Israel, **until the fulness of the Gentiles be come in. And so all Israel shall be saved...**

There shall come out of Sion the Deliverer, and shall turn away ungodliness from Jacob: For this is my covenant unto them, when I shall take away their sins.

Why does the fullness of the Gentiles have to come in for all Israel to be saved? Because the lost tribes are mixed in with the Gentiles. We read that in HOS 7:8. How could God sort them out and keep His covenant with Abraham? Only by leading them to Jesus, and hiding them in the Church. There may be other peoples in the Gentile Church besides the physical seed of Israel. But rest assured that all of the physical seed of Israel are in the church. How do we know? Because God says that all Israel will be saved! If that is not true, we better tear ROM 11:25-27 out of our Bibles, because that is what it says.

ROM 11:27 goes on to say that God made this covenant with the children of Israel. A covenant they didn't even know about. That a deliverer (Jesus) was going to save them. Believe it or not, many would like to spiritualize ROM 11:25-29, and claim this is only about the church. But they have a logical paradox there is no avoiding. In Romans 11:25-29 a definite distinction is made between Israel and the church:

ROM 11:25 For I would not, brethren, that ye should be ignorant of this mystery, lest ye should be wise in your own conceits; that **blindness in part is happened to Israel,** (one group) **until the fulness of the Gentiles** (another group) **be come in.**

ROM 11:28-29 **As concerning the gospel, they** (the first group) **are enemies for your** (the second group) **sakes: but as touching the election, they are beloved for the fathers' sakes.** For the gifts and calling of God are without repentance.

In the verses above we see two personal pronouns, "they," and "your." Language is meant to communicate. It is contrary to the rules of language to call "we," and "them," one group. Secondly, who are these people that are enemies of the gospel for our sakes, (the gentile church's sake) and yet are still elect for the sake of the fathers? Who are the fathers? Are they not the patriarchs of the children of Israel, and are not the "they" their physical descendants? The author understood Israel from this perspective for years before he had the courage to teach it. He did not want to pay the price in lost friends and fellowships that he knew it would cost. That is OK, just so he doesn't displease the Lord.

In Romans 11:25 the Jews and gentiles are addressed as two separate entities. So Romans 11:25-29 is about an Israel separate from the Gentile Church!

How the ten lost tribes of Israel migrated to Europe is a story recorded by others. But however well analyzed, this secular evidence is not conclusive.[54] Suffice to say that the heraldic symbols used by the great houses of Europe have their roots in the titles Jacob gave his children. If you question that, ask any authority on heraldry. Those coats of arms which people so proudly hang on their walls are straight out of GEN 49:1-27.

God's true servants have not always been the rulers in the land. Throughout the whole Christian Era the true saints of God were hounded all over Europe. The chronicles of the oppression of the middle ages have to be read to be believed. "Fox's Book of Martyrs," the Mennonite record in "Martyr's Mirror," and Broadbent's "The Pilgrim Church" record the sufferings of our forefathers in detail. The true Christians had no settled home, and their very lives were continually at stake. They wandered from place to place or were in hiding from persecution. The valley of Achor in the middle ages. The Lord told us it would be like that:

> HEB 13:13-14 Let us go forth therefore unto him without the camp, bearing his reproach. **For here have we no continuing city, but we seek one to come.**

---

[54] To avoid any suggestion that the author is using material which is conjectural or lacks red-letter accreditation, only common historic knowledge and the Bible itself were used to support the conclusions in this chapter.

Then they cried unto the Lord. The Lord hid them from their persecutors and planted them in a very pleasant land. It was rich and fruitful, and flowing with milk and honey. The New World was such a land, and the United States was founded by Christians fleeing religious persecution. God also told us exactly how that was going to happen:

> REV 12:15-17 And the serpent cast out of his mouth water as a flood after the woman, that he might cause her to be carried away of the flood. And the earth helped the woman, and the earth opened her mouth, and swallowed up the flood which the dragon cast out of his mouth. And the dragon was wroth with the woman, and went to make war with the remnant of her seed, which keep the commandments of God, and have the testimony of Jesus Christ.

In these verses in REV 12 following the time, times, and half a time, we read that Satan was going to try to destroy Israel, and the Church, with a flood of people. REV 17:15 defines "waters" as peoples, and tongues, and nations. But the Lord separated them from their enemies by the Atlantic Ocean. This country grew and prospered and became the hub of the western world. West, West, where have I heard that before:

> HOS 11:10-11 (excerpts) They shall walk after the LORD...**then the children shall tremble from the west**...and I will place them in their houses, saith the LORD.

This hemisphere is as far West as you can get. Go any further and it is called the Far East.

Then, like the Levites, the church is called to be priests and to come out from the world, 2CO 6:14-18, 1PE 2:5-9, REV 1:6, REV 5:10. God called Levi to be directly in the Lord's service. As priests, they were separated from the rest of the people. God even gave them special cities to live in:

> NUM 35:7 So all the cities which ye shall give to the Levites shall be **forty and eight cities:** them shall ye give with their suburbs.

The Levites had 48 cities, we had 48 states. It was not until after that pivotal year of 1948 that other states were added.  We too began to mix ourselves with the nations.  Also, it was after that year that the United States lost its influence as the Christian lighthouse of the world.

Occasional coincidences happen.  But is all this just random chance which by some fluke just happens to fit the Bible?  That is hard to swallow, even for a wide eyed tourist like me.  Here is another couple of "coincidences" of interest.

(1) The Lord Gave Abraham the covenant of circumcision.  Until the last decade, babies were routinely circumcised in the United States.  This was the only nation on Earth, besides Israel, to do so.  Why us?  There is no sound medical reason for this practice.

(2) The United States was the first nation to have a five day work week, thus observing the sabbath as well as Sunday.

(3) Though Jacob had only 12 sons, Joseph's two sons actually became two tribes.  Counting Ephraim and Manasseh, there were then thirteen tribes.  In America there were only 12 colonies, but the Carolinas were too large to govern in horse and buggy days.  So the Carolinas were split into two states, North and South Carolina.  Result: As Israel's twelve sons became thirteen tribes, so our twelve colonies became thirteen states.

But that was long ago.  Since then we have fought a half dozen foreign wars.  Bringing our "children forth for slaughter," as Hosea foretold.  We have become rich and complacent.  Then in 1948 this country began its slide into apostasy.  Now there are witches covens and Satan worshippers in every major city in America, and immorality and drug abuse is epidemic.  1948 is also when major spiritual problems began in the rest of the world.  It was after then that false religions and satanism increased in Europe and England.  It was after that year that violence broke out in places so remote that we had never even heard of them before.  People all over the globe who had been peaceful for centuries suddenly became almost ungovernable. Revelation's final beast, the Leopard-Bear-Lion, has come back to life, and the middle east has been set on fire.[55]  Is 1948 an important date?  In that year the new nation of Israel came into being, and the time of the two witnesses ended.  Are we up to the task ahead?  No.  Nonetheless, the Lord will take this stick of Ephraim and unite it with Judah for the final days.  This verse was quoted before, but now our eyes can be opened to understand it:

> EZE 37:19   Say unto them, Thus saith the Lord GOD; Behold, I will take the stick of Joseph, which is in the hand of Ephraim, and the tribes of Israel his fellows, and will put them with him, even with the stick of Judah, **and make them one stick, and they shall be one in mine hand.**

That verse tells us that Judah will have only one ally. Ephraim!  We know Judah is the Jews, now back in the Holy Land.  The United States is the only ally Israel presently has. So we are the only candidate in the world for the job.  We win the title of Ephraim by default.  Black man, white or oriental, if you are a Christian and in the United States, you are my brother, and are probably a physical descendant of Abraham. Now that's really exciting!

But our traditions blind us.  We laugh and point our fingers at the blindness of the Pharisees of Jesus' time, and we are no better ourselves.  As it was with them, so it is with us:

> JOH 12:40   He hath blinded their eyes, and hardened their heart; that they should not see with their eyes, nor understand with their heart, and be converted, and I should heal them.

It is not because of our military might that this nation has never lost a war.  It is because we trusted in the Lord our God. But our future is not so rosy.  From Isaiah to Revelation, the trouble ahead is spelled out in great detail.  If the Lord does not intervene we will probably be totally destroyed, and here is why.

---

[55] Through the rest of the book, the initials LBL are used for the Leopard-Bear-Lion Beast when he is referred to more than once in a single paragraph.

We have as much armed might as any nation on Earth. Our technology is unsurpassed. Our computer aided tactics are a wonder to behold. Our atomic stockpile is large enough to blow any potential enemy back to the stone age. Our missiles are so accurate that we can drop one into a teacup eight thousand miles away...but...but...

> PSA 127:1 Except the LORD build the house, they labor in vain that build it: **except the LORD keep the city, the watchman waketh but in vain.**

The condition of the church and the nation has already been voiced so clearly that it needs no repetition. We have turned away from the Lord of Glory. This final conflict will not be won by our might, nor by military power, but by Jesus standing on Mount Zion...

From the context of the Ezekiel verse quoted above, it is apparent that God will wield the stick of Ephraim and Judah in this last of all wars. The next question has to be...who will God wield this stick against? We will go into that at length in Book 3.

# Chapter 17

# *The Stepladder Effect*

In the chapter entitled "Mystery's End," we saw that the last trumpet blew in REV 11:15. That last trumpet is the end of all things, so what do we do with the rest of Revelation? If everything ends in REV 11:15, what do we do with chapters 12 through 22? The answer is hidden in Hebrew poetry.

If you are not interested in learning how Hebrew poetry works, skip to book three, and refer back to these chapters as you need to. They are a bit technical, but these concepts are too important to leave out. Some of the prophetic conclusions we come to later on, are proven by holding them up against Hebrew poetic forms. Hebrew poetry is parallel in nature. A Hebrew poet says something, then he says it again in different words. All Bible poetry, and many major prophecies, were written in this repetitive way. This repetition can be a sentence, a paragraph, or even several chapters long.

Just as the four gospels gave four views of the life of Jesus; so there are duplicate prophecies which give us different views of the same event. The same prophetic story told in different words.

But, how can we spot a repeat when we see one? By recognizing Hebrew poetic structure when we read it. There are only two styles which are prophetically significant, the Bifid, and the Chiasm.

The most elegant of the Old Testament prophets is Isaiah. He wrote in exquisite classical Hebrew. His poetic form is unsurpassed. Right away we spot something unusual. Isaiah is divided into two almost equal parts, and is repetitive.[56]

---

[56] The liberals see this division and like to claim that the last half of Isaiah was not written by Isaiah at all. Missing no chance to discredit the Scripture if they possibly can, in their "higher criticism" they willfully disregard well known Hebrew poetic forms, and invent a shadow author they call deutero-Isaiah. There is no historic basis for their contention. The Jewish Rabbis have always attributed the whole book of Isaiah to Isaiah.

Isaiah 1 through 33 is parallel to Isaiah 34 through 66, not just in a general way but in actual content:[57]

| 1st Half<br>Chapters | Content | 2nd Half<br>Chapters |
|---|---|---|
| 1-5 | Ruin and Restoration | 34-35 |
| 6-8 | Biographical Information | 36-40 |
| 9-12 | Blessings and Judgments | 41-45 |
| 13-23 | About Gentile Nations | 46-48 |
| 24-27 | Redemption and Deliverance | 49-55 |
| 28-31 | Ethics and Sermons | 56-59 |
| 32-33 | Restoration of Israel | 60-66 |

Scholars call this the "bifidic" form. The definition of Bifid is to split or divide into two halves or hemispheres. The last half of Isaiah contains a different description of the same subjects that are covered in the first half. This bifidic structure is not always as clear as it is in Isaiah, but in Daniel it stands out like a sore thumb. Daniel was written in two languages. DAN 2:4 through DAN 7:28 is in High Syriac (early Aramaic), while DAN 8:1 through 12:13 is in Hebrew.

Why two languages? Besides proving that the book is in two sections (bifidic), this is because The Lord always speaks to a people in their own language. In Daniel, God is addressing two different audiences, the Gentile nations and the Jewish people. God is telling them both about the time of the Gentiles. The first half of Daniel is to and about the Gentiles, the second half to and about the Jews. So the first and last halves of Daniel are parallel, and are about the same Gentile times!

Now we notice a kind of sub-parallel, in three steps, within the first half of Daniel, the half which is to the Gentile nations:

---

[57] Packer-Tenny-White, *The Bible Almanac*, 1980, p349.

| DAN 2<br>DAN 7 | Both chapters are about the Gentile empires which are to rule in the Holy land during the time of the Gentiles. |
|---|---|
| DAN 3<br>DAN 6 | Both chapters are about God's people in tribulation. |
| DAN 4<br>DAN 5 | Both chapters are about judgment on Gentile rulers. |

Daniel 2 and Daniel 7 are parallel, 3 and 6 are parallel, and 4 and 5 are parallel. A kind of poetic stepladder. This isn't exactly like the bifid, so this must be another poetic form in operation here. Maybe Isaiah will again come to our aid. Isaiah 55:8 is a verse we all know, which says something in an unusual repetitive way:

ISA 55:8 **For my thoughts are not your thoughts, neither are your ways my ways, saith the LORD.**

If we were to say that in normal English, we would say, "Your ways and thoughts, are not like my ways and thoughts." But in this Hebrew poetic form it is My-your=your-My, for a stepladder like this:

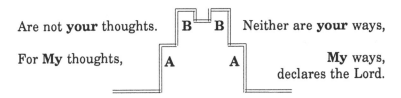

Are not **your** thoughts.   **B** — **B**   Neither are **your** ways,

For **My** thoughts,   **A**   **A**   **My** ways, declares the Lord.

This **AB=BA** stepladder is called a Chiasm.[58] Sometimes a chiasm can have more steps. It can be **ABC=CBA** or even **ABCD=DCBA.** Pronounced kee-ah-zum, chiasms appear in Scripture all the way from Genesis to Revelation. What the author declares in the steps going up, He repeats in the steps going down. Here are a couple of more examples. They have

---

[58] Packer-Tenny-White, *The Bible Almanac*, 1980, p364.

been shortened, and the central words have been bold faced for
clarity.  The full text can be found in your Bible:

> PSA 68:15-16   **(A)** The **hill of God** is as the hill of
> Bashan;
>        **(B)** an **high hill** as the hill of Bashan.
>        **(B)** Why leap ye, ye **high hills?**
>        **(A)** this is the **hill which God desireth**
> to dwell...

> MAR 5:3-5   **(A)** Who had his dwelling **among the
> tombs;**
>        **(B)** and **no man could bind him,**
>        **(C)** no, not **with chains:**
>        **(C)** he had been bound **with chains,**
>        **(B) neither could any man tame him.**
>        **(A)** And always he was **in the tombs...**

Now here is the point: In the above **AB=BA** chiasm there
are not four concepts, but two concepts about the same subject,
and they are repeated in different words.  In the **ABC=CBA**
chiasm there are not six concepts, but three concepts about the
same condition, and they are repeated in different words.

If Daniel and Revelation are chiasmic, they should be
understood to contain prophecies which are parallel.  Daniel
would be 10 parallel prophecies, about the time of the Gentiles,
stated in different ways.  Revelation, would be 12 parallel
prophecies, about the Christian Era, stated in different ways.
Let's first overlay Daniel, and then Revelation, with this little
hypothesis, and see if it fits.

### Stepladder in Daniel

In Daniel 12:4 God commanded the prophet to seal the
book.  Then five verses later, Daniel 12:9, God states that the
book was sealed.  Now Daniel was a very saintly man who did
what he was told.  So after DAN 12:4 was written, but before
DAN 12:9 was written, Daniel must have done something to
seal his prophecies.  He could not change the content of the
visions he had seen, nor change the historic incidents he had

written about; so he must have done something else. The question is, what?

Daniel scrambled his prophecies. He put them out of chronological order. Chapter 5 was actually written after Chapter 8, and Chapter 6 was actually written after Chapter 9.[59] This is easy enough to prove, because Daniel dated most of the episodes. In this shuffling of the visions, the book of Daniel was sealed until our Sovereign God wanted it opened. Now let's find out how. Look at the graph of the chapters in the order they now appear. The chapters with the star are the ones that are out of place:

|  |  | Prophecy | Subject |
|---|---|---|---|
| **(A)** | ch.2 | The Great Image | 4 Gentile Nations |
| **(B)** | ch.3 | The Fiery Furnace | God's People in Tribulation |
| **(C)** | ch.4 | Nebuchadnezzar Insane | Gentile King Judged |
| **(C)** | * ch.5 | Belshazzar Killed | Gentile King Judged |
| **(B)** | * ch.6 | The Lions Den | God's People in Tribulation |
| **(A)** | ch.7 | The Four Beasts | 4 Gentile Nations |
|  | ch.8 |  |  |

**\* ch.5 was actually written here**

ch.9

**\* ch.6 was actually written here**

ch.10

Chapter 5 was actually written after Chapter 8, and Chapter 6 was written after Chapter 9. Look at the subject column on the right. In their new order the subjects of each

---

[59] The dating of ch.5 after ch.7 is stated in text. The dating of ch.6 after ch.9 is determined by the address form Daniel used when a new king ascended to the throne of Babylon. Both ch.6 and ch.9 were written in the 1st year of Darius, In ch.9 the correct introductory form for Darius is used, while it is omitted in ch.6. Daniel was a master of court protocol, it is unlikely that he would have ignored it here.

As an aside, the Lord has not permitted the author to fathom what the book means when it is put back into it's correct chronological order. However he senses that there is a message there for someone.

chapter form a three step chiasm! Do you see it? Isn't that great. If Daniel had not put his book out of order, there would be no **ABC-CBA** chiasm here.

Something as complex as this chiasm didn't happen by accident. It was deliberate, and chiasms are repetitive. So, the Lord did this to give us a proof positive clue that Daniel is a series of repetitive prophecies. When viewed in its entirety the Message of Daniel's 1st chiasm is:

> **During the time of the gentiles there will be four major empires** (and their descendants) **who will rule in the Holy Land. Also, during that time, Gods people will suffer great persecution. But at the end, God will judge those nations which have made His land a desolation, and made captives of His people.**

Now let's go into a little detail. There are two kinds of reports in Daniel: visions and historic incidents. The question arises, what are these historic incidents doing in an apocalyptic book? The prophecies of the Gentile kingdoms in DAN 2 and 7 are straightforward enough, and easy to understand; but can the historic incidents also have prophetic meaning? Most of us don't think overly long on the fiery furnace, or the lions den; but they are also prophecies of the time of the Gentiles, **in symbolic language!** Now in the Christian Era, with Daniel fulfilled, we can walk up and down the chiasmic stepladder to see the messages of both types of prophecy.

**(A) Four Kingdoms:** DAN 2, DAN 7. Straight allegories: the Great Image, and the Four Beasts. During the time of the Gentiles there would be only four major empires (and their descendants) who would rule in the Holy Land. History bears this out. After the fall of Judah, there was Babylon, Medo-Persia, Greece, and then Rome who ruled in the Holy land. Since those four, there have been no great world empires ruling there; but the descendants of those domains continued to rule Jerusalem until 1948AD. These kingdoms will be discussed in detail in a later chapter. *(Charts No.21 and 22 at the end of Book 3)*

**(B) Tribulation:** DAN 3, DAN 6. Symbolic Incidents: The Fiery Furnace, and the Lions Den. Throughout the time of the

Gentiles, God's chosen people would suffer great tribulation; but if they continued to stand in the Lord, He would deliver them. Does anyone question the almost continuous persecution of world Jewry during the time of the Gentiles? Yet they are still here, just as the Lord said they would be.

Now let's look at the symbolic message hidden in the account of Daniel in the lion's den, DAN 6. Daniel was in captivity to Babylon for most of his life. Though God blessed him there, he was still a captive in a godless empire. At close to the end of his life, some of the rulers of the land accused him to Darius the King about his worship of God. Because of the unchangeable laws of the Medes and Persians, even though Darius did not want to, he had to throw Daniel to the lions. The Lord protected Daniel, and shut the mouths of the lions. Next morning the king took Daniel up out of the lions den, and threw his accusers in.

The interpretation: Throughout the time of the Gentiles, God's people have been in a godless world. Like the laws of the Medes and Persians, God's laws are unchangeable. When we are in disobedience, Satan accuses the brethren before the Lord. Because of His unchangeable law, God has to allow tribulation to fall on us; we go through a famine, or persecution, or war, or a Holocaust. But if we rely on Him, the Lord protects us through it all. Exactly like Darius, at the end of it all, the Lord gives orders for us to be "taken up" out of our trials; and the "accuser of the brethren is cast down." That is exactly what has happened to the brethren since the time of Daniel, but at the end, Jesus will cry, "Come out, and come up here, ye servants of the Most High God." Isn't that one of the most blessed of the hidden truths in Daniel?

(C) **Judgment:** DAN 4, DAN 5. Symbolic Incidents: Nebuchadnezzar goes insane, and Belshazzar's Feast. At the end of the time of Gentile rule, God will judge those nations who have persecuted His people, and made His land a desolation, DAN 2:35. Babylon symbolizes all the economies of this world, REV 18:24. Nebuchadnezzar represents the leaders of great kingdoms of the known world. Belshazzar ruled for a short time at the end of the Babylonian Empire, and he represents the final rulers of this world. There were great kingdoms before the Cross, and they rejected the witness of the Jews (Nebuchadnezzar goes insane). Then the world recognized the God of heaven, and Christianity became the faith of the whole known world. Like Nebuchadnezzar after his repentance, surpassing glory was added to the Western Christian Nations. Then, these nations also turned away from the Lord. As in Babylon with Belshazzar, we have the Word of God (the handwriting on the wall), and the witness of the saints (the candlestick, REV 1:19), yet the nations again blaspheme God, and turn away from all knowledge of Him. Now is as the time of Belshazzar. It is the end of Babylon, and Belshazzar dies. Thus the kingdoms of this earth go to final Judgment. In our own time, the ungodly will have no reprieve. Armageddon, the Judgment Seat of Christ, and the second death.

Have you read anything like this in any book written before the time of the Gentiles ended in 1967? Not very likely. These insights were not available to us before then. We just learned about chiasms in the last few years. That is one of the ways Daniel was sealed until the time of the end. This 1st chiasm was primarily to and about Gentile nations, but the second one is about what has happened to God's people over the 2500 years since the Babylonian Empire. This second chiasm is an **AB=BA**. It's central message is:

**After the Jews returned from captivity, there will be two major empires (and their descendants) who will rule in the Holy Land into the very distant future. During that time Messiah will come, be killed; and the temple will be desolated.**

The DAN 8 through 12 chiasm begins with (**A**) the vision of the Ram and the He Goat, DAN 8. This vision tells us of Medo-Persia and Greece. This Ram and He Goat is fulfilled in part before the Cross, but it also contains information about the ultimate time of the end, DAN 8:17,19,23. A different vision about Medo-Persia and Greece is given in the last (**A**) as the kings of the North and South, DAN 10-12. They are parallel to each other. First let's look at a graph of this chiasm, and then we will discuss it:

|  | Prophecy | Subject |
|---|---|---|
| **(A)** ch.8 | Ram and He Goat | 2 Gentile Powers |
| **(B)** ch.9:24-26 | 69 Sevens | Messiah dies in Time of the Gentiles |
| **(B)** ch.9:26-27 | 70th Seven | The Time of the Gentiles |
| **(A)** ch.10-12 | North & South | 2 Gentile Powers |

**(A) Two Gentile Powers:** DAN 8, DAN 10-12. Except for the time of Roman rulership, Jerusalem and the Holy Land have been under the influence of the Medo-Persian and Greek Empires, their Moslem descendants, and the satanic princes of those countries. These princes have controlled the governments of the Holy Land from Daniel's time until 1967. Here is the Scripture to back that up:

> DAN 10:20 ...now will I return to fight with the **prince of Persia**: and when I am gone forth, lo, the **prince of Grecia** shall come.

> DAN 8:17,19 (excerpts) Understand, O son of man: for **at the time of the end shall be the vision**...Behold, **I will make thee know what shall be in the last end of the indignation:** for at the time appointed the end shall be.

DAN 8:17-19 informs us that the latter half of this vision of the Ram and the He Goat is a vision of the very end, and DAN 10:20 tells us who is behind the scenes. The angelic being who was speaking to Daniel was not battling some mere mortal. As we discussed earlier, these are satanic princes! At the very end of time, out of the area controlled by those princes, a little horn (ruler) will come who will lead the enemy's forces at Armageddon, but he will be brought to ultimate defeat when Messiah returns.[60]

---

[60] Many try to identify the little horn of DAN 8:9-11 and 8:23-25 as Antiochus Epiphanies, the Greek king who desecrated the temple in 165BC. The problem with that interpretation is that 165BC was not "the time of the end" v.17, or "the appointed time of the end" v.19. Scripture declares this to be an end time vision, and to date it remains unfulfilled.

"Finally," you say, "there is your antichrist, I knew there was one all along." Not at all. This will be another **political and military leader**, but now he will be from the Middle East. We did not recognize Adolf Hitler as the little horn of DAN 7 (more on Hitler later). What makes us think we will recognize the little horn of DAN 8 when he appears? He could be Arafat the Palestinian, Hussein of Iraq, Libya's Maummwar Khadaffy, one of those crazy mullahs from Iran. He could even be someone acting behind the scenes that we don't think is very important, like the hidden Ali Akbar Mohatashimi, secret leader of the terrorists:

> DAN 8:9-11 And **out of one of them came forth a little horn,** which waxed exceeding great, toward the south, and toward the east, and toward the pleasant land. And it waxed great, even to the host of heaven; and it cast down some of the host and of the stars to the ground, and stamped upon them.

> DAN 8:23-25 And **in the latter time of their kingdom, when the transgressors come to the full,** a king of fierce countenance, and understanding dark sentences, shall stand up. And **his power shall be mighty, but not by his own power:** and he shall destroy wonderfully, and shall prosper, and practice, and shall destroy the mighty and the holy people. And through his policy also he shall cause craft to prosper in his hand; and he shall magnify himself in his heart, and **by peace shall destroy many:** he shall also stand up against the Prince of princes; but he shall be broken without hand.

This is the vision of the end, and this little horn does not come out of the Roman Empire, but out of the lands once ruled by Greece. The Grecian Empire of Alexander the Great covered the whole Near East. Notice that this final ruler is going to use peace talks to put people off their guard. Sound familiar? Read today's newspaper.

There is so much Scripture for the location and behavior of the final enemy that it is difficult to avoid duplication. All end time prophecy points to these countries. The final enemy of God's people will come from the Mohammedan world. Note at the very end that it won't be our weaponry, but the Prince of princes who will defeat him.[61]

**(B) Messiah and Gentile Times:** DAN 9:1-25, DAN 9:26-27 Straight allegory. The 69 Weeks, and the 70th Week. Hear Oh Israel, Messiah is coming. He is coming during the time of Gentile control of Jerusalem. Why? Because He is the Savior who died for the sins of the whole world, Jew and Gentile alike, 1JO 2:2. This is the cardinal message of the 2nd chiasm. The Cross of Jesus at the end of the 69 Sevens is the central event of all creation. The Cross is the primary message to God's chosen people, and the whole world.

The 70th Seven tells the Jews that from 536BC, in the 1st year of Darius, until 1948AD, the land will be controlled by Gentiles for 2484 more years. In the middle of that time, the temple mount will be desecrated, but in the fullness of time, the Lord will restore the Holy People to their precious land. Then, soon after the Jews are restored, He will destroy the satanic beings who caused that desecration. Daniel does not tell us how much time will pass between the restoration of the land and the destruction of the enemy. Luke 21:24-32 states that it will not be longer than a generation.

Now that we understand the pattern, let's go to Revelation. The following chapter is not intended as a full exegesis of that book. It is only an outline and study guide, but it is a foundation which will help students of prophecy understand almost every verse. Some of the allegories are still sealed. The Lord has left them for others to unravel.

---

[61] Included in this prophecy is a time period of 2300 evenings and mornings, DAN 8:14. From Scripture and history we know that evenings and mornings are not days, and not times. The author confesses that he is not sure what they mean. The Lord has left that time period for someone else to decipher.

# Chapter 18

# *More Parallels*

In REV 5:1 God the Father holds a scroll sealed with seven seals. It is written on both sides. That was very unusual in the prophet John's time of 95AD. Most 1st Century scrolls were written on only one side. There must be a reason for this two sided scroll. Let's see if we can discover it:

> REV 5:1 And I saw in the right hand of him that sat on the throne **a book written within and on the backside**, sealed with seven seals.

> REV 5:5-6 (excerpts)...in the midst of the throne...and in the midst of the elders, stood a **Lamb as it had been slain, And he came and took the book** out of the right hand of him that sat upon the throne.

This "little book" is the book of Revelation itself. It was given to the Lord Jesus who then opened the Seven Seals, the Seven Trumpets, and the Two Witnesses. Before the Seventh Trumpet blows, the Lord tells us what He is going to do with the part of the book He has not read. In the verse quoted above the book was sealed, but in the verse below it is opened:

REV 10:1-2 And I saw another **mighty angel** come down from heaven, clothed with a cloud: and a rainbow was upon his head, and his face was as it were the sun, and his feet as pillars of fire: **And he had in his hand a little book open:** and he set his right foot upon the sea, and his left foot on the earth,

As used in Revelation, "angel" can refer to several different beings. He can be one of God's angelic messengers, or a fallen angel, or Satan, or a human messenger, or the Holy Spirit, or Jesus. Context reveals his identity. A careful reading of the description of the Lord Jesus in REV 1 and elsewhere, will show the angel of REV 10:1-2 is the Lord Jesus Himself. The Lord Jesus gives this little open book to John.

REV 10:10 **And I took the little book out of the angel's hand,** and ate it up; and it was in my mouth sweet as honey: and as soon as I had eaten it, my belly was bitter. **And he said unto me, Thou must prophesy again before many peoples, and nations, and tongues, and kings.**

Ahh...now that verse explains it all. The little book is now open because the Lord has broken all the seals. Then He tells John, "you must prophecy again!" In other words: Listen here John, turn this two sided book over and read the other side. Repeat in different words what has just been read in the Seven Seals and the Seven Trumpets. Isn't that delightful! It was written on both sides because the Lord willed to read one side, and John was to read the other. "Out of the mouth of two or three witnesses..." But prophecy to and about what? The verse itself tells us, about peoples, nations, languages and kings. So the second half of Revelation will cover those subjects.

The Seventh and last Trumpet blows in REV 11:15, which begins the eternal kingdom of God. If it is all over in REV 11, then chapters 12 through 20 must be a repeat of 1 through 11. So that is why the Lord told John, "You must prophecy again!" Plain as day, the Lord is telling us that John is going back to square one, and Revelation is bifidic!

If Revelation is like Daniel in other ways, we should also see a chiasm in both halves. Let's find the parallels: ch.2-3 are about churches, and now that we know who the Two Witnesses are, so is ch.11. Ch 6 is Seven Seals, and ch.8-9 is Seven Trumpets. The first half of ch.7 is the Jewish saints, the second half the Gentile saints. That is a perfect **ABC=CBA** chiasm:

|        |          | Prophecy | Subject |
|--------|----------|----------|---------|
| **(A)** | ch.2-3 | The Seven Churches | The Church |
| **(B)** | ch.6 | The Seven Seals | World Judged |
| **(C)** | ch.7:4-8 | The 144,000 | Old Testament Saints |
| **(C)** | ch.7:9-14 | The Great Multitude | New Testament Saints |
| **(B)** | ch.8-9 | The Seven Trumpets | World Judged |
| **(A)** | ch.11 | The Two Witnesses | The Church |

Just like in Daniel, in Revelation we can find the overall message of the book by understanding the central idea of the chiasm itself. Also, the 1st chiasm will be written to different people than the second. This first chiasm is spiritual in nature. It is totally allegorical and can only be understood by extensive cross referencing with other passages of Scripture which use the same language. It is primarily to the church. It is about the role of God's people in a rebellious world. The central message of this first chiasm is:

**During the Christian Era there will be Seven different church periods, and seven different kinds of churches. The Jews and the Church will be God's two witnesses on Earth. Trials, plagues, famines, tribulation and wars will take**

place. But the dead in Christ, both Jew and
Gentile, will be with the Lord. At the end, God
will set up His eternal kingdom

**(A) The Seven Churches and the Two Witnesses:** REV
2-3, REV 11. In the Seven Churches of REV 2-3, the Lord tells
us what the church will be like during the whole Christian Era,
sometimes good, sometimes fair, and sometimes bad. In REV
11, God has placed His Two Witnesses on the Earth to stand
against the enemy and preach the gospel. Throughout the
Christian Era the church will be in great tribulation, but it will
also be victorious. The record of the persecution of the church
in the Christian Era is unassailable. But, though mighty
empires have fallen around it, the true church of Jesus still
stands. The chart following shows how the Seven Churches of
REV 2-3 parallel church history in the Christian Era. At the
end of the time of the Two Witnesses, 1948, the Church and the
Jews will lose their spiritual power. Though there will always
be a faithful remnant, in the last days Jesus will spit the
lukewarm churches out of His mouth; and the enemy will
destroy them, REV 3:16 and REV 11:7. *(Chart No.20)*

**(B) The Seven Seals and the Seven Trumpets:** REV 6,
REV 8-9. During the Christian Era, God will pour out His
wrath upon the unbelievers. Because of His Two Witnesses, the
world will be without excuse. To bring the unsaved to repentance, many terrible things will happen. Anarchy, wars, famines
and natural disasters will abound, REV 6:1-8. At the end there
will be a mighty war with 200,000,000 horsemen fighting, REV
9:16. Not until this generation could we field armies of that
size. Remembering that Revelation is allegorical, in Chapter 27
we discuss these "horsemen" further. Man will hide in the caves
in the ground and under mountains. But he will not repent of
his rebellion, and his sorcery, and his idolatry, REV 9:20-21.

**(C) The 144,000 and the Great Multitude:** Central to it
all, are the redeemed. Those for whom the Lord shed His blood,
and reconciled to the Father, from this great tribulation. They
are the children of Israel REV 7:4-8, and the Gentile Church,
REV 7:9. The seal on the heads of the 144,000 is the name of
Jesus and God the Father, REV 14:1 NASB. The fifth seal, REV
6:9, describes these brethren who have gone on before. They are
clothed in white robes, which is the righteousness of Christ, and

stand beneath the Cross (the altar is a symbol of the Cross).
They do not cease to cry, "how long Oh Lord, how long..."

> REV 7:13-17  And one of the elders answered, saying unto
> me, What are these which are arrayed in white robes? and
> whence came they?  And I said unto him, Sir, thou knowest.
> And he said to me, These are they which came out of great
> tribulation, and have washed their robes, and made them white
> in the blood of the Lamb.  Therefore are they before the
> throne of God, and serve him day and night in his temple: and
> he that sitteth on the throne shall dwell among them.  For the
> Lamb which is in the midst of the throne shall feed them, and
> shall lead them unto living fountains of waters: and God shall
> wipe away all tears from their eyes.

Now that we understand the chiasmic pattern, the last half
of Revelation is very open; most of these later visions can be
related to world history.  It is not the author's intent to belabor
the chiasmic form, but it is one of the major tools to show that
Revelation is repetitive in an organized way.  That it contains
12 concurrent prophecies about the history of Israel, and the
Christian Era.  Remember in Daniel, how half of that book was
to Gentile nations, while the other half was to the Jews?
Though the audiences are different, the pattern in Revelation is
the same.  The central message of this 2nd chiasm is:

**There will be seven major kingdoms throughout
history.  They will be ruled by Satan.  Concurrent with those visible kingdoms, God will have
a spiritual kingdom on Earth composed of the
Jewish people and the Gentile church.  Then
Jesus will return to reward the saints and judge
the wicked.**

Earlier in this chapter, we saw that the first chiasm of
Revelation is to and about the church's spiritual role.  This
second chiasm is about kingdoms.  The Jews and the church are
the Lord's earthly kingdoms.  The beasts and Babylon are
within the satanic kingdom of the enemy.  Babylon centers on
the world economic system, while the beasts are governmental.

In fact the beasts are Satan himself, and he appears to us in two guises.

(1) As the Scarlet beast he is the embodiment of the sin which deceives the world.

(2) Through the Leopard-Bear-Lion he displays his control of the world's kingdoms, and his earthly throne.

Even Revelation's last two chapters are kingdom oriented. They are about the new heaven and the new Earth, and God's eternal kingdom.   This **AB=C=BA** structure is a little more complicated, but careful study will support it:

| | | | |
|---|---|---|---|
| **(A)** | ch.12 | Woman with 12 Stars | Israel |
| **(B)** | ch.13 | Leopard, Lion, Bear Beast | Satanic Kingdom |
| | ch.14 | 144,000 & The Gospel | The Saved Within It |
| | ch.15 | Song of Moses and Lamb | Victory for Redeemed |
| **(C)** | ch.16 | Bowls of Wrath | Wrath for the Wicked |
| **(B)** | ch.17 | Seven Headed Beast | Satanic Kindoms |
| | ch.18 | Babylon | Satanic System |
| | ch.19 | King of Kings | Destruction of Wicked |
| **(A)** | ch.20 | The Thousand Years | The Church |

Sometimes man's chapter breaks are in the wrong place, or don't belong in the passage at all. They can interfere with the flow of scripture. This last half of Revelation is an example. REV 13, 14, and 15 is all one continuing story. REV 17, 18, and 19 is another. As the reward for the saints stands alone in the middle of the 1st chiasm, REV 7:10-17;  so God's wrath on the kingdoms that have rejected His Son stands alone in the second, REV 16.

   **(A) Israel and the Church:** REV 12, REV 20.  Straight allegory.  The Woman with Twelve Stars, and the Reign of Christ.  Many take REV 20 literally, the so-called millennium, because it appears to use literal language. The last trumpet, the chiasm, and context, make that view very difficult to support. More probably, this is the whole body of Christ, all the redeemed, Old Testament and New. From the time of Moses, Israel has been the caretaker of the oracles of God, ROM 3:2. Israel was the line through whom the Savior of the world would come. After Jesus was glorified, Israel and the church (the spiritual kingdom over which the Lord now reigns, REV 20:4), would be persecuted, but not destroyed. Satan would be bound so as not to deceive the nations during the Christian Era, REV 20:2, MAT 12:29, JOH 12:31.[62] At the end of the Christian Era Satan would be released for a little season, REV 12:12-13 and 20:7. Jesus is the first and only resurrection. There is no other. Blessed indeed are those who have part in Him as born again believers. Over them the second death has no power, REV 20:6. In the culmination of all things on this present Earth, there is Armageddon, REV 12:17 and 20:7-9. Please notice how the account in REV 12 parallels REV 20, and that the many parallel verses indicate that they are about the same time and events.

**(B) The Beast with Seven Heads, and Leopard, Bear, Lion:** REV 13, REV 17. Straight allegory. Throughout all history there will be only seven major empires (and their descendants) who will rule in the Earth. They will be satanically empowered, REV 17:3, for they are in his domain, LUK 4:6. Out of the Middle East will come an empire that is the combination of three ancient ones, Babylon, Medo-Persia, and Greece. That geographic area is Iraq, Iran, and Syria, now the radical Shiite headquarters of the Mohammedan world. They are combined by a common religion, and a satanically inspired hatred of the church and Israel. They will always be at war with the spiritual kingdom of the Lord Jesus, REV 13:12 and 17:14.

**The 144,000, the Eternal Gospel and Babylon:** REV 14-15, REV 17-19. Straight allegories. All the servants of the Lord are compared with servants of the enemy. After the Cross, the

---

[62] The Greek word used for thousand here is "chilioi" (Strong's 5507). It is the indefinite plural form of the word for thousand,"chiliad." Consequently, though thousand is a correct translation, it can not be proven that this is only one thousand. Instead it is an indefinite number of thousands. Scripturally this time can refer to the Christian Era regardless of length.

Old Testament Saints sing about Jesus.[63]   For them it is a new song, REV 14:3. Then the eternal gospel is preached to the church, REV 14:6. The trials of the Christian Era are foretold, followed by the Lord coming in the clouds to reap the Earth of the saints, REV 14:14-16. In the Grapes of Wrath, more is told about Armageddon, REV 14:17-19. The battlefront will be 200 miles long, from Jerusalem northward.   Knowing that the prophecies in Revelation are parallel makes this a lot easier. The various little pieces at the end of each prophecy, about a great battle, are about the same great battle: Armageddon.

Mighty Babylon falls, REV 18. She is the haunt for every evil beast and bird and creeping thing. Who is she?

> REV 18:24  And **in her was found the blood of prophets, and of saints, and of all that were slain** upon the earth.

Since every death on Earth is attributed to her, from the prophets of the Old Testament to the saints of the church, Babylon is far broader than one single empire or city, no matter how great and long lasting.  Babylon is every unsaved and rebellious person, land, and empire, that has ever existed on Earth.   She began when Cain shed the blood of his brother Able, and will continue until the last Christian is bludgeoned to death in some dark and nameless dungeon.  Babylon means confusion. Satan is the author of confusion.  Babylon is Satan's world.  We have been commanded throughout Scripture to separate ourselves from her.  We haven't listened very well so the Lord reminds us here:

> REV 18:4-5  And I heard another voice from heaven, saying, **Come out of her, my people, that ye be not partakers of her sins, and that ye receive not of her plagues.**  For her sins have reached unto heaven, and God hath remembered her iniquities.

---

[63] That the 144,000 are the OT Israelites is provable by comparing their identification as "first fruits," REV 14:4 with JER 2:3 and other Scriptures.

Soon the light of the Word will be heard in her no more, nor the voice of Jesus our bridegroom, nor the witness of the church, the bride of Christ and Babylon will be no more...

> REV 18:23, 19:1 **And the light of a candle shall shine no more at all in thee; and the voice of the bridegroom and of the bride shall be heard no more at all in thee:** for thy merchants were the great men of the earth; for by thy sorceries were all nations deceived...
> And after these things I heard a great voice of much people in heaven, saying, Alleluia; Salvation, and glory, and honor, and power, unto the Lord our God:

**The Songs of Moses and the Lamb and the return of the King:** REV 19. Straight Allegory. In the return of Jesus and in the song of the redeemed, the Lord closes the doors on the great beasts of Revelation. For the world it is all over. As is true in the rest of Revelation, a dual address is made to distinguish between the Old Testament saints and the church. The song of Moses is sung by Israel, while glory to the Lamb is sung by the church.

**(C) The Seven Bowls:** REV 16. Straight allegory. The judgment of the bowls is a terrible intensification of the seven trumpets. The plagues are similar. The fifth bowl is directed at only one geographic location, the throne of the beast. Spiritual in nature, this bowl tells us of the spiritual darkness which now engulfs the Middle East, and that it will intensify. The only other threefold enemy of the Lord mentioned in Revelation is the Leopard-Bear-Lion beast, so these three unclean spirits (like frogs) are probably the satanic princes who spiritually control those lands. Though these spirits remained in the Mid-East throughout the Christian Era, now the black poison of Islam is spreading over the whole world. As is true of the other prophecies which tell us of man's final rebellion, this one also ends with Armageddon.

Here in Book 2 we have seen how the Lord planned the Christian Era. All along there have been two churches: the Jews and the Gentile church. The Lord has not forgotten His chosen people, the Jews; and through the Gentile church untold numbers of Ephraim have unknowingly returned to the Lord.

Through bifids and chiasms we understand that both Daniel and Revelation are repetitive in an organized way. Daniel contains 10 parallel prophecies about the time of gentile domination of the Holy Land. Since the time of the Gentiles was over in 1967AD, Daniel, for the most part, is fulfilled. Using the same bifidic and chiasmic style as Daniel, Revelation continues on where Daniel left off. With 12 parallel prophecies in two chiasms, Revelation reviews the Old Testament Era, and amplifies what Daniel told us about the time of the Gentiles. Then the Lord expounds on the satanically controlled empires of the world, and defines who the final enemies of his dual church will be. Revelation then closes with a brief description of the glorious eternal kingdom of God.

The author realizes that the last two chapters were the bearest of sketches, but he did not know how to fill in the blanks without losing the reader's interest. However, the beasts of REV 13 and 17 relate to our own time. In Book 3 we will study these beasts, and identify the final nations who will stand against the Lord.

# Chart No.12

## The Great Trumpet
### MAT 24:21,29,31

MAT 24:21 For then shall be **great tribulation**, such as was not since the **beginning of the world** to this time, no, nor ever shall be.

MAT 24:29 **Immediately after the tribulation** of those days shall the sun be darkened, and the moon shall not give her light, and the stars shall fall from heaven, and the powers of the heavens shall be shaken:

MAT 24:31 And he shall send his angels with a great sound of a trumpet, and **they shall gather together** his elect from the **four winds**, from one end of heaven to the other.

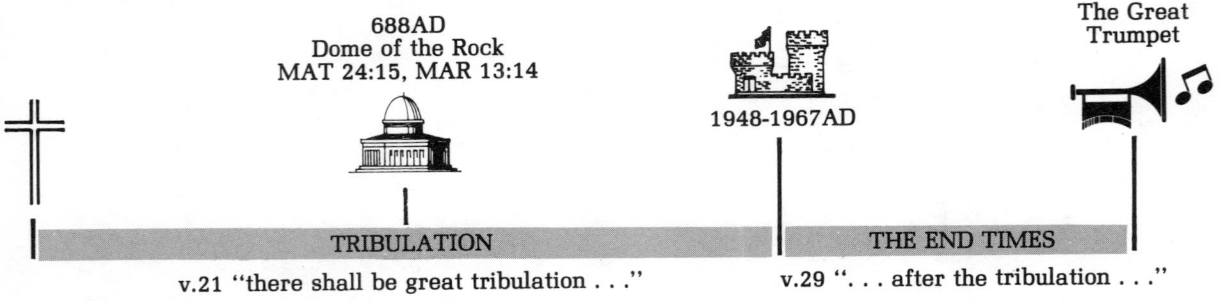

The Great
Trumpet

688AD
Dome of the Rock
MAT 24:15, MAR 13:14

1948-1967AD

TRIBULATION

THE END TIMES

v.21 "there shall be great tribulation . . ."

v.29 ". . . after the tribulation . . ."

NOTE: The Great Tribulation is foretold in v.21. A period after the tribulation is spoken of in v.29. The Great Trumpet sounds and the elect are gathered in v.31.

That "THE" tribulation started in the 1st Century is provable by Scripture. REV 1:9, "I John, who also am your brother, and companion in tribulation (**THE** tribulation, NASB and NIV), and in the kingdom and patience of Jesus Christ..." 37 times the Greek word for tribulation "thlipsis" is used in the New Testament. In all but one, thlipsis is addressed to the Christians! Tribulation is promised for the saints, JOH 16:33 and 2TI 3:12. Wrath is for the unsaved. Tribulation for the saints has continued unabated throughout the whole Christian Era.

## Chart No.13    Is the "Great Trumpet" the Last Trumpet?
### MAT 24:31, 1TH 4:16 and 1CO 15:52

1TH 4:16 For the Lord himself shall descend from heaven with a shout, with the voice of the archangel, and with **the trump of God:** and the dead in Christ shall rise first:

1CO 15:52 In a moment, in the twinkling of an eye, at **the last trump:** for the trumpet shall sound, and the dead shall be raised incorruptible, and we shall be changed.

MAT 24:31 And he shall send his angels with a **great sound of a trumpet,** (the sound of a Great Trumpet, NASB) and they shall gather together his elect from the four winds, from one end of heaven to the other.

Since our trumpet is the **LAST** trumpet All other trumpets must come before it!

The "Great Trumpet" of Mat 24:31 must either be our trumpet, or our trumpet would have to come after it!

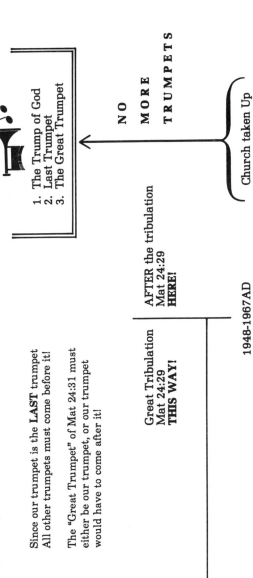

1. The Trump of God
2. Last Trumpet
3. The Great Trumpet

NO MORE TRUMPETS

Church taken Up

Great Tribulation
Mat 24:29
**THIS WAY!**

AFTER the tribulation
Mat 24:29
**HERE!**

1948-1967 AD

## Chart No.14

## The Last Trumpet
### 1CO 15:52, REV 10:6-7 and 11:15

1CO 15:52 In a moment, in the twinkling of an eye, **at the last trump:** for the trumpet shall sound, and the dead shall be raised incorruptible, and we shall be changed.

REV 10:6-7 ...that there **should be time no longer: But in the days of the voice of the seventh angel, when he shall begin to sound, the mystery of God should** be finished, as he hath declared to his servants the prophets.

REV 11:15 And the **seventh angel sounded;** and there were great voices in heaven, saying, **The kingdoms of this world are become the kingdoms of our Lord, and of his Christ; and he shall reign for ever and ever.**

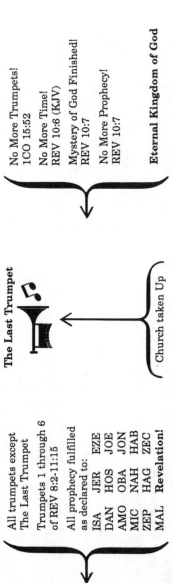

The Last Trumpet

All trumpets except
The Last Trumpet

Trumpets 1 through 6
of REV 8:2-11:15

All prophecy fulfilled
as declared to:

| | | |
|---|---|---|
| ISA | JER | EZE |
| DAN | HOS | JOE |
| AMO | OBA | JON |
| MIC | NAH | HAB |
| ZEP | HAG | ZEC |
| MAL | **Revelation!** | |

Church taken Up

No More Trumpets!
1CO 15:52

No More Time!
REV 10:6 (KJV)

Mystery of God Finished!
REV 10:7

No More Prophecy!
REV 10:7

**Eternal Kingdom of God**

NOTE: The addressee of 1CO 15:52 is "WE". So, the Last Trumpet is to us. It is not to "great tribulation" believers after the church is taken out.

Our trumpet is the **LAST** trumpet; therefore trumpets one through six of REV 8 through 11 must come before it. At the 7th trumpet, there is no more time, and the mystery of God is finished!

When the 7th trumpet sounds in REV 11:15, note that the Lord reigns for ever and ever. This signifies that the 7th Trumpet ushers in the eternal kingdom of God!

# Chart No.15

## The Two Witnesses
### REV 11:3-4, 1:20, ROM 11:24-25

REV 11:3-4 And I will give power unto my two witnesses, and they shall prophesy a thousand two hundred and threescore days, clothed in sackcloth. These are the two olive trees, and the two candlesticks standing before the God of the earth.

REV 1:20 The mystery of the seven stars which thou sawest in my right hand, and the seven golden candlesticks. The seven stars are the angels of the seven churches: and the seven candlesticks which thou sawest are the seven churches.

ROM 11:24-25 For if thou wert cut out of the olive tree which is wild by nature, and wert graffed contrary to nature into a good olive tree: how much more shall these, which be the natural branches, be graffed into their own olive tree? For I would not, brethren, that ye should be ignorant of this mystery, lest ye should be wise in your own conceits; that blindness in part is happened to Israel, until the fulness of the Gentiles be come in.

1. Two Witnesses for 1260 days (years)
2. Identified by the Bible as two candlesticks and two olive trees.
3. Rev.1:20 identified candlesticks as churches!
4. Rom.11:24-25 identifies olive trees as Jew and Gentile believers.

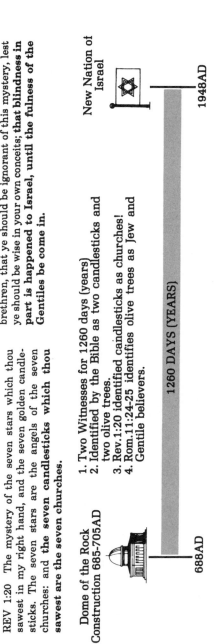

**Dome of the Rock Construction 685-705AD** — 688AD

**1260 DAYS (YEARS)**

**New Nation of Israel** — 1948AD

NOTE: The 1260 days started AFTER 688AD. Why? Before then both Jews and Gentiles could freely worship in Jerusalem. History shows that it was the home of the great Coptic Church. Only after the Mohammedan Jihad of the 7th Century were Christians and Jews prevented from worshipping on the old temple site.

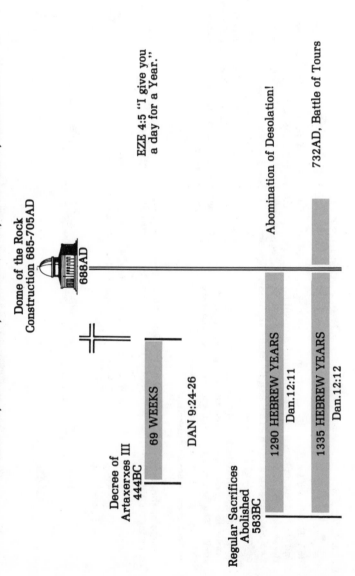

**Chart No.16**      Summary Of Prophetic Day Years
EZE 4:5, DAN 9:24-26, DAN 12:11-12, REV 11:2-4, REV 12:6

Dome of the Rock
Construction 685-705AD

688AD

EZE 4:5 "I give you
a day for a Year."

Abomination of Desolation!

732AD, Battle of Tours

Decree of
Artaxerxes III
444BC

69 WEEKS

DAN 9:24-26

Regular Sacrifices
Abolished
583BC

1290 HEBREW YEARS
Dan.12:11

1335 HEBREW YEARS
Dan.12:12

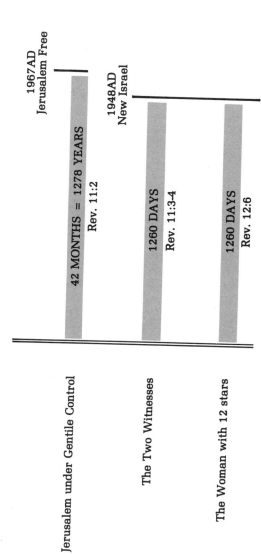

1967AD
Jerusalem Free

1948AD
New Israel

42 MONTHS = 1278 YEARS
Rev. 11:2

1260 DAYS
Rev. 11:3-4

1260 DAYS
Rev. 12:6

Jerusalem under Gentile Control

The Two Witnesses

The Woman with 12 stars

NOTE: Since God gave us the definition of a day for a year, it is counter to the Word to interpret prophetic days in any other way. To do so we would need Scriptural support rather than suppositional theology.

## Chart No.17

### Time, Times And Half A Time
### DAN 7:25, DAN 12:7, REV 12:14

DAN 7:25 And he shall speak great words against the most High, and shall wear out the saints of the most High...and they shall be given into his hand until a time and times and the dividing of time.

DAN 12:7 ...it shall be for a time, times, and an half; and when he shall have accomplished to scatter the power of the holy people, all these things shall be finished.

2PE 3:8 But, beloved, be not ignorant of this one thing, that one day is with the Lord as a thousand years, and a thousand years as one day.

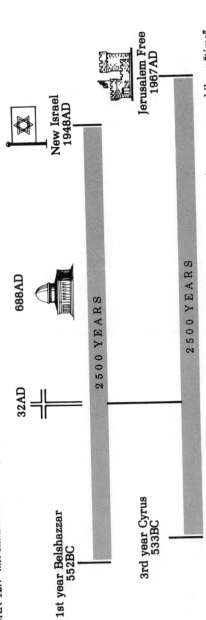

1st year Belshazzar
552BC

3rd year Cyrus
533BC

32AD

688AD

2500 YEARS

2500 YEARS

New Israel
1948AD

Jerusalem Free
1967AD

NOTE: The definition for "time" is in 2 Pet.3:8 "...be not ignorant of this one thing, that one day is with the Lord as a thousand years, and a thousand years as one day." The Greek word used here for day is "hemera," (Strong's 2250) which may be translated as day, year, age, while, or "time" depending upon context. The translation "time" is acceptable here.

## Graph Of Divided Israel
### From the Exodus to the Cross

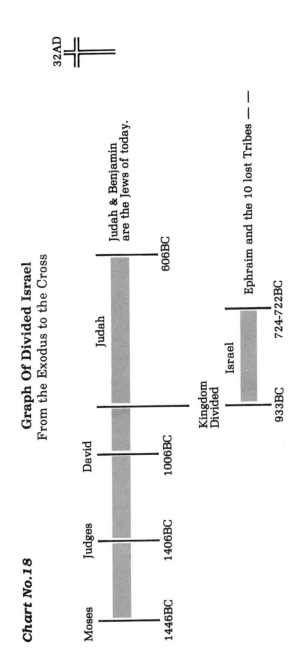

Moses    Judges    David    Judah

1446BC    1406BC    1006BC    606BC

Judah & Benjamin
are the Jews of today.

Kingdom
Divided

Israel

933BC    724-722BC

Ephraim and the 10 lost Tribes — —

32AD

NOTE: The ten northern tribes are: Reuben, Simeon, Zebulun, Issachar, Dan, Gad, Asher, Naphtali, Ephraim, and Manassah. Levi was not counted in the Old Testament because the Lord separated them out as His tithe and to be priests. Levi, however, is counted in Revelation, and Dan is left out. Over the next 200 years, the northern kingdom grew to have a strong economy and powerful army.

## *Chart No.19*

# Time, Times And Ephraim
## REV 12:14

REV 12:14  And to the woman were given two wings of a great eagle, that she might fly into the wilderness, into her place, where she is nourished for a time, and times, and half a time, from the face of the serpent.

2PE 3:8  But, beloved, be not ignorant of this one thing, that one day is with the Lord as a thousand years, and a thousand years as one day.

United States
1776AD

688AD

32AD

2500 YEARS

Captivity of Israel
724BC

NOTE: It is possible, but not likely, that this "time, times, and half a time" overlays one of those in Daniel. But in Daniel's time, northern Israel had been dispersed for over 150 years. Consequently, the addressee of Daniel's prophecies was the Jew in captivity. In Revelation, Israel is again spoken of as twelve tribes, REV 7:1-9 and REV 14:1-5. So the addressee of the REV 12:14 prophecy is all Israel.

## THE SEVEN CHURCHES

There are three interpretations of these churches; all are correct...

1. They were seven literal churches in Asia Minor whom John encouraged or exhorted.

2. They are an allegorical picture of all the churches of the Christian Era. All seven kinds of churches exist today.

3. They represent seven different periods of church history. These seven churches accurately portray the changing spiritual condition of the church throughout the Christian Era.

| | | |
|---|---|---|
| 32-95AD | **Ephesus** | *"Lost your first love..."* MAR 12:29-30. Heresy enters church: Marcionites, Gnostics, Nicolaitans, etc. |
| 95-321AD | **Smyrna** | *"Persecuted 10 days..."* Ten major persecutions under ten Roman Emperors: (1) Domitian (2) Trajan (3) Hadrian (4) Antonius Pius (5) Marcus Arelius (6) Septimus Severus (7) Maximin (8) Decius (9) Valerian (10)Diocletian |
| 321-450AD | **Pergamum** | *"Where Satans throne is..."* Constantine makes Christianity state religion. Church hierarchy begins. |
| 450-950AD | **Thyatira** | *"That Woman Jezebel..."* Beginning of Mary worship. Idols brought into the churches. Bishops rise to power. |
| 950-1450AD | **Sardis** | *"But you are dead..."* Dead Catholic formalism. Bible taken from the people. Persecution of the brethren intensifies. |
| 1450-1948AD | **Philadelphia** | *"Have kept MY Word..."* The Reformation, the Protestant church begins, the Puritan movement, foreign missions founded. |
| 1948- ?? | **Laodecia** | *"You are neither hot nor cold..."* Lukewarm church of today. Great church organizations and works, but spiritually poor. |

BOOK 3

# The Final Hours

# Chapter 19

# *Leopards, Bears, Goats & Others*

For decades, students of prophecy have been pointing their fingers at the Russians, and from the 38th and 39th chapters of Ezekiel, "positively" naming them as the final enemy of the Christian World. That identification is as premature as the belief that Napoleon was the antichrist. Even though Ezekiel 38-39 speaks of the kings from the uttermost parts of the north, those chapters are only one small piece in the total prophetic picture. The Russians will be at Armageddon, sure enough; but regardless of the popularity of that view, they will not be the central driving nation in Satan's forces.

We now know who will be fighting on Israel's side at Armageddon, Ephraim and no one else. But against what group of nations will Israel and Ephraim be fighting? As the key to understanding Revelation's day=years was in Daniel, so the key to understanding the beasts in Revelation is in Daniel. When we walk back into history this time, we are going to place ourselves almost two decades before the fall of Babylon. King Nebuchadnezzar, who turned to the Lord after "seven seasons" of insanity, DAN 4:34-37, has been dead for nearly 10 years. A couple of sons, and a son-in-law, have succeeded Nebuchadnezzar to the throne in rapid succession.[64] The Babylonian kingdom was in confusion.

At that time, Daniel was the second ruler in the land. Daniel has now been in Babylon for almost 50 years. He knew the 70 years captivity prophesied by Jeremiah still had almost 20 years to run.[65] As Babylon's acting Prime Minister,

---

[64] Evil-Merodach, Nergal-Sharezer, and Labashi-Marduk are those rulers.

[65] DAN 9:2 In the first year of his reign I Daniel understood by books the number of the years, whereof the word of the LORD came to Jeremiah the prophet, that he would accomplish seventy years in the desolations of Jerusalem.

JER 29:10 For thus saith the LORD, That after seventy years be accomplished at Babylon I will visit you, and perform my good word toward you, in causing you to return to this place.

keeping the empire together under those unstable conditions must have taxed even Daniel's awesome capabilities. Something like this must have been going through his mind, "If Babylon falls apart now, what will happen to my kinsmen in captivity with me?"

Then in 555BC, Nabonidus seized the throne. Three years later, in 552BC, he named Belshazzar as his regent; and under him, the empire endured for 16 more years. No doubt Daniel knew of Belshazzar's wanton ways before he came to power. The young prince hosted riotous parties and did not honor the Lord the way his forefather Nebuchadnezzar had. From DAN 5:11-12, it is apparent that the saintly Daniel was now out of favor in the court. In that unfriendly environment, Daniel must have been deeply concerned for the safety of his people.

So far, the only prophecy in which Daniel had been personally involved was Nebuchadnezzar's dream of the Great Image, DAN 2:31-45. Though Daniel did not have that dream himself, the Lord gave him insight, not only to recall the king's dream, but to interpret it for him:

DAN 2:31-34 (excerpts) Thou, O king, sawest, and behold a great image....**This image's head was of fine gold, his breast and his arms of silver, his belly and his thighs of brass, His legs of iron, his feet part of iron and part of clay. Thou sawest till that a stone was cut out without hands, which smote the image upon his feet** that were of iron and clay, and brake them to pieces.

DAN 2:35 Then was the iron, the clay, the brass, the silver, and the gold, **broken to pieces** (at the same time NASB) **together**, and became like the chaff of the summer threshingfloors: **and the stone that smote the image became a great mountain, and filled the whole earth.**

That Great Image of DAN 2 is a pretty complex prophecy, with many details not central to our subject. But from that dream, Daniel knew that four Gentile empires and their descendants were to rule in the Holy Land far into the future. They were first Babylon, then empire X, then empire Y, and finally empire Z. From history, after Babylon fell: Medo-Persia, Greece, Rome, and their descendants are recognized as the following empires.  Of course, Jesus is the stone cut out without hands who is going to put an end to all this. *(Chart No.21)*

But before that happens, the feet of the image tell us about our own times.  The feet came out of the legs of iron, which are generally accepted to represent the Roman Empire. Those feet were of mixed iron and clay which did not cling to each other, and they had ten toes...

> DAN 2:36-44 (excerpts) ...we will tell the interpretation ...Thou art this head of gold (Nebuchadnezzar of Babylon). And after thee shall arise another kingdom inferior to thee, and another third kingdom of brass, which shall rule over all the earth.  And **the fourth kingdom** (Rome) **shall be strong as iron...  thou sawest the feet and toes, part of potters' clay, and part of iron, the kingdom shall be divided**; but there shall be in it of the strength of the iron...And as the toes of the feet were part of iron, and part of clay, so the kingdom shall be partly strong, and partly broken...**they shall mingle themselves with the seed of men: but they shall not cleave one to another**, even as iron is not mixed with clay.  And in the days of these kings shall the God of heaven set up a kingdom, which shall never be destroyed ...but it shall break in pieces and consume all these king-doms, and it shall stand for ever.

Rome fell in 476AD, and Europe divided into roughly ten nations.  They have been politically divided ever since.  Daniel knew that Messiah (the stone cut out without hands, DAN 2:34,44-45) would return during the time of those ten toes, and put an end to all of the Gentile nations at one time, v35.  But what about right now in Babylon?  With the empire in a stew, he and his people were in deep trouble.

In the 1st year of Belshazzar, the Lord affirmed the dream of the Great Image, by giving Daniel the vision of the four beasts rising up out of the sea[66], DAN 7:1-24.  He tells

---

[66] The sea is the peoples of the world.  REV 17:15 "And he saith unto me, The waters which thou sawest, where the whore sitteth, are peoples, and multitudes, and nations, and tongues."

Daniel that these four beasts are four kings (or kingdoms) which will rule in the earth.

> DAN 7:3-7  And four great beasts came up from the sea, diverse one from another. **The first was like a lion, and had eagle's wings:** I beheld till the wings thereof were plucked, and it was lifted up from the earth, and made stand upon the feet as a man, and a man's heart was given to it. **And behold another beast, a second, like to a bear,** and it raised up itself on one side, and it had three ribs in the mouth of it between the teeth of it: and they said thus unto it, Arise, devour much flesh. **After this I beheld, and lo another, like a leopard, which had upon the back of it four wings of a fowl; the beast had also four heads;** and dominion was given to it. After this I saw in the night visions, **and behold a fourth beast, dreadful and terrible, and strong exceedingly;** and it had great iron teeth: it devoured and brake in pieces, and stamped the residue with the feet of it: and it was diverse from all the beasts that were before it; **and it had ten horns.** I considered the horns, and, behold, **there came up among them another little horn, before whom there were three of the first horns plucked up by the roots:** and, behold, in this horn were eyes like the eyes of man, and a mouth speaking great things.

> DAN 7:17  **These great beasts, which are four, are four kings** (or kingdoms), which shall arise out of the earth.

Since these Four Beasts sound just like the empires of the Great Image, let's lay this vision over DAN 2:31-45. Guess what, they are exact parallels. Using different words, the Lord is telling us of the same empires, but in much more detail. Here, instead of ten toes coming out of Rome, it is ten horns, and the Lord gives us something extra. Out of these ten horns of the broken up Roman Empire, another king was to come, a little horn:

> DAN 7:20-21  **And of the ten horns that were in his head,** and of the other which came up, and before whom three fell; **even of that horn that had eyes, and a mouth that spake very great things, whose look was more stout than his**

**fellows. I beheld, and the same horn made war with the saints, and prevailed against them...**

This last king was very powerful and evil, and conquered the peoples around him. He spoke boastfully, but the Most High overthrew him. In 1933 the Nazis destroyed the German Republic, and under the man Adolf Hitler, the Roman Empire was reestablished. Hitler conquered the major powers in Europe; and after the death of Mussolini, controlled Italy. Hitler also seized Poland, Yugoslavia, Greece, and all of North Africa, except Egypt. In fact, Nazi Germany subdued almost all of the old geographic Roman Empire! This Third Reich (or third Roman empire) was supposed to last for 1000 years. Instead, it lasted only 12. "A little season," as REV 17:10 tells us. The corollary between the Roman Empire and Nazi Germany is astonishing. Look at some similarities:

| | | |
|---|---|---|
| 1. The Roman Eagles | = | The German Eagles |
| 2. The Roman Legions | = | The German Legions |
| 3. Hail Caesar | = | Heil Hitler |
| 4. Caesar Worshipped | = | Hitler Deified |
| 5. Military State | = | Military State |
| 6. War Glorified | = | War Glorified |
| 7. Great Public Works | = | Great Public Works |
| 8. Christians Slaughtered | = | The Gas Chambers |

Nowhere in this prophecy are we told that the vision of the Four Beasts is about the ultimate time of the end. This little horn came out of the Roman Empire, and Hitler was the last of its emperors.[67] Why does the Lord tell us so much about him? Well, who was this vision given to, and what is it about? It was to Daniel, and is about the time of Gentile dominion over the Jews, and the Holy Land. In telling Daniel

---

[67] There are two distinct little horns in Daniel. One in DAN 7, and one in DAN 8. One out of the Roman Empire, and one out of the Greek Empire. They are not the same person! The little horn out of Rome is NOT the ruler of the ultimate time of the end. But, the little horn of out of Greece is, DAN 8:17,19,23. The old Greek empire covered from Greece itself, through Turkey, Syria, Lebanon, the Holy Land and Egypt, to beyond Babylon. So the little horn of DAN 8 will come from that area.

about the long term future of the Jews, it is unlikely that the Lord would leave out a horrendous event like the Holocaust.

Since this little horn (ruler) is within the time, times and half a time, he would have to come before it ends, i.e., before 1948AD. He had to come on the scene while the Jews were still in the nations. Of all the conquerors in the Christian Era, Hitler had the greatest impact on the Jews. So from this angle also, Hitler is heir apparent to the title of: The Little Horn of Daniel 7! *(Chart No.22)*

Now, let's look at the "time, times, and half a time" again. As you remember from Chapter 15, one of them was fulfilled in 1948, at the founding of new Israel. Well, here it is in context, at the end of the prophecy of the Four Beasts. Many have interpreted this verse to be about "the" tribulation, and in a way it is; but it is about the tribulation the Jews have suffered ever since the Babylonian captivity.

> DAN 7:25 And he shall speak great words against the most High, and shall wear out the saints of the most High, and think to change times and laws: **and they shall be given into his hand until a time and times and the dividing of time.**

Because of where this prophecy is in Scripture, we can see that God knew, all along, that those beasts and their descendants would only rule the Holy Land until 1948AD. A time incidentally, which equals the time of the Gentiles. That is what the time of the Gentiles is all about. It is the time these nations were to dominate the Holy Land. Looking back now, we can see that all day=years, times, Gentile times, and the Christian Era, are concluded in new Israel. We are in a unique time now, the Time of the End. *(Refer again to Chart No.16 at the end of Book 2)* Please forgive the author for being repetitive, but these prophecies are like a vast mosaic. As we lay each new tile, we need to relate it to other tiles we already have in place.

After this prophecy, Daniel has little more to say about the Roman Empire, Europe, and the West. Why? Because after the little horn of Nazi Germany, the Jews are back in Israel; and Europe no longer plays a central role in God's overall plan for His people. Instead, we are left with ten

horns, and ten toes, which don't stick together, and this
startling little verse:

> DAN 7:12 As concerning rest of the beasts, they had their
> dominion taken away: **yet their lives were prolonged for a
> season and time.**[68]

So who are the rest of the beasts? Daniel 7 lays it all out
for us: the Lion, Bear, and Leopard! This verse is after the
little horn of Hitler is destroyed, so it should be about events
which take place after Nazi Germany falls. If we look at the
lands of those ancient empires today, we see their descendants
as:

| | | | |
|---|---|---|---|
| Lion | = | Babylon | = **Iraq** |
| Bear | = | Medo-Persia | = **Iran** |
| Leopard | = | Greece | = **Syria/Lebanon**[69] |

Today, there is no restructuring of the Roman Empire
(unless NATO or the Common Market can loosely be classed as
one); but Lion (Iraq), Bear (Iran), and Leopard (Syria/Lebanon)
have come back in to world view, and **they do not have
world dominion.** Now that is truly marvelous. An exact
word for word fulfillment of DAN 7:12! Also these beasts are
the center of the radical Shiite wing of the Moslems, the

---

[68] If time here is also 1000 years, and a season is 1/4 of that time, we
have roughly 1250 years. This may be another reference to the 1260 year
Mohammedan domination of the Holy Land, from the Dome of the Rock to
new Israel.

[69] After Alexander the Great died in 323BC, his empire was divided
among his four generals, Ptolemy, Seleucus Nicator, Lycimicus, and
Cassander. They formed four Greek sub-empires. This explains the four
wings and four heads on the Leopard of DAN 7:6, and the four horns out
of the He-Goat of DAN 8:8. The geographic center of the Seleucid Empire
was Syria/Lebanon. The Seleucid's were Greek, so Syria/Lebanon was
Greek. The Seleucids, ruling from Antioch and Damascus, were the
dominant gentile oppressors of the Holy Land between the Medo-Persian
and Roman Empires. That is why we may identify the Syria/Lebanon area
today as Greek.

Palestinians, the Jihad, and the terrorists. They are now center stage in Bible prophecy!

In Daniel, beasts are defined as kings or empires. Since Beasts are empires in Daniel, beasts are also empires in Revelation, unless the Bible itself gives us a later definition. The author could find no later definition. So unless there is one, the beasts in Revelation are empires. Are the short hairs beginning to rise on the back of your neck, yet? If not, they should be; for a major beast in Revelation looks like a **Leopard, Bear, and Lion,** REV 13:2! We don't need to guess anymore. Now we can know who that beast is:

**SYRIA, IRAQ, IRAN, and the radical Mohammedan world!**

We have forgotten our history. The militant Mohammedans have been at the throats of the Christians all the way back to the 7th Century. If we don't believe they are still our enemies, it is because we can't hear what they are saying. They tell us so as plainly as they know how! They scream their malice at the top of their voices. We don't listen. We don't believe the hatred in their eyes, and their shaking fists, which we so eagerly show on national TV. They call us the "Great Satan" while they maim and kill each other on impulse. They bomb our sleeping young men in Beirut. They take our people hostage and murder them out of hand.

But we keep dancing. While we shuffle our feet, Hussein of Iraq has seized a peaceful neighbor. He holds our people hostage, and calls for a holy Arab war against the West. These are murderous men. Soon they will have nuclear weapons, and the systems with which to deliver them.

A strong nation can handle adversaries without, but what do we do about the vipers within? Wanting to show these assassins our "good will," we try to appease them. After all, we want to be reasonable. We take some of their better educated radicals, and make them professors in our colleges. With our own tax dollars, they subvert our children. We invite them to speak on public radio, where in silky tones they explain to us how reasonable their terrorist acts are. These radical Mohammedans proclaim that they are only doing these horrible things to get our attention. It's just good clean advertising and public awareness that they are after. Our "loyal" press whitewashes what these heathen do, but the blood and gore keeps seeping through for all to see.

The radical Mohammedans only want us to betray Israel a little bit, and of course, they want the Holy Land back. Thus, they try to win by diplomacy what the Sovereign God will not let them win by force of arms. God help the United States to have the will to remain on Israel's side as the end approaches, for the Lord will always honor His ancient promise:

> GEN 12:3 And I will bless them that bless thee, and curse him that curseth thee: and in thee shall all families of the earth be blessed.

If we ever abandon Israel, we are finished. That one promise could be all that stands between us and our own destruction. The Israelites are our brethren in arms against a common enemy. We are simpletons, indeed, if we try to make treaties with those who would go against that Sovereign decree.

However, as we stand firm in our commitment to Israel, the United States will become more and more politically isolated from Europe and the rest of the world. At the end, Europe itself will side with the radical Mohammedans for two weeks, REV 17:12. The much advertised political reunification of Europe in 1992 may not take place. But even if Europe does unite, it won't be a long standing relationship. Daniel said outright, that the ten toes of the old Roman Empire would not cling to one another, DAN 2:43.

Up to now, we have looked at the prophetic milestones in the Christian Era. We have identified the Beasts in Daniel, and the end of the time of the Gentiles. So much for the past. Let's use what we now know to decipher the beasts in Revelation. This should give us an inkling of what still lies ahead.

# Chapter 20

# *Scarlet Beast*

It never ceases to amaze the author, that in most of the books written about Revelation, the identity of the beasts is never thoroughly analyzed. We have four beasts in Daniel which can be historically identified as Babylon, Medo-Persia, Greece, and Rome. Therefore, the biblical definition of beasts is empires. But when we get into Revelation, we go off on some wild tangent and say, "Oh, the beast is the antichrist." The logic of that conclusion escapes me. Nowhere in Scripture has the Lord done away with beasts = empires, or heads and horns = nations and kings. So let's try another one of our little exercises. Let's take the Scarlet Beast of REV 17; lay its heads and kings over world history, and see if there is a match:

REV 17:3  So he carried me away in the spirit into the wilderness: and I saw a woman sit upon **a scarlet coloured beast, full of names of blasphemy, having seven heads and ten horns.**

From REV 18, it is apparent that the woman sitting on the beast is spiritual Babylon (more on this later).  The Babylon of Revelation represents the world's economic and monetary systems, REV 18:11-15.  But the seven heads grow out of the beast itself.  In ISA 1:14 we see that sin is referred to as scarlet, so the scarlet color of this beast well describes Satan's sinful nature.  Since the beast has blasphemous names written on it, sin also rules over the seven heads.

In Daniel, beasts were empires, and heads were kings or kingdoms.  Scripture hasn't changed that definition.  In REV 17, the beast is Satan's spiritual empire exhibiting itself through world rulers, and his throne is somewhere on Earth, Rev 16:10.  The seven heads would represent the seven great empires of the world, which the enemy has controlled down through the ages, LUK 4:6.  Out of one of them came ten nations.  On the next few pages, we will show how we can biblically come to these conclusions.

Daniel tells us that ten horns came up out of his fourth beast, DAN 7:7.  Ten horns also came out of this scarlet beast.  Consequently, it is probable that the ten horns of REV 17:3 are those same European nations, but not necessarily just the common market.  Separate European nations have existed since the Roman Empire fell.

REV 17:7-8  And the angel said unto me, Wherefore didst thou marvel? I will tell thee the mystery of the woman, and of **the beast that carrieth her, which hath the seven heads and ten horns.**

**The beast that thou sawest was, and is not; and shall ascend out of the bottomless pit,** and go into perdition: and they that dwell on the earth shall wonder, whose names were not written in the book of life from the foundation of the world, when they behold **the beast that was, and is not, and yet is (and will come, NASB).**

Another consideration: a beast which comes after the seven heads, "was, and is not, and yet is (and will come, NASB)." What can that mean? It means that before John's time there was a satanically controlled empire which did not exist while John was alive. It was a beast which existed before John's time, and would return after his time. Which one of the Old Testament empires could it be? The secret is to place ourselves in the time of the prophet John, and look backwards into history. Study the world empires that existed before John's time; and read on...

> REV 17:10-11 And **there are seven kings: five are fallen, and one is, and the other is not yet come;** and when he cometh, he must continue a short space. And **the beast that was, and is not, even he is the eighth,** and is of the seven, and goeth into perdition.

Now we are going to try to use the lessons we learned from Daniel to decipher the above verses. From John's time, there had already been five world empires. Rome was during his lifetime, so Rome is the 6th. Another would follow, the 7th, and last a little while. *(Chart No.22)* Nazi Germany almost duplicated the old Roman Empire. Earlier, this was covered in detail. As Hitler and his Nazi regime was the little Horn of Daniel 7, so he is also the number one candidate for this Seventh King. He lasted 12 years, "continued a short space." **However, this seventh king is not the last kingdom in this prophecy. "Then Cometh The Eighth."**

So who is this Eighth beast? Here is a way to figure that one out. The five which were, refers to those kingdoms which dominated the Holy Land before John's time. Those empires were Egypt, Assyria, Babylon, Medo-Persia and Greece, by historic record. Nonetheless, the first of those empires is a little uncertain. The first ought to have been Egypt, but there is a historic fly in the ointment.

Before the Assyrian empire, the Holy Land was inhabited by a collection of independent city states. These cities were directly ruled by the Canaanites, who were only loosely controlled by Egypt. They were also influenced by the declining Hittite Empire, which was centered in what is now Turkey.

1400 years later, during the time of Mark Anthony of Cleopatra fame, Egypt became a vassal state under Rome. However, Egypt still existed as an subordinate nation during John's time. Since the 8th Beast "is not" in John's time, it is unlikely to be Egypt. Consequently, that first "king" is probably the Canaanites. They are all that is left. So leaving out Egypt and Rome, this 8th Beast, which is "of the seven," has to come out of the following: Canaan, Assyria, Babylon, Medo-Persia or Greece.

> REV 17:8 The beast that thou sawest was, and is not; and shall ascend out of the bottomless pit, and go into perdition...and they shall wonder...**when they behold the beast that was, and is not, and yet is.**
>
> REV 17:11 And **the beast that was, and is not, even he is the eighth, and is of the seven,** and goeth into perdition.

The King James quote above is slightly different than the more modern translations. The NASB translates REV 17:8, "was, and is not, and will come," and 17:11, "he is *one* of the seven," If *one* appears in your Bible, the *one* is in italics, which means *one* is not in the original texts. So the Bible is not saying that this final beast is ONLY one of the seven kings. Instead, Revelation is declaring that he is composed of one, some, or even all of the seven.

| "The Beast Which Was" | "And Is Not" | "And Will Come" |
| --- | --- | --- |
| 1  Canaanites or Egypt? | During John's time | ?? |
| 2  Assyria | ROME IS. | |
| 3  *Babylon | | |
| 4  *Medo-Persia | | |
| 5  *Greece | | |

* Lion (Iraq), Bear (Iran), Leopard (Syria/Lebanon), DAN 7.

In the rest of this chapter, and in the next, you are going to read a very few "definites," and a lot of "maybes." Much of Revelation is not open yet (at least to this author), and one thing is for sure; if we start being definite about Revelation before it is open, we will wind up definitely wrong! The church has had enough of that to last us, so please bear with the author's caution.

REV 17:8 makes the descendants of the Canaanites a strong possibility to be at least part of this final beast. In that verse, the King James reads "was, and is not, and yet is." The Palestinians today, were a people, are not a real nation, and yet they exist. What's more, they are spiritually, and perhaps physically, the descendants of the Canaanites.70

Unfortunately, it looks like the Palestinians are not all there is to the final beast. REV 17 only zeroes in on one aspect of this satanic beast. REV 13 gives us a wider geographic view of that evil animal. Besides, this 8th Beast will not be going it alone; he will have some allies from afar:

> REV 17:12-14 And **the ten horns which thou sawest are ten kings, which have received no kingdom as yet; but receive power as kings one hour with the beast. These have one mind, and shall give their power and strength unto the beast.** These shall make war with the Lamb, and the Lamb shall overcome them: for he is Lord of lords, and King of kings: and they that are with him are called, and chosen, and faithful.

As mentioned earlier, this verse shows that the descendants of the old Roman Empire will throw their full support to the final beast for "one hour."71 Notice also that these leaders are "as kings," and not real kings by blood line. That is the way some European nations are run today, figurehead royalty, while elected officials have the real power.

But what is an hour? In day=years, an hour is about two weeks. There are more "hours" in Revelation. The "hour of trial" of REV 3:10 equals two weeks. "In that same hour" of

---

70 It is sad to think that the Near East is in the turmoil it's in today, because 3300 years ago, the Israelites did not completely destroy the Canaanites as the Lord commanded Joshua. If that is so, half way obedience sure has long term consequences. The author wonders if there is a lesson for us in this.

71 Despite the European nations' current displeasure with Iraq, they are so close to a total accommodation with the Mohammedan religion that one wonders if this book will be published before the final hour.

REV 11:13 equals two weeks. "The hour of judgment" of REV 14:7 equals two weeks. "In one hour" is recorded three times in the destruction of Babylon, REV 18:10, 18:17, and 18:19. Because of these "hours," the author concludes that Armageddon will be fought for about two weeks. The carnage would continue on; but to save the few elect who are still hanging on, Jesus will put a stop to it. With today's weaponry, two weeks is long enough. If it were any longer, there probably wouldn't be a planet left, nor a Mount Zion for the Lord to stand on, when he returns.

As of this writing, the United States is the only nation consistently supporting Israel in the United Nations. This also appears to fulfill EZE 37:16-20. The Europeans are gradually sliding into the Middle Eastern camp.72 Mohammedanism is the fastest growing religion in Europe. They are even taking over the physical facilities of many Christian churches, and using them as mosques.73

After the shooting starts, it is the author's firm conviction that the European nations will be on the side of the enemy! This from REV 17:12-13 quoted above. About now, we would just as soon avoid reading the prophecy of the earth's destruction recorded in Isaiah 24. The Lord commanded us to be sober and vigilant for a reason. This is serious business:

> ISA 24:1-20 (excerpts) **Behold, the LORD maketh the earth empty, and maketh it waste, and turneth it upside down, and scattereth abroad the inhabitants thereof.** The earth mourneth and fadeth away, the world languisheth and fadeth away, the haughty people of the earth do languish. The earth also is defiled (polluted) under the inhabitants thereof; because they have transgressed the laws, changed the ordinance, broken the everlasting covenant. Therefore hath **the curse devoured the earth, and they that dwell**

---

72 If EZE 37:16-23 is to be fulfilled literally, we may expect conditions in the United States to become so intolerable for the true church that we will have to flee to Israel.

73 From a personal letter by another Christian writer, Franz Zegers of den Helder, Holland. This letter is in the authors file.

**therein are desolate: therefore the inhabitants of the earth are burned, and few men left.**

The city of confusion (Babylon means confusion) **is broken down: every house is shut up, that no man may come in. Fear, and the pit, and the snare, are upon thee, O inhabitant of the earth.** And it shall come to pass, that he who fleeth from the noise of the fear shall fall into the pit; and he that cometh up out of the midst of the pit shall be taken in the snare: for the windows from on high are open, and the foundations of the earth do shake.

The earth is utterly broken down, the earth is clean dissolved, the earth is moved exceedingly. **The earth shall reel to and fro like a drunkard, and shall be removed like a cottage; and the transgression thereof shall be heavy upon it; and it shall fall, and not rise again.**

What a somber passage of Scripture that is; and since the church is going to be on Earth until all prophecy is fulfilled, REV 10:7, "those who are alive and remain" will see it. Our flesh cringes from these things, and makes us wish that "Happy, happy, happy, we're all going to be raptured out" had some credibility. But our God is on the throne, and we can place our trust in Him. In times as trying as these are going to get, there will be nowhere else to turn. He will not suffer the righteous to stumble, nor to beg for bread.

If it were not for REV 13, the Palestinians would be all there was to the final beast, and the author would be thinking of ways to wrap up the book. but because of that prophecy, we have more to go on...

# Chapter 21

# *The Hidden Beast*

Because of what we are going to discuss in this chapter, it is time for a little review.  From the time of the Babylonian empire, Daniel looked down through the centuries and saw that four Gentile nations and their descendants were going to rule in the Holy Land for thousands of years.  Though the Lord told him the duration in the time, times; he did not understand DAN 12:8.  The Lord only permitted him to see a little past the Dome of the Rock, in 688AD.  But he correctly identified the major Middle Eastern empires as a Lion, Bear, and Leopard: or Babylon, Medo-Persia and Greece.  In REV 17 we ran into those same empires again as three of the "five are fallen."  We found that the final beast would come out of those five fallen empires.  This final beast would be "of the seven" and "was" before Rome.  That puts to rest the idea that Rome, the United States, Russia, or any of the latter day empires could be the final beast.

Now is when understanding the chiasmic form is import-ant.  From it, we can see that REV 17 equals REV 13 as the **B=B** of the second chiasm.  They are repetitive.  These two chapters give us two different pictures of the same time.  The Scarlet Beast of REV 17 tells us the future of the West.  REV 13 tells us of the Leopard-Bear-Lion beast: the beast from the

East. Scripturally, there can be only one identity for this LBL, the historic Mohammedan world! In this chapter we talk a lot about the radical Mohammedans, but there is a lot in Revelation about them.[74]

> REV 13:1  And I stood upon the sand of the sea, and saw **a beast rise up out of the sea, having seven heads and ten horns,** and upon his horns ten crowns, and upon his heads the name of blasphemy.

> REV 13:2  **And the beast which I saw was like unto a leopard, and his feet were as the feet of a bear, and his mouth as the mouth of a lion:** and the dragon gave him his power, and his seat, and great authority.

Remember allegorical language?  In allegorical language the key words which tell us a vision is symbolic are: "as," "like," and "like unto."  Now look at the above verse again. This beast looks "like" a Leopard, with feet "as" Bear's feet, and a mouth "like" a Lion's.  Allegorical language, for sure. From the standpoint of Revelation, there is only one beast, the satanic empire; but here the beast is revealed to us wearing a different costume.  In this vision, Satan's Empire looks "like" part Leopard, part Bear, and part Lion.  Daniel defined the Lion, Bear, and Leopard as the three Middle Eastern empires, Babylon, Medo-Persia, and Greece.  Their descendants continued on down through the Christian Era.  Today those empires are the geographic center of the Mohammedan world.

Though Islam started in Arabia, a location evidently foretold by the prophet Zechariah in ZEC 5:5-11, the military and political headquarters of that religion has always been in the fertile crescent.  Within those states which we now know as Syria, Iran, and Iraq.  With the decline of the Caliphs in the 9th Century AD, the Mohammedan world broke into individual states.  The last great central ruler of the Moslem Empire was Haroun Al-Raschid who made peace with the Christian nations

---

[74] It is not the author's intent to prejudicially pick on the whole Arab race, nor on all the Mohammedans.  There are many who are kind and honest and of good will.  But the radical Middle East is of that faith, and it is the evil powers among those people that Revelation addresses.

in 786AD. Though they remained unified in purpose, shortly after his reign, the Middle East, and North Africa divided into individual states, just as the Roman Empire had almost 500 years earlier.

As was true of the Scarlet Beast, the account of this Leopard-Bear-Lion is also partly historic. Since the Scarlet Beast and LBL are just different views of the same beast, we can lay these seven heads over world history just as we did the seven heads on the Scarlet Beast, and another historic fit appears:

REV 13:3   And **I saw one of his heads as it were wounded to death; and his deadly wound was healed:** and all the world wondered after the beast.

Of the seven world empires of REV 17, a major one had a deadly wound, and then came back to life. Rome! Under Adolf Hitler, the Third Reich restored the Roman Empire to very close to its 1st Century boundaries. But the Leopard-Bear-Lion beast is about empires in the Middle East, so LBL should be mostly about that geographic area. Because of that possibility, let's put the Canaanites into the equation.

1400 years before Christ, Joshua also gave them a deadly wound of the sword, and the Holy Land became the home of the children of Israel. After the Dome of the Rock, the Jews and Christians were driven from the land by the Moham-medans. The people left in the land were some imports, and the descendants of those people Joshua did not drive out. **Now they have come back to life as the Palestinians.** This second interpretation fits the remainder of REV 13 very closely, so we will pursue it. Some will argue that the Pales-tinians are of uncertain ancestry, and may not be the direct descendants of the Canaanites. Ah, but they are their spiritual "image." As there were pagans in the land in Joshua's time, which the Israelites failed to drive out; so these Palestinians are pagans in the land, which New Israel has failed to drive out. The problem within Israel's borders today, stems from their making the same mistake the early Israelites did before them:

REV 13:4-6 And **they worshipped the dragon** which gave power unto the beast: and they worshipped the beast, saying, Who is like unto the beast? who is able to make war with him? And there was given unto him a mouth speaking great things and blasphemies; **and power was given unto him to continue forty and two months. And he opened his mouth in blasphemy against God, to blaspheme his name, and his tabernacle,** and them that dwell in heaven.

The above verse should relieve anyone of the delusion that it is possible for the Moslems to be coming to God through another door, "they worship the dragon."[75] That should not be too hard to believe, seeing their fruits. But here is something we can sink our teeth into. In the above verse there is another "forty two months." If we also interpret this 42 months as day=years, and lay this 1278.4 years over world history, we get the same results we always have. From the Dome of the Rock to a free Jerusalem is 1278.4 years. But here is the bonus! This forty two months is within the passage which tells us about the Leopard-Bear-Lion, so we now have positive proof that LBL is the Mohammedan world! This forty two months is a parallel look at the Arab control of Jerusalem.

Dome of the Rock            Jerusalem Free
688AD                          1967AD

Forty Two Months = 1278.4 days=years

---

[75] The Mohammedans worship "Allah," which is an offshoot of an early Arabic cult idol. The war in the Middle East is a conflict between deities. The God of the Bible against the god of this world. Jesus said, "Verily, verily, I say unto you, He that entereth not by the door into the sheepfold, but climbeth up some other way, the same is a thief and a robber. I say unto you, I am the door of the sheep. I am the door: by me if any man enter in, he shall be saved, JOH 10:1-9 (excerpts). The Moslem's condition is not the same as that of the Jew blinded by God. Mohammedans have been blinded by the enemy, 2CO 4:3-4, and though they are aware of the ministry of Jesus, they deny Him as the Messiah, and make war with all who accept Him.

Indeed the Mohammedans have blasphemed God's tabernacle. They have built a monument to the false prophet on it! As far as "those who dwell in heaven" is concerned, Ephesians declares that we presently dwell in the heavenlies with Christ. But to continue on:

> REV 13:7-10 And **it was given unto him to make war with the saints, and to overcome them:** and power was given him over all kindreds, and tongues, and nations. And all that dwell upon the earth shall worship him, whose names are not written in the book of life of the Lamb slain from the foundation of the world. If any man have an ear, let him hear. He that leadeth into captivity shall go into captivity: he that killeth with the sword must be killed with the sword. Here is the patience and the faith of the saints.

After the Mohammedans took Jerusalem in 637AD, they continued an unremitting war with the Christian nations. They swept through North Africa, the Middle East, and even into India. They destroyed the great Coptic Church which covered that whole area. In 786AD they made peace with the Christian nations, but were not too ecstatic about keeping it. They continued to attack the Eastern Orthodox Church, and finally, in the 15th Century, Constantinople fell. That city (renamed Istanbul) was the Eastern bastion of the whole Christian world. The great Christian church of Santa Sofia, built by the Christian emperor Justinian, was turned into a mosque. Throughout the ensuing centuries, the West kept the Mohammedans at bay by force of arms. Now we have forgotten our history, and can't hear the hatred the radical mullahs are screaming at us.

Remember the "was, and is not, and yet is" of REV 17:8? Within those Islamic states today, there lives a phantom empire. In that hidden empire are the secret Guardians of the Islamic Revolution, the May 15 group, Abu Nidal, the Islamic Jihad, or "holy war," and the Hezbollah, or "party of god." These are only the most visible of many murderous groups. They too "are not, yet they are." Behind some of most violent groups is a homicidal Iranian mullah, the secretive Ali Akbar Mohtashemi. *(Chart No.23)*

Mohtashemi and others could be gone tomorrow. They might be caught or killed; but regardless of who is pulling the trigger, the prophetic finger still points at the radical Moslems ot the Middle East. These are the international terrorists and supporters of the conflicts with Israel. They will work with anyone who will fight against the Jews; be it the Palestinians, the Syrians, the Iraqis, or the Iranians; to them it doesn't matter. Their hatred of the Christian world transcends national boundaries.

To a fundamental Shiite, religion and nationalism are interchangeable. His government is just an arm of Islam. To them, there is no separation between church and state. The church is the state. If it serves a Shiite's religious interest, it also serves his national interest. A radical Mohammedan's loyalty to Islam is the same entity as his loyalty to his country. In a terrorist's eyes, all Islam is united against the infidel (translate that Christians and Jews). That is why these killers can find refuge and support in one Moslem country after another. These nations are all together in the same "holy" war against the West.

In their clandestine bands, they have guerrillas, assassins, kidnappers, and explosives experts; and they are stationed all over the world. They proudly take "credit" for the violent destruction of life and property in the West. They are even in our ghettos and prisons. The inmates in many of our penitentiaries are controlled by them, and they grow stronger everywhere.[76]

The leaders of this world-wide shadow empire are shrouded in mystery. They are funded by Haphez el Asaad of Syria, Saddam Hussein of Iraq, Maummwar Khadaffy of Libya, the mullahs of Iran, and other visible governments; but are they controlled by them? That is doubtful. They have their own agenda; but **they are part of the final beast**. When they come out of hiding to capture, and murder, and burn, we

---

[76] To our peril, we de not take our own Black Muslims seriously. They hate the Christians with a fierce and undying hatred. England's cities are now being terrorized by roving bands of violent blacks. Many British citizens are immigrating to this country because of the increasing unrest in their own land. How long can the West maintain cohesion under this growing anarchy?

are looking into the face of the enemy; for the dragon gives them their power, REV 13:4. Whether they will come out into the open and take over these countries, or just influence them from undercover is uncertain. The Bible has yet to tell us. But they are so powerful that many governments dare not go against them. For instance, 60% of Jordan's population is Palestinian, which makes the Jordanian government powerless to control them. Their goals, the goals of the Iraqis, and of the Iranian mullahs are the same, regardless of what each individual leader might say. All wish to conquer Israel. All of them together are the Hidden Beast! Some strong man, a Middle Eastern Hitler, will eventually unite them for war; and that will be Armageddon. Listen to these verses from Daniel again:

> DAN 8:23-25 And in the latter time of their kingdom, when the transgressors are come to the full, **a king of fierce countenance, and understanding dark sentences, shall stand up.** And his power shall be mighty, but not by his own power: and he shall destroy wonderfully, and shall prosper, and practice, and shall destroy the mighty and the holy people. **And through his policy also he shall cause craft to prosper in his hand; and he shall magnify himself in his heart, and by peace shall destroy many:** he shall also stand up against the Prince of princes; but he shall be broken without hand.

Again someone will say, "There is the antichrist, I knew it all along." This passage speaks of an end-time king indeed, but his aims are military and political. He is out there smiling at us right now; as our newsmen give him a face full of microphones. Over our own media he will sell us his latest deception. Only he, and a few trusted lieutenants, know what his plans are. He will destroy many, by deceit, and peace talks are also his weapons. Read DAN 8:23-25 again. When Leopard-Bear-Lion sends envoys around seeking a peaceful solution, it will be a lie, and time to hide. That is a major sign that Armageddon is imminent! Interestingly enough, Scripture seems to indicate that Jordan, Syria, Egypt, and possibly Arabia will not be on the enemy's side during this final conflict, ISA 19:14-25 and DAN 11:41.

A hundred years ago, Christians were the most powerful force on Earth. Today there are many more militant Moham- medans than there are Christians, and bless our kindly and unsuspecting little hearts, the West has been selling them sophisticated weaponry. Now, the radicals in the Middle East are again exhibiting their hatred for the West. Most Europeans don't care, because they aren't Christian any more, and because it helps to support their munitions industry. Brethren, Israel is in trouble, and so are we! Praise God that Jesus is coming, because we will lose this war without Him.

> REV 13:11-13  And **I beheld another beast coming up out of the earth; and he had two horns like a lamb, and he spake as a dragon.** And he exerciseth all the power of the first beast before him, and **causeth the earth and them which dwell therein to worship the first beast, whose deadly wound was healed.** And he doeth great wonders, so that he maketh fire come down from heaven on the earth in the sight of men,

This two horned beast comes while Leopard-Bear-Lion exists.  The Mohammedan world is a religious entity, so probably this two-horded beast is also.  The western nations make a great show of their "Judao-Christian" ethical standards (as the faith is popularly called today); but we have become more degenerate than the third world.  We have two major political and military power blocs, East and West; and we have two major churches, the Protestants and Catholics.  Unlike the prior beasts which came out of the sea, this two horned beast comes out of the Earth.  The Eastern bloc and the West have no visible kings, but claim to be ruled "by the people."

We all speak peace like a lamb, but are lying like the dragon.  We have the most terrible weapons ever invented by man, and seek more.  With our bombs and missiles we cause fire to come out of the sky for all to see.  Our science is so mind boggling, that to some, it appears miraculous.  As one of today's intellects has put it: "If a science is sufficiently advanced, it is indistinguishable from magic."  Then also, in Europe's bondage, and our greed for Middle Eastern petroleum, we bow before the Leopard-Bear-Lion, and in so doing we honor their Mohammedan forefathers who destroyed the Coptic church.

> REV 13:14  And **deceiveth them that dwell on the earth by the means of those miracles which he had power to do in the sight of the beast;** saying to them that dwell on the earth, that they should **make an image to the beast, which had the wound by a sword, and did live.**

And what is this "image" of the beast? A popular conception is that it is a stone carving in the likeness of Satan, or of "the" antichrist placed on the old temple site. People are then supposed to bow down and worship it. Knowing this beast to be Leopard-Bear-Lion (the Mohammedan World), if that image is to be interpreted literally, it would have to be a stone carving of a map of the Middle East. Idolaters round the world have bowed down to a lot of strange things in the past, but I doubt if a map has been one of them.[77] So this likeness is probably also allegorical. If beasts are empires, an image of that beast would be a later empire which was like it. It would be some new empire with the same nature as the first, coming out of the same geographic area. Since REV 13 is about Leopard-Bear-Lion, this could be a likeness of the first Mohammedan Empire.

After Mohammed died in 634AD, his followers began a "holy war" to conquer the Christian nations. By the power of the sword, they intended to make the whole world Islamic. The Moslem armies were victorious for almost a hundred years. They defeated the Spanish only two decades after they built the Dome of the Rock. Then in 732AD they entered France where Charles Martel stood against them with a much smaller force of knights and peasants. Some of those peasants were armed with nothing but the scythes they used for reaping their grain. But that day, the unseen forces of the Lord stood

---

[77] In a manner of speaking, the Palestinians make an idol of what they think their homeland to be. On the surface, that is what the fighting is all about. But underneath, Satan wants to destroy the Jews as he always has: REV 12:17 "And the dragon was wroth with the woman, and went to make war with the remnant of her seed, which keep the commandments of God, and have the testimony of Jesus Christ."

with that little band of Christian knights, for they won a great and impossible victory.  If it had not been for that victory, Christianity could have been swept from the Earth, for there were no armies left in all Europe which could have withstood the Mohammedans.

Did the Lord predict this victory?  Since this prophecy is about those who desecrated the temple, and it is pinned to the abolition of sacrifices, God gave the prophecy to Daniel:

> DAN 12:12  Blessed is he that waiteth, and cometh to the thousand three hundred and five and thirty days.

Sacrifices Abolished                                      Battle of Tours
    583BC                                                      732AD

    1335 Hebrew Days = 1315 Solar Years
          - 583BC = 732 AD

The Battle of Tours gave a "wound of the sword" to the Moslems from which they did not recover until this generation. Now a "likeness" of that beast has come to life.  A new Jihad is again rising in the East.  It is just like the old beast, killing Christians and Jews.  It respects little but force, and has the same goals.  They again try for an Islamic world by the power of the sword.  If the Europeans do not bow down before them, they "can neither buy or sell" the oil they so desperately need for their industrial machine.  So we speak peace where there is no peace, and try to sign treaties with those who respect no law but deceit and violence.

> 1TH 5:3  For when they shall say, Peace and safety; then sudden destruction cometh upon them, as travail upon a woman with child; and they shall not escape.

Do we have the moral courage to stand by Israel, and clean out that nest of assassins?  The longer we wait the stronger they get, and their increasing strength leads them to think they can defeat Israel.  One of these days, a little border war in the Holy Land, or a terrorist action, or a madman in power over there will draw the rest of the world into conflict. That's how the Lord told Ezekiel that Armageddon would start:

> EZE 38:4-7 (excerpts) ...and **I will...put hooks into thy jaws, and I will bring thee forth, and all thine army...Persia, Ethiopia, and Libya with them; all of them with shield and helmet:** Gomer, and all his bands; the house of Togarmah of the north quarters, and all his bands: and many people with thee.

It is generally believed that before this happens, the beast will show its dominion by a distinctive mark. Since the beast is Satan's world wide physical and spiritual empire, what can that mark be? It has to be one by which the whole world will be influenced:

> REV 13:16-18 And he causeth all, both small and great, rich and poor, free and bond, **to receive a mark in their right hand, or in their foreheads: And that no man might buy or sell, save he that had the mark,** or the name of the beast, or the number of his name. Here is wisdom. Let him that hath understanding count the number of the beast: for it is the number of a man; and his number is Six hundred threescore and six.

This one passage is the only Scripture which defines the "mark of the beast."[78] Yet with no more to go on than that, whole doctrinal systems have been invented. In the face of that library of speculations, let's see if we can find some Bible which might give us some insight into the meaning of 666. Since the Lord did not spend a great deal of time on 666, neither will the author. The next chapter will be short.

---

[78] The other verses which mention this satanic mark, are about the judgments which will fall on those who have it, or the victory of the saints who did not: REV 14:9, 15:2, 16:2, 19:20 and 20:4.

# Chapter 22

# Two Marks

God's message to us in the Bible is spiritual. This is particularly true in Revelation. The Lord had a wonderful way of explaining spiritual truths so that we could understand them. He used illustrations of natural things to explain spiritual principles: seals and marks, for example. In Bible times, everyone understood the seals and marks which were struck on parchments and merchandise. They appeared on everything from a jug of wine, to orders for a governor. To make spiritual truths understandable to us, the Lord uses seals and marks to describe similar things which are taking place in the unseen spiritual world.

If we look at ancient methods of sealing things, we note that hot wax was dropped on the edge of a scroll, and an authorizing signet was stamped into it. A mark was struck into a seal. The seal prevented tampering, **and the mark specified the sealing authority**, be it a king, or a general, or some other delegated personage. An official seal was untouchable; and on pain of death, no unauthorized person could break one. When we read about biblical seals and marks, we need to place ourselves in the historic position of the writer and ask, "What did a seal or mark mean to him?" It meant that the sealed document or merchandise was under the authority and protection of the one who sealed it.

The beast is Satan's empire, spiritual and physical. He seals his servants with a seal, into which he strikes his mark. Satan's mark is the spiritual badge of someone who is under the protection and authority of that evil king. That is what sealing was all about.

Since Revelation is spiritual in nature, 666 could be an unseen spiritual seal. Satan's servants have not been visibly marked in the past, so it is improbable that they will be so marked in the future. Furthermore, 666 could be spiritual characteristics. If we can discover what 666 spiritually means, we ought to be able find out who has the mark, and what it is. If a person displays the attributes of 666, we should be able to recognize that individual as belonging to the beast. How can we confirm this? By looking at spiritual marks as described for us in Bible prophecy, and by studying biblical examples of sixes. Besides Revelation, there are only two other places in Scripture where 666 is used:

1KI 10:14 Now the weight of gold that came to Solomon in one year was **six hundred threescore and six talents of gold,**

2CH 9:13 Now the weight of gold that came to Solomon in one year was **six hundred and threescore and six talents of gold;**

In the 1KI and 2CH quotes above, gold, the medium of exchange, is shown as 666. The nations surrounding Israel were in bondage to Solomon, and had to give him gold. They were in economic bondage to him to the tune of 666 talents. Looking at REV 13:17, we note "no man might buy or sell" unless he has the mark. Neither can a man "buy or sell" if he does not deal in gold, or some substitute medium of exchange. So this mark is related to a person's economic bondage. Let's say it again. The mark of the beast shows an economic bondage.

Daniel is such a marvelous book. It always has so much hidden away in it. In DAN 3 Nebuchadnezzar built an image of, guess what? Gold! He decreed that all should bow before this image or be thrown into the fiery furnace. The image was 6 cubits wide by 60 cubits high. That is eleven sixes or 66666666666 which, from a symbolic standpoint, is a lot of 666's. This concept would be guesswork if we didn't have the following verses from the same chapter:

> DAN 3:5 That at what time ye hear the sound of the **cornet, flute, harp, sackbut, psaltery, dulcimer**, and all kinds of musick, ye fall down and worship the golden image that Nebuchadnezzar the king hath set up:

> DAN 3:10 Thou, O king, hast made a decree, that every man that shall hear the sound of the **cornet, flute, harp, sackbut, psaltery, and dulcimer**, and all kinds of musick, shall fall down and worship the golden image:

> DAN 3:15 Now if ye be ready that at what time ye hear the sound of the **cornet, flute, harp, sackbut, psaltery, and dulcimer**, and all kinds of musick, ye fall down and worship the image which I have made; well: but if ye worship not, ye shall be cast the same hour into the midst of a burning fiery furnace; **and who is that God that shall deliver you out of my hands?**

Well, our God was able, and did deliver Shadrack, Meshack, and Abed-nego; but did you count the number of musical instruments. There are six, and they are repeated three times. There is another listing of musical instruments in v7, but it has only five. Now the Lord did not have Daniel repeat six musical instruments three times as an exercise in penmanship. If six is repeated three times, we have another 666.

Sixty years pass, now that is a strange coincidence. Then on the night Babylon fell, Belshazzar the king held a great feast for a thousand or so of the empire's dignitaries. He invited all the Babylonian court nobles and their ladies to attend. After they had partied a bit, in a supreme act of defiance, he had the vessels of the Temple of the Lord brought before him, so he and his friends could drink a little wine from them:

DAN 5:2-4  Belshazzar, whiles he tasted the wine, commanded to bring the golden and silver vessels which his father Nebuchadnezzar had taken out of the temple which was in Jerusalem; that the king, and his princes, his wives, and his concubines, might drink therein. Then they brought the golden vessels that were taken out of the temple of the house of God which was at Jerusalem; and the king, and his princes, his wives, and his concubines, drank in them. They drank wine, and praised the gods of **gold, and of silver, of brass, of iron, of wood, and of stone.**

Count the number of gods. There are six. So we see another six, this time six false gods. These gods are made of the major building blocks of all manufactured goods: gold, silver, brass, iron, wood, and stone. Music is a call to worship them. Throughout the Old Testament, gold, music, and revelry are associated with worship of idols. Aaron's calf was made of gold; and after sacrificing to it, "the people sat down to eat and to drink, and rose up to play," EXE 32:6.

God hated these idols; and the idolatry of the Israelites was the central reason the Lord sent them into captivity. These multiple sixes in the Old Testament are not there by accident. Let's see if we can put them together with other Scriptures to uncover what they might mean.

Did you know that God puts a mark on His people? To understand the enemy's mark, maybe we need to understand what God's mark is. He first told us about it through Ezekiel. Just before Jerusalem fell to Babylon, the Lord gave that prophet a vision of the coming destruction of the city and the massacre of its inhabitants. In that vision, the Lord stood at the gate of the city, accompanied by angels of destruction with shattering weapons in their hands. Then the Lord (as the man clothed in linen) marked His people that were in the city:

EZE 9:4,9  And the LORD said unto him, Go through the midst of the city, through the midst of Jerusalem, and **set a mark upon the foreheads of the men that sigh and that cry for all the abominations that be done in the midst thereof.** Slay utterly old and young, both maids, and little children, and women: but come not near any man upon whom is the mark; and begin at my sanctuary.

Here we read about what took place in the unseen spirit world while Nebuchadnezzar was physically destroying Jerusalem. The Babylonians sacked Jerusalem three times, and killed or took captive most of its inhabitants. We have ample record of those invasions. 2KI 24:13, 25:9-17, JER 27:19-22, and 2CH 36:6-21 are the primary references, and there are others.

Now the above verse was written by a prophet who could see what was going on in the spiritual world. The 2CH verse quoted below was written by someone who did not. Because of the similarity between the EZE prophecy above, and 2CH account below, these two references probably refer to the same incident. Compare the almost identical wording of the two quotations:

> 2CH 36:17 Therefore he brought upon them the king of the Chaldees, **who slew their young men with the sword in the house of their sanctuary, and had no compassion upon young man or maiden, old man**, or him that stooped for age: he gave them all into his hand.

In none of the historic records of this incident is there the first word about a visible mark suddenly appearing on the foreheads of some of the people. Not even a hint of one. If something as spectacular as an angelic mark had started glowing on some Jewish foreheads, Jeremiah and the writers of 2 Kings and 2 Chronicles would have gotten so excited they could not have avoided recording it. They saw no mark, so this mark was only visible in the spiritual world.

Now, even though that mark was spiritual, it was a very real mark. Its being spiritual did not nullify its reality. It was a real mark given by an angelic being, to be visible to angelic beings. This seal had a definite function. **It was given to protect the saints who belonged to the Lord from destroying angels.**

In Revelation, we find another marking of the Lord's people. It was given to them just before another group of destroying angels was loosed on the earth, REV 7:2-3. It is reasonable to conclude, that this mark was given to them for the same reason. **To protect the Lord's servants from destructive angelic beings.** Since God's mark in Ezekiel was invisible, we have every reason to believe that God's mark in Revelation is also invisible:

> REV 7:2-3 And I saw another angel ascending from the east, having the seal of the living God: and he cried with a loud voice to the four angels, to whom it was given to hurt the earth and the sea, Saying, Hurt not the earth, neither the sea, nor the trees, **till we have sealed the servants of our God in their foreheads.**

> REV 14:1 And I looked, and, lo, a Lamb stood on the mount Sion, and with him an hundred forty and four thousand, **having his Father's name written in their foreheads.** (His name and the name of His Father, NASB)

REV 14:1 identifies God's mark as the name of the Lord. In the NASB, both God the Father's and Jesus' names are included in that mark. Without getting into a lengthy theological debate; right now, today, we are "sealed by the Holy Spirit" of promise, and marked with Jesus' name, EPH 1:13. The Holy Spirit has placed Jesus' mark on us. It is a real seal, but it is invisible to the natural world. This seal is also on us for a definite reason. **We are sealed to show that we are under the protection and authority of God the Father, and the Lord Jesus!**

Since God's real mark is invisible in the natural world, it is reasonable to conclude that Satan's mark of REV 13:16 is invisible in the natural world; unless we can find Scripture which says differently. The author can find no such Scriptures, so from a biblical standpoint, Satan's mark is an invisible spiritual mark. Now let's put it all together:

> REV 13:16-18 And he causeth all, both small and great, rich and poor, free and bond, **to receive a mark in their right hand, or in their foreheads: And that no man might buy or sell,** save he that had the mark, or the name of the beast, or the number of his name. Here is wisdom. Let him that hath understanding count the number of the beast: **for it is the number of a man; and his number is Six hundred threescore and six.** (i.e.,666)

We need to go back to Daniel for a moment. Babylon was the center of world commerce, worshiping the almighty gold daric.[79] The seat of governmental authority in Babylon was Nebuchadnezzar the king. He was an absolute monarch. At the sound of 6x6x6 kinds of music, he commanded everyone in his empire to bow down and worship his 6x6666666666 image of gold. The king was in essence saying, "I order you to worship this gold. I have made an idol of it. I worship it, you make it your god, too. I support it with my authority, and I'll make it sound pretty for you." Governments today, bow before their economies, and order their citizens to support their systems.

Ever since God marked Cain who slew his brother Abel, there has been a mark, in fact two marks. One for God's servants, and one for those belonging to the enemy. Through the ages, Satan has tried to turn man away from God. He has used false gods, disguised as materialism of every kind. Gods of gold, silver, brass, iron, wood and stone.

We have them with us today. They are wrapped in prettier packages of course, and have more interesting labels. We are too sophisticated to bow down to any old stone idol. So instead, we call our images automobiles, airplanes, jewelry, furniture, televisions, and boats. We bow down to these present-day gods without any problem at all. Same gods, western society names. We worship them, so they are a stumbling block to us also. Using music, Satan has made them sound pretty. Advertising jingles, and spotlights on the rich and famous market the world's goods in abundance, financial success, power, and sexual prowess. We are told: In this life, that's all there is of any importance. Oh Lord, how has Satan been able to blind the people so?

When someone turns himself totally over to these things and excludes the Living God from his life, he has a mark on him that angelic beings see. It may be hidden in his hand as a credit card, or struck between his eyes as the consuming thoughts of a depraved mind. He is under the authority of the ruler of this world, and has become his blind slave. If he becomes openly evil, that mark even becomes visible to

---

[79] The daric was an early gold coin used throughout the Middle East.

Christians. The greed and wanton pleasure seeking, the drugs, the immorality and egocentricity becomes a spiritual "mark of the beast" on him that won't wash off. You can see the sin in his face. It is a brand that sears his soul. Though you hope desperately that it isn't there, if you look carefully you can see it. He is without hope, and his final end is eternal fire:

> REV 14:9-11 And the third angel followed them, saying with a loud voice, **If any man worship the beast and his image, and receive his mark in his forehead, or in his hand,** The same shall drink of the wine of the wrath of God, which is poured out without mixture into the cup of his indignation; and he shall be tormented with fire and brimstone in the presence of the holy angels, and in the presence of the Lamb: And the smoke of their torment ascendeth up for ever and ever: and they have no rest day nor night, who worship the beast and his image, and whosoever receiveth the mark of his name.

# Chapter 23

# *The Sun, Moon & Stars*

Most of the pieces are now in place. We need to stand back for
a moment and take the long view. The Bible teaches that the
Lord planned three major epochs for the world He has made.
The first epoch was from Adam to the flood and records 2000
years of history. Examples like Seth, Enoch, and Noah show
that men before the flood (with precious little doctrine) could
be pleasing in God's sight. Man looks at someone's doctrinal
position, but the Lord looks on the heart. When that early
world became so evil that God could no longer tolerate it, He
destroyed it with a flood:

> GEN 6:5-7 And GOD saw that the wickedness of man was
> great in the earth, and that every imagination of the thoughts
> of his heart was only evil continually. And it repented the
> LORD that he had made man on the earth, and it grieved
> him at his heart. **And the LORD said, I will destroy man
> whom I have created from the face of the earth; both
> man, and beast, and the creeping thing, and the fowls of
> the air; for it repenteth me that I have made them.**

Yet He saved righteous Noah and seven others. Between
the flood and the birth of the Lord another 2000 years was
recorded.[80] Moses, David, and Isaiah are examples of men of
God after the flood. Through faith, they obeyed the Lord and
were found pleasing in His sight. They trusted in their coming
Messiah even though they did not know who He was. The
Lord inspired the Old Testament writers to record these
examples, for us. They were for our learning, so that we too,

---

[80] The exact time which elapsed between Adam and Noah, and Noah and
the birth of Jesus has been the subject of much debate among evangelicals.
The Early Israelites did not always include every generation when they
recorded a genealogical line. This in no way suggests that the Bible
account is in error, any more than someone telling his life story would be
accused of error because he failed to include the moment he learned to
swim. What is important is that the time the Lord willed to record in both
eras was about 2000 years.

could walk in a way that would be pleasing in His sight.[81] Over the following centuries the Children of Israel drifted away from God and became ineffectual witnesses. It was time for the next step of God's eternal plan. God sent His own beloved Son.

Three times the Lord gave epochal signs to turn this world from its rebellion against its Creator. First, there was Noah and the flood. Second, there was Moses and the law. Third, He sent His Son. But we killed His Son. As the reason for the death of Jesus was spread around the world, millions of people came to the Lord. The whole Roman Empire was turned upside down. The Lord Jesus brought salvation to all who received Him. Jesus tore the veil of the temple from top to bottom that we might have access to the Father through His blood; but now, in our becoming like the heathen around us, the Christian nations have invoked the following:

> HEB 10:28-31 He that despised Moses' law died without mercy under two or three witnesses: **Of how much sorer punishment, suppose ye, shall he be thought worthy, who hath trodden under foot the Son of God,** and hath counted the blood of the covenant, wherewith he was sanctified, an unholy thing, and hath done despite unto the Spirit of grace? For we know him that hath said, Vengeance belongeth unto me, I will recompense, saith the Lord. And again, **The Lord shall judge his people. It is a fearful thing to fall into the hands of the living God.**

Notice who the judgment is falling upon: God's people. But it is now 1990, and we prefer a more ear-tickling, modern theology. The God of the universe having died for our sins is thought to be an old shopworn tradition we have outgrown. The Christian nations have turned away from God, and there is little left for the Lord to do:

---

[81] This is not suggesting that salvation is by works, or through the deeds of the law. We are saved by grace through faith in Jesus, and that faith only. But that faith will produce works of righteousness in which we were foreordained to walk, EPH 2:10, JAS 2:17, 1JO 2:4.

LUK 20:14-16 Then said the lord of the vineyard, What shall I do? I will send my beloved son: it may be they will reverence him when they see him. But when the husbandmen saw him, they reasoned...saying...let us kill him, that the inheritance may be ours. So they cast him out of the vineyard, and killed him. What therefore shall the lord of the vineyard do unto them? **He shall come and destroy these husbandmen...**

The parable above primarily refers to the Pharisees of Jesus' time, but we are guilty of the same sin. The consequences will be the same. Luke 21:24-32 gives us not longer than one generation after the restoration of Jerusalem until the Lord returns. The Christian Era will have also lasted about 2000 years. Then cometh destruction. The final participants are now all in place. A lukewarm church, an uninvolved Europe, the emerging Islamic beast, and the new nation of Israel, about which there is this startling statistic.

Before 1948 there were Jews spread all over the Middle East. The World Organization of Jews from Arab Countries lists the number of Jews in Moslem countries before 1948 and now:

| | | | |
|---|---|---|---|
| Morocco | - | 285,000 in 1948, | 10,000 now. |
| Syria | - | 18,000 in 1948, | 4,000 now. |
| Tunisia | - | 110,000 in 1948, | 3,500 now. |
| Yemen | - | 55,000 in 1948, | 1,200 now. |
| Iraq | - | 140,000 in 1948, | 300 now. |
| Egypt | - | 75,000 in 1948, | 200 now. |
| Lebanon | - | 2,000 in 1948, | 200 now. |
| Libya | - | 38,000 in 1948, | 4 now. |
| Jordan | - | | none now.[82] |

When Israel became a state there were about 856,000 Jews living in Arab states. Within the next two decades, 90% of them left. They were not always persecuted, so what motivated them to tear up their roots, leave their homes and

---

[82] Wesley Pippert, *Land of Promise, Land of Strife*, pp 171-172.

successful businesses, and immigrate to Israel? The Lord God did. Here is the scripture which makes that data relevant:

> ISA 11:11-12 (excerpts) ...**the Lord shall set his hand again the second time to recover the remnant of his people**, which shall be left, from Assyria, and from Egypt, and from Pathros, and from Cush, and from Elam, and from Shinar, and from Hamath, and from the islands of the sea...he shall set up an ensign for the nations...and shall assemble the outcasts...from the four corners of the earth.

The names in ISA 11:11-12 are the ancient names for many of the modern lands in the list above. That verse further states that this will be fulfilled when the Lord restores His people the 2nd time. Besides the restoration decreed by Cyrus in 536BC, there has been no other Jewish restoration in history, except 1948. Later in Isaiah, there are more verses which refer to this same time:

> ISA 27:12-13 ...in that day...ye shall be gathered one by one, O ye children of Israel. And **it shall come to pass in that day, that the great trumpet shall be blown**, and they shall come which were ready to perish in the land of Assyria, and the outcasts in the land of Egypt, and shall worship the LORD in the holy mount at Jerusalem.

So when the Lord restores Israel from the nations "the great trumpet" will be blown. Now how many great trumpets are there? There is only one other great trumpet in Scripture, the one at which the saints are gathered in MAT 24:31! The sequence of events from now until that "great trumpet" is somewhat speculative, but there are scriptural guideposts scattered throughout the Bible which give us some direction. All of them show that we are holding on to a lighted stick of dynamite with a very short fuse:

> JOE 3:1-2, (NASB excerpts) For, behold, **in those days, and at that time, when I restore the fortunes of Judah and Jerusalem, I will gather all the nations...Then I will enter into judgment with them**...on behalf of My people and My inheritance, Israel, whom they have scattered among the nations; and they have divided up my land.

The dating of the prophet Joel is uncertain, but there is a peculiarity about it which points us to 1948. "When I restore the fortunes of Judah..." The Lord did not say the fortunes of Israel, but Judah! Judah is the Jews. They went home in 1948, and freed Jerusalem in 1967. The great war foretold in the surrounding verses did not take place anywhere near the 536-516BC restoration under Zerubbabel and Ezra; so these "fortunes of Judah" have to refer to new Israel. Look at some further quotes from that same chapter:

> JOE 3:9-15 **Proclaim ye this among the Gentiles; Pre-
> pare war, wake up the mighty men, let all the men of
> war draw near;** let them come up: Beat your plowshares
> into swords and your pruninghooks into spears: let the weak
> say, I am strong. Assemble yourselves, and come, all ye
> heathen, and gather yourselves together round about: thither
> cause thy mighty ones to come down, O LORD. **Put ye in
> the sickle, for the harvest is ripe: come, get you down;
> for the press is full, the fats overflow;** for their wickedness
> is great. Multitudes, multitudes in the valley of decision: for
> the day of the LORD is near in the valley of decision. **The
> sun and the moon shall be darkened, and the stars shall
> withdraw their shining.**

The Lord declares through the prophet Joel that when the fortunes of Judah are restored, He will bring all the nations forth for war. As of this writing, this prophecy is still unfulfilled, but there are storm clouds on the horizon. Look carefully at the bold face of the above quote. Sounds very much like the Revelation quote below:

> REV 14:17-18 ...And another angel came out from the altar,
> which had power over fire; and cried with a loud cry to him
> that had the sharp sickle, saying, **Thrust in thy sharp
> sickle, and gather the clusters of the vine of the earth;
> for her grapes are fully ripe.**

Any question that these two passages refer to the same incident? Remarkably, they were written about 800 years apart, yet they sound the same. This is Armageddon, and it will take place in the same generation that the fortunes of Judah are restored. Any question that their fortunes were restored in 1948 and 1967AD? If not, most of us will be alive during Armageddon. Joel states that sun, moon, and stars would not shine. Revelation declares:

> REV 6:12-13 And I beheld when he had opened the sixth seal, and, lo, there was a great earthquake; and **the sun became black as sackcloth of hair, and the moon became as blood; And the stars of heaven fell unto the earth...**

These are puzzling pictures, and many believe that they will be fulfilled literally. But, there are good scriptural reasons to think them allegorical. First, in prophesying the fall of Babylon, ISA 13:10 uses the same pictorial language to describe the event. Ezekiel uses the same language to foretell the fall of Egypt, EZE 32:7-8. AMO 8:9 uses similar language to tell of the destruction of Israel, as MIC 3:6 does about the prophets. Yet in none of those events do we have a record of any astronomical phenomenon being observed like the darkening of the sun, moon or stars. Furthermore, read Acts 2:19-20 where Joel is quoted at length in the New Testament. Here again is blood, fire, smoke, and sun turned to darkness and the moon to blood. Peter declares this blood, fire, smoke, and the moon turning to blood was fulfilled at Pentecost; yet Acts does not report that these signs literally took place then.[83]

If these terms are allegorical in one passage in Joel, they should be interpreted allegorically in another in the same book, unless there is strong biblical evidence not to. The author could find none, so let's look at sun, moon, and stars as possibly allegorical, and look for biblical definitions. Jesus is "as the sun shining in His strength," REV 1:16, and the stars are messengers both earthly and angelic, REV 1:20. The root meaning of the Greek word "aggelos," from which we get angel, is messenger. Angel = messenger, remember that, it's important:

> MAL 4:2 But unto you that fear my name shall **the Sun of righteousness arise with healing in his wings...**

---

[83] Some believe that Peter is referring to the miraculous events which surrounded the Crucifixion. That is a possibility, I suppose. Even so, there is no record of fire, or smoke, or of the moon turning to blood.

REV 1:16 ...and **his countenance was as the sun shineth in his strength.**

REV 1:20 **The mystery of the seven stars which thou sawest in my right hand...The seven stars are the angels** (the messengers) **of the seven churches...**

All agree that MAL 4:2, quoted above, is a prophecy of the coming of the Lord Jesus. Note how "sun" is spelled. The Hebrew word used here is "shemesh." This same word is translated "sun" over 100 times in the Old Testament. So Jesus is not only the Son of God, but also the "Sun" of righteousness. This is one of God's pictorial ways of describing the radiant glory of His righteous Son.

What about the stars? Churches have ministers and teaching elders. They are "messengers" of the Lord to this world, and to brethren. They are the stars, REV 1:20.

But the moon, what is that? Well, the moon has no light of its own. All it has is the reflected light of the sun. In the same way, the church has no light source of its own. All it can do is reflect the light of the Son.

Now to the interpretation: The world has become so spiritually darkened and blinded by sin, that it can no longer see the brilliant light of the Sun of righteousness. That Light is covered in a black sackcloth made of the hair of iniquity. The light of the Lord is not diminished, but man is separated from the light by his sin. He prefers darkness rather than light.

As for the stars, the author would prefer to leave this whole subject out, but it is too important. Ministers and evangelists are falling all over the place. They no longer teach the Word of Truth, and the Lord permits them to be discredited, to lose their "ministries" and be brought before the judgment seats of this world. Many of them are not truly God's servants, but are servants of the enemy in masquerade. Here is the scripture:

2CO 11:14-15 ...for Satan himself is transformed into an angel of light. Therefore it is no great thing if **his ministers also be transformed as the ministers of righteousness;** whose end shall be according to their works.

This is not theoretical. There are Bible and theology teachers, and men in the ministry with big names, who are false counselors. They write popular books, and all men speak well of them, but they belong to the enemy. They are real flesh and blood false prophets among the sheep.

> LUK 6:26 Woe unto you, when all men shall speak well of you! **for so did their fathers to the false prophets.**

We would like to believe that the pastor we listen to, and lean on for our spiritual support, is not one of these. But if he departs from the Word of God by even one verse, he is! For to what ever degree a church leader leads the brethren astray, he serves Satan. In most cases we don't need to look at the church down the street to find these wolves. The chances are better than 80% that you just need to look straight ahead from your own pew.[84] If you think that excessive, see if your own pastor teaches a balanced gospel: That God indeed loves us, but if man turns away from Him, judgement will fall. If we disobey, He will discipline. Brrrrrrr! That is "negative" and we don't want our pastor to teach that. Nonetheless, it is the balance of Scripture; and by our disregarding this balance we face a troubled future.

The church is the moon. It sheds no light of its own. The church's only purpose is to reflect the glory of the Lord Jesus by teaching the Gospel, and by so doing, being a light to the world, MAT 5:14. We are to mirror the light of the Lord in our lives. Since 1948 the church has lost its zeal; and we are in the period of time when MAT 24:29 is being fulfilled, the days after the tribulation, the days when the moon is turned to blood, REV 6:12. Blood is useless for reflecting light.

You see, "All those who desire to live godly in Christ Jesus shall be persecuted," 2TI 3:13. The tribulation is over in the West, because much of the church isn't doing anything to get persecuted for. These are the signs in the sun, moon, and

---

[84] From a 1984 trans-denominational survey of protestant pastors polling them on the five basic tenants of the Christian faith. For an in depth study read David Hunt's, *The Seduction of Christianity*.

stars today, but our spiritual hearts are darkened, and we can't see them.

Now refer to *Chart 24* at the end of Book 3, which also quotes three verses of Scripture from an earlier chapter. Look at them in the light of what we now know. That graph looked crazy when you first saw it, didn't it?  But now it makes perfect sense.  Throughout the Christian Era the Church has grown and spread until it covered the whole Earth.  Saints by the millions were tortured and killed for the Lord, but the gates of hell did not prevail against them.  The records of their faithful deeds were dutifully recorded by the surviving brethren, and passed down to us in books such as "Martyrs Mirror," "The Pilgrim Church," and "Fox's Book of Martyrs."  Few read those works today, and the terrible slaughter of the saints is almost forgotten.  The great tribulation of the church is over. Now the church's central concern is not sharing the gospel, or surviving through persecution, but (can you believe it) the Christian and his money.

Like the holocaust was to the Jews, at the very end, trouble will also come upon us.  The harassment of the true church has already begun here, and it will get worse.  By our complacency we have allowed a minority of power seeking godless men to control our government, businesses, and media. They, too, tell us to worship the image of the beast, and be the slave of his mark.  Now it is too late.  These economic power brokers are entrenched, and a fearful Ephraim may yet have to flee this land and go to the only place on Earth where the Lord has promised him safety: Israel!

# Chapter 24

# *Children Of Deception*

Sometimes to look forward in time, all we need to do is look back a few centuries. The author could not write about what is going to happen to us, and why, if Jesus were not standing as a light at the other end of this dark tunnel. This is like having a loved one who is terminally ill. Do you tell him of the pain he will soon suffer, or do you hide it from him?

One of Satan's major goals has always been to silence the witness of the church, and prevent the lost from hearing the gospel. To accomplish this he uses several primary weapons.

(1) Get sin into the camp, any kind will do.
(2) Get the church interested in secular pursuits, like a building fund.
(3) Get the Word of God out of the church, use commentaries instead.
(4) Persecute the brethren. This persecution intensifies if a nation turns away from God.

If Satan is permitted to gain control in a country, he will attempt to destroy the Christians within it. Why? Because Christians do such things as praying, and leading the Lost to Jesus. They stand against the enemy who is trying his best to turn people away from the Lord. At no time in history were the saints left untroubled when the land around them became violent and sinful.

The 20th Century is no different. Despite our so-called "civilization," we have had the Nazis, Pol Pot, the Viet Cong, Idi Amin, Stalin, Abu Nidal, Hussein of Iraq, and the

Guardians of the Islamic Revolution as modern examples. Christians and Jews have suffered terribly at their hands. Today, the true saints are persecuted in every godless land. That is a fact of life foretold in the Bible, 2TI 3:12 and elsewhere. But it couldn't happen here, right? Let's look at the short history of a modern democracy.

One of the most civilized nations on Earth was a German Republic formed out of the ruins of the 1st World War. It had a constitution not unlike our own. It was considered by many to be a worker's paradise. That country was the home of the Knights Templar of Crusader fame, the seat of the Reformation, the home of Martin Luther, and the Lutheran church, and a center of religious and scientific thought for all Europe.

In the 1930's roving bands of violent youths began to terrorize the cities. Does that ever sound familiar. To stand against this anarchy, a charismatic leader was elected. Adolf Hitler was that leader. He was an occult figure, strong in the mysticism and mythology of the middle ages. He sold a germanic "New Age" philosophy. He romanticized the supremacy of the Aryan race. He even built a cult around it, complete with secret rites, and special signs and uniforms. Then he enlisted those same violent breakers of the law to enforce his new laws, and the persecution of Jews and of the church began. His symbol was the satanic double serpentine swastika, a variation of one of today's New Age symbols.

A few short years after Hitler came to power, Nazi Germany had Adolph Eichmann, the Gestapo, the SS, and the gas chambers. The Nazi's killed 6,000,000 Jews, and numberless Christians. Estimates vary, but the death toll for the Second World War, in Europe alone, was in excess of 20,000,000 people. That number is so large that it loses meaning; but it comes into focus if you think of your own death, and the deaths of your loved ones as a few of them.

Now, we again have a nation going astray, this time it is our own. Prayer, Bible reading, and creation science are no longer permitted in our public schools. Our college campuses are floating in Hari Krishna, Hindu gurus, and the New Age. What a paradox; the Bible on which this nation was founded is forbidden to our children, but Far Eastern mysticism may be studied for college credits. To see the error of far eastern mysticism, all one needs to do is compare the conditions in

Christian lands with the conditions in the lands those religions came from. One cannot divorce the misery of those people from the religious systems on which they rely. In the United States, abortion clinics have butchered over 22,000,000 babies since Roe vs. Wade. That is more than three times as many people as the Nazis slaughtered in their death camps. One van was found in California which contained the remains of 16,500 unborn infants. Some cosmetic companies are even using parts of these aborted babies in the preparation of their beauty aids. God will not forget, nor forgive. Though there will be a far more terrible reckoning later on, the Lord is now bringing this sin down on our heads in an unusual way. Did you know that an increasing number of healthy young American couples are unable to have children?

> HOS 9:16   Ephraim is smitten, their root is dried up, they shall bear no fruit: yea, though they bring forth, **yet will I slay even the beloved fruit of their womb.**

Violent youth gangs, and desperate drug addicts, have made the streets of many of our cities unsafe to walk on, or even drive through. There are many neighborhoods of inner cities where the police are afraid to go, and do not patrol. It is too dangerous. In Washington D.C., our nation's capitol, the quiet of almost every night is broken by sporadic bursts of gunfire, from fully automatic weapons, as young drug lords battle to expand their "turf."[85] In our public schools, 125,000 teachers are threatened monthly, and there are 525,000 attacks and robberies monthly. Some are for school lunch money, but a high percentage are drug related. One year, in Detroit schools alone, there were over 120 shootings and hundreds of stabbings and other violent crimes. 70% of our high school students go to school armed, and their major fear is not nuclear war, but a breakout of school violence.[86] To top it off, the truancy laws force parents to expose their children to this environment. Not one of us would deliberately send a

---

[85] *U.S. News and World Report*, April 25, 1989

[86] *National Review*, Dec. 13, 1985

child to a place where there are ongoing robberies, murders, prostitution, violence, drugs, profanity, and obscene language. So what do we do? We send impressionable Christian children into public schools where even teachers are afraid for their own safety.

Armed gangs of marijuana growers roam freely over many of our National Forests, and make them unsafe to hike in. Campers have been attacked and beaten. Our park rangers are not the Marines, and they are too outnumbered to drive these violent lawbreakers out.[87] To compound the problem, our "loyal" citizenry supports these felons by buying and using the drugs they grow. It is estimated that 40% of our young adult population uses marijuana on a regular basis, and cocaine abuse is epidemic. If you are robbed or your house is broken into, there is a 72% chance that the person involved is a drug addict.[88] Coupled with that, violent crime is on the increase.

Our pop music industry is dominated by drug-using rock stars who have become the cult leaders of our youth. Some of them are openly demonic, laying hands on recordings, and asking for the devil's blessing on it. The songs they sing glorify rebellion against parents, drug abuse, sexual promiscuity, violence, homosexuality, sadism, murder, and satanism. Every imaginable degeneracy. Our children know every lyric, and sing along with every word. The image these rock groups portray is one of utmost depravity, and some of the lewd and obscene acts they perform on stage are too degenerate to record here.

Satanic symbols and slogans can be found on almost every graffiti littered wall in America. The witchcraft and satanism marketed to our children through rock music, and the broadcast media, has influenced a new crime wave. Almost every major high school in the nation has a satanic cult operating within it.

It is virtually impossible to get a police official to go on record about the satanists; but it has been estimated by law

---

[87] *Readers Digest,* Nov. 1987

[88] Letter from *Citizens for a Drug Free America,* Dec. 1988.

enforcement authorities, that one out of every five missing children is probably the victim of these cultists. The satanists sacrifice, and eat infants in their black masses, and drink their blood. Some of the women in these cults even act as breeders. They deliberately become pregnant, by anyone, and have babies for the express purpose of sacrificing them. Many Metro Squads are afraid to investigate these satanists. They fear that the investigating officers will either be turned into satanists themselves; or if their "cover is blown," that they will be murdered.

This is not happening in some dark and far-off jungle. All this malevolence is being committed by the offspring of doting American mothers who blindly believe in their children's innocence: ignoring the heavy metal and beat of drums, with black light on satanic posters, radiating from their teenager's room...long into the night.

How can this be happening here? Violent and demonic TV, movies, video games, and drugs, have spawned a generation of Americans that we do not know. A generation not unlike the Hitler youth of the 30's. Old Testament and New, God saw the same sins and foretold their consequences:

> ISA 57:4 ...are ye not children of transgression, a seed of falsehood. **Enflaming yourselves with idols under every green tree, slaying the children in the valleys under the clifts of the rocks?**

> EZE 8:10 So I went in and saw; and behold every form of creeping things, and abominable beasts, and all the idols of the house of Israel, **porturayed upon the wall round about.**

> EZE 18:10-13 (excerpts) If (a man) beget a son that is **a robber, a shedder of blood...and defiled his neighbour's wife, Hath oppressed the poor and needy, hath spoiled by violence...**hath committed abomination...**shall he then live? he shall not live: he hath done all these abominations; he shall surely die; his blood shall be upon him.**

What about our own Babylon, our financial institutions? By lending money to undeveloped countries our banks have ruined Third World economies. In many of these countries, the average yearly income, for a whole family, is far less than the average American teenager has for his spending allowance. But, rather than forgiving their debt, we demand repayment from those who have nothing but a little plot of ground, and the rags on their back. To get our pound of flesh, we buy their food at prices their own people cannot afford to pay. This so inflates their local food prices, that the natives can not afford to eat the very food they grow. In this way we literally starve their poor. Then our banks lend them more money, to pay just the interest on their debt, which gets them deeper in debt. We pride ourselves on our social programs here, ignoring the fact that we have built them on the struggling backs of the peasants of the Third World. We are our brother's keeper, and God will not forget:

AMO 8:4-6 Hear this, O ye that swallow up the needy, even to make the poor of the land to fail, Saying, When will the new moon be gone, that we may sell corn? and the sabbath, that we may set forth wheat, making the ephah (bushel) small, and the shekel (dollar) great, and falsifying the balances by deceit? **That we may buy the poor for silver, and the needy for a pair of shoes; yea, and sell the refuse of the wheat?**

JAM 5:1-5 **Go to now, ye rich men, weep and howl for your miseries that shall come upon you.** Your riches are corrupted, and your garments are motheaten. **Your gold and silver is cankered; and the rust of them shall be a witness against you, and shall eat your flesh as it were fire. Ye have heaped treasure together for the last days.** Behold, the hire of the labourers who have reaped down your fields, which is of you kept back by fraud, crieth: and the cries of them which have reaped are entered into the ears of the Lord of sabbaoth. Ye have lived in pleasure on the earth, and been wanton; ye have nourished your hearts, as in a day of slaughter. Ye have condemned and killed the just; and he doth not resist you.

Our 30,000 churches are strangely silent on these and other issues. Many of them are playing with eastern religions disguised as meditation, positive imaging, visualizing, and the New Age. Some have even gone so far as to condone abortion, homosexuality, divorce, pre-marital sex, and the monetary practices for which the Lord destroyed the Israelites before us:

EZE 22:26-29, NASB  Her priests have done violence to My law and have profaned My holy things; they have made no distinction between the holy and the profane, and they have not taught the difference between the unclean and the clean; and they hide their eyes from My sabbaths, and I am profaned among them. **Her princes within her are like wolves, tearing the prey by shedding blood and destroying lives in order to get dishonest gain.** **And her prophets have smeared whitewash for them seeing false visions and divining lies for them,** saying, "Thus says the Lord God," when the Lord has not spoken...

Whitewashing over evil is not new. It has been around since Israel's time and longer. Will all this go unpunished? Not if our God is who He says He is! As Israel did before us, we have become more wicked than the nations round about us. We have turned from light to darkness, just like Satan did. In all history, God has never allowed these conditions to last for long. When the widow, and the poor, and the needy cry to Him, will He not hear? He will surely answer their cry, and that right speedily.

How painful this is to those who sigh and groan over the abominations committed in our midst. Much of what is happening is beyond the power of the individual Christian to change. What are we to do? To answer that question, we need to take a look at the walled cities of Judah, and the ancient methods of waging war.

# Chapter 25

# The Crumbling Walls

The major defense of Judah's cities was their strong high walls. They were made of stone and usually set on a hill with the foundations set in bedrock. Most of the great siege engines had not been invented yet; so a relatively few defenders could protect a good sized city from an enormous army. When a heathen army besieged a city of Judah, there were three primary ways the attackers tried to defeat it.

(1) Starve them out. That could be a long term project lasting several years. The cities were prepared for that option, having many storehouses full of food to tide them over. Sometimes it was a case of who ran out of supplies first.

(2) Cut off the city's water supply. That was easier said than done. Most cities had huge cisterns, or other hidden water sources. The most famous of these was Hezekiah's incredible tunnel to a major spring outside the walls of Jerusalem. Other cities had wells within the walls.

(3) Breach the walls, and invade the city. This was the quickest, but by no means easy. To do this, the invading general would locate the weakest section of the wall. Then with battering rams and fire, he would smash a hole in the wall, through which his armies could attack. The city was also prepared for this option. They would defend the wall with boiling oil and stone missiles. But if the attackers were determined and a breach was made, the defenders would send their strongest warrior into the gap. It was a suicide mission; for while he held the enemy at bay, the stone masons would build a new wall behind him. Ezekiel tells us of this man in the gap:

> EZE 22:29-31 (NASB) The people of the land have practiced oppression, and committed robbery, and they have wronged the poor and needy and have oppressed the sojourner without justice. **And I searched for a man among them, that should build up the wall and stand in the gap before Me for the land, that I should not destroy it: but I found no one.** Thus I have poured out My indignation upon them with the fire of my wrath; their way I have brought upon their heads, saith the Lord GOD.

We have many breaks in our spiritual walls today, and it would take many men, in many gaps, to stand while the walls were being built behind them. What would the Lord have us do in this New (dark) Age? Pray the Lord to make us men in the gap. It is a suicide mission to be sure; but every true servant of the Lord has to be willing to pay that price. The only offensive weapon we have is the Sword of the Spirit, the Word of God, but it is powerful enough, even "mighty to the tearing down of fortresses." Brother, it is lonely out there. If you don't love Jesus, trust the Holy Spirit, and cling to the Bible, you will wonder if you are doing the right thing; but any real stand for Jesus is a stand alone, for Scripture says:

> HEB 13:12-13 Wherefore Jesus also, that he might sanctify the people with his own blood, suffered without the gate. **Let us go forth therefore unto him without the camp, bearing his reproach.**

Be willing to stand against the complacency and false doctrine within our churches. Be one who speaks against the abominations which have caused the Lord to hide His eyes from us. Maybe, if a few stand, the church, and then the country, would repent; and the Lord could yet withhold the evil that He has decreed upon our land:

> JON 3:8-10  But let man and beast be covered with sackcloth, and cry mightily unto God: yea, **let them turn every one from his evil way, and from the violence that is in their hands. Who can tell if God will turn and repent, and turn away from his fierce anger, that we perish not?** And God saw their works, that they turned from their evil way; and God repented of the evil, that he had said that he would do unto them; and he did it not.

By the so-called "good life" we have become so spiritually weakened that we are little prepared to "fight the good fight," or "to endure hardship as a good soldier." Still, as a good soldier, the man in the gap must try. If he doesn't, here are some other Words of God which will also stand:

> HEB 12:4-8  **Ye have not yet resisted unto blood, striving against sin.** And ye have forgotten the exhortation which speaketh unto you as unto children, My son, despise not thou the chastening of the Lord, nor faint when thou art rebuked of him:  **For whom the Lord loveth he chasteneth, and scourgeth every son whom he receiveth. If ye endure chastening, God dealeth with you as with sons; for what son is he whom the father chasteneth not? But if ye be without chastisement, whereof all are partakers, then are ye bastards, and not sons.**

If we are God's children as we claim, then these verses also apply to us. God will yet discipline the Western Church. Because of when we are in relation to Bible prophecy, that discipline will most likely come to us as Armageddon. Right now that war seems far away. We hear of peace talks here, and treaties there. Peace, and treaties, but under the surface there is a gut-wrenching fear of what is to come upon the earth, for the Bible says:

1TH 5:3 **For when they shall say, Peace and safety; then sudden destruction cometh upon them, as travail upon a woman with child; and they shall not escape.**

JER 14:13-14 Then said I, Ah, Lord GOD! behold, the prophets say unto them, Ye shall not see the sword, neither shall ye have famine; but I will give you assured peace in this place. Then the LORD said unto me, **The prophets prophesy lies in my name**: I sent them not, neither have I commanded them, neither spake unto them: they prophesy unto you a false vision and divination, and a thing of nought, and the deceit of their heart.

How Armageddon will start is uncertain. REV 20:8-9 is a synopsis of Ezekiel ch.38-39 which is considered to be the classic description of this battle. There are literally hundreds of verses about this final war. All nations will be involved, REV 3:12, and the eye of the storm will be in the valley of Megiddo, which is just to the West of the Sea of Galilee, in northern Israel, REV 16:16. The generals of the world will be hidden in their underground command centers, REV 6:15. The Battlefront at Megiddo will be 200 miles long, REV 14:20.

200,000,000 horsemen will be fighting, REV 9:16. More on these horsemen in a later chapter. Because of the size of those armies it is unlikely that they will all be fighting in that valley. Just moving that many troops into one valley would be a logistical nightmare. It is more probable that this will be another world war, with Israel in the center. Tactical nuclear weapons weigh about 100 pounds, and it is likely that they will be used, REV 16:21. Chemical agents and germ warfare are also likely, ZEC 14:12. This fire storm will be so great that it is probable that ICBM's will also be employed, ISA 24:6.

One third of the world's population will be killed, REV 9:18. The rest will not repent, REV 9:20-21. That is the whole world. Now if two thirds did not repent, who is the third that will be killed? They must be those who do repent, the church. Thank you Lord that we too will be counted worthy to suffer for your Name. After we have been tried as if by fire, then Jesus will end it with a Word, REV 19:21.

All the above references are now quoted in paragraph style. The context of each verse may be located from the above references. It may seem a long quote without interruption by the author for explanation, but none is needed. The description is dreadfully clear. Some verses are literal, while some are in allegorical language. These allegories picture modern warfare as it must have looked to the ancient writers who had never heard of gunpowder, much less of a mortar, tank or nuclear weapon:

And when the thousand years are expired, Satan shall be loosed out of his prison, And shall go out to deceive the nations which are in the four quarters of the earth, Gog, and Magog, to gather them together to battle: the number of whom is as the sand of the sea ...**the hour of temptation, which shall come upon all the world, to try them that dwell upon the earth.** And he gathered them together into a place called in the Hebrew tongue Armageddon.

And the kings of the earth, and the great men, and the rich men, and the chief captains, and the mighty men, and every bondman, and every free man, hid themselves in the dens and in the rocks of the mountains; And said to the mountains and rocks, Fall on us, and hide us from the face of him that sitteth on the throne, and from the wrath of the Lamb:

And the winepress was trodden without the city, and blood came out of the winepress, even unto the horse bridles, by the space of a thousand and six hundred furlongs (200 miles). And the number of the army of the horsemen were two hundred thousand thousand (200,000,000): and I heard the number of them.

And thus I saw the horses in the vision, and them that sat on them, having breastplates of fire, and of jacinth, and brimstone: and the heads of the horses were as the heads of lions; and out of their mouths issued fire and smoke and brimstone. By these three was the third part of men killed, by the fire, and by the smoke, and by the brimstone, which issued out of their mouths. And there fell upon men a great hail out of heaven, every stone about the weight of a talent (100 pounds): and men blasphemed God because of the plague of the hail; for the plague thereof was exceeding great.

And this shall be the plague wherewith the LORD will smite all the people that have fought against Jerusalem;

Their flesh shall consume away while they stand upon their feet, and their eyes shall consume away in their holes, and their tongue shall consume away in their mouth.

And the rest of the men which were not killed by these plagues yet repented not of the works of their hands, that they should not worship devils, and idols of gold, and silver, and brass, and stone, and of wood: which neither can see, nor hear, nor walk: Neither repented they of their murders, nor of their sorceries, nor of their fornication, nor of their thefts.[89]

And they went up on the breadth of the earth, and compassed the camp of the saints about, and the beloved city: and fire came down from God out of heaven, and devoured them. Therefore hath the curse devoured the earth, and they that dwell therein are desolate: therefore the inhabitants of the earth are burned, and few men left.

And the remnant were slain with the sword of him that sat upon the horse, which sword proceeded out of his mouth: and all the fowls were filled with their flesh.

That is Armageddon. There is little the author could add to make it sound more appalling. Since we are here until the last trumpet, and there is no more time, REV 10:6-7, most of us will be on earth during this conflict. It does not sound like anyone could live through it, but some Christians will. The Bible tells us there will be "we who are alive and remain."

Now we can understand why Satan has gone to the effort to get false teachings like the pre-tribulation rapture, and the pre-millennial views into the church. With those doctrines, we can relax in judgment deferred. Sort of a "someone else has to pay the bill" outlook. If this Laodecian church will not be here for this war, there is no reason to fear discipline for our lukewarmness.

In our hearts we say, "Who needs to worry about being worldly or disobeying the Lord. God is love, and all is forgiven

---

[89] Sorcery, spoken of several times in Revelation, is the usual translation of the Greek word "pharmekia." That is the word from which we get pharmacy, or drugs. This must have mystified the translators of the King James who never heard of amphetamines, morphine, or cocaine. Still, drug addiction was addressed in Scripture.

in Christ Jesus isn't it? We don't need to live sanctified lives, or lead the lost to Jesus. What does it matter what we do? We're saved, and we're going to be raptured out before all this happens, aren't we? So let's enjoy ourselves while it lasts..." And that is exactly what the church is doing. We start to believe that the terrible end of this world is for the other guy. We have developed an eat, drink, and play Bingo on Wednesday night mentality. There are many verses which show that this line of reasoning is questionable:

> 1PE 4:17 **For the time is come that judgment must begin at the house of God:** and if it first begin at us, what shall the end be of them that obey not the gospel of God?

> HEB 12:28-29 Wherefore we receiving a kingdom which cannot be moved, let us have grace, whereby we may serve God acceptably with reverence and godly fear: **For our God is a consuming fire.**

> 1PE 1:14-17 As obedient children, not fashioning yourselves according to the former lusts in your ignorance: But as he which hath called you is holy, so be ye holy in all manner of conversation; Because it is written, Be ye holy; for I am holy. And if ye call on the Father, who without respect of persons judgeth according to every man's work, **pass the time of your sojourning here in fear:**

Fear! Many will say that fear is not for the New Testament believer, but all of the above are New Testament quotes. Notice that judgment begins with us, and it is our God who is a consuming fire. What does a Christian do in these circumstances? Where is safety? It is in obeying God's Word, and remaining in the center of His will. What about when the bombs start falling, and all around us is in turmoil? In His Word, God has told us exactly what to do when that time arrives:

> ISA 26:20-27:1 Come, my people, enter thou into thy chambers, and shut thy doors about thee: **hide thyself as it were for a little moment,** until the indignation be overpast. For, behold, the LORD cometh out of his place to punish the inhabitants of the earth for their iniquity: the earth also shall disclose her blood, and shall no more cover her slain. **In**

**that day the LORD with his sore and great and strong
sword shall punish leviathan the piercing serpent, even
leviathan that crooked serpent; and he shall slay the
dragon** that is in the sea.

ZEP 2:2 Before the decree bring forth, before the day pass
as the chaff, before the fierce anger of the LORD come
upon you, before the day of the LORD'S anger come upon
you. **Seek ye the LORD, all ye meek of the earth, which
have wrought his judgment; seek righteousness, seek
meekness: it may be ye shall be hid in the day of the
LORD'S anger.**

Where is that hiding place?   For Joshua's spies it was in
a harlot's house.  For Shadrack, Mesheck, and Abednago it was
in the fiery furnace, for Daniel it was in a king's palace.  For
Paul it was in prison, and for Corrie TenBoom it was in a flea
infested barracks in a Nazi concentration camp.  They were
right where God wanted them, and not a hair on their heads
perished.  So your hiding place is wherever the center of the
Lord's will is for you, be it in your basement, or hiking in a
forest.  Fear not, brethren, the Lord has not forgotten how to
protect the righteous.  The only fear we should have is of being
out of God's will.  Trust in the Holy Spirit to lead you, and
God's Word to guide you, for that hiding place may be different
for every saint on earth.

But meanwhile, stand in the gap.  Prepare the brethren
for the coming hour of trial.  Lead the lost to Jesus.  If
everyone who reads this book leads just one more person to the
Lord, think of the joy that would bring to the angels in heaven,
not to mention to the Lord Jesus, Himself:

ISA 27:13 And it shall come to pass **in that day, that the
great trumpet shall be blown,** and they shall come which
were ready to perish in the land of Assyria, and the outcasts
in the land of Egypt, and shall worship the LORD in the
holy mount at Jerusalem.

# Chapter 26

# *The Apantesis*

Six references in Revelation relating to the end speak of it as that "hour." As a result, the author believes that Armageddon will be allowed to continue for about two weeks. An hour in day=year is exactly 15.22 days, and that could be the exact time from the first shot until the Lord's return. We know not when that "day nor the hour" might be, but from the time that "hour" of Armageddon begins until Jesus stands on Zion won't be long. We are taken to be with the Lord at the Last Trumpet at which there is no more time. Consequently, our being caught up in the clouds will coincide with the end of that battle. To get the whole picture, we look first in Acts at Jesus' ascension in 32AD, and then in 1TH at His return:

> ACT 1:9 ...while they beheld, he was taken up; and a cloud received him out of their sight. And...behold, two men stood by them in white apparel; Which also said, Ye men of Galilee, why stand ye gazing up into heaven? this same Jesus, which is taken up from you into heaven, **shall so come in like manner as ye have seen him go into heaven.**

> 1TH 4:16-17 **For the Lord himself shall descend from heaven with a shout, with the voice of the archangel, and with the trump of God:** and the dead in Christ shall rise first: Then we which are alive and remain shall be caught up together with them in the clouds, to meet the Lord in the air: and so shall we ever be with the Lord.

Study those verses carefully. First, Jesus will return just like we saw him go. This will be a physical reality, not just some spiritualized fulfillment in the church. The "like manner" is how we can be so sure. "Like manner" means exactly the same. It was a physical reality for the Apostles, it will be a physical reality for us. We will be standing on Earth and will see Him appear in the sky. The chronology of events will be as follows.

(1) Armageddon will be in progress.
(2) Jesus returns from heaven with a shout and a trumpet.
(3) During His descent, we will be caught up to meet Him in the air.
(4) With us escorting Him, the Lord will continue His descent to stand on Mount Zion.

How can we know that this is the correct sequence? By looking at other examples in history and in the Bible of what happened when a king returned to a city, and by understanding the definition of the Greek word "apantesis."[90] That word appears only four times in Scripture. In MAT 25:1 and 6; ACT 28:15, and in reference to the return of Jesus, 1TH 4:17. So what is an apantesis?

When a king or high official approached a city, the people would go forth to welcome him several miles from town. They did not stay out there. This reception committee would turn around, and singing and dancing they would escort the monarch all the way back to the city. When he went to get the Ark of the Covenant, David did not stay out there with it, but accompanied it back to Jerusalem singing and dancing, 2SA 6:12-15. When Jesus was approaching Jerusalem, the people of the city "went forth to meet Him," JOH 12:12-13. They did not stay out there, but immediately escorted Him back into the city singing "Hosanna in the highest. Blessed is He that cometh in the name of the Lord," MAT 21:8-10, MAR 11:9-10.

---

[90] We have George E. Ladd, in his book *The Blessed Hope*, pp 89-92, Eerdman's, to thank for this understanding. F.F. Bruce also did a lengthy study on the subject which has escaped the author's file.

In ACT 28:15 we see the Roman brethren going forth from the city to meet Paul, and then escorting him back to Rome. "Apantesis" was the Greek word used to identify this custom.

We know Jesus is the bridegroom, and the church is the bride. With those definitions in mind, the best New Testament example of an "apantesis" is the parable of the ten virgins, the bridegroom, and the wedding feast, of MAT 25. In this parable, Jesus likened the kingdom of heaven to a Jewish wedding. The author has taken the liberty of leaving the original Greek word "apantesis" in the following quote rather than "meet" which is the usual English translation:

> MAT 25:1-10 (excerpts) Then shall the kingdom of heaven be likened unto ten virgins, which took their lamps, and went forth to apantesis the bridegroom. And at midnight there was a cry made, **the bridegroom cometh; go ye out to apantesis him. Then all those virgins arose, and trimmed their lamps...the bridegroom came; and they that were ready went in with him to the marriage: and the door was shut.**

Note the chain of events:

(1) The virgins prepared to go forth to meet the bridegroom.
(2) They left the house where the wedding was to take place, and went forth to apantesis him.
(3) They returned to the wedding with him.

The bridegroom and the virgins did not stay out in the street, but returned immediately to the wedding feast. The Greeks used a word which by definition means "an encounter" or "to meet" for this custom. It was an "apantesis." This was a common way to greet an honored guest who had traveled a distance to see you. We sometimes do it today. When someone comes to see us, we go out to greet them, and walk back into the house with them. Later the Romans also accepted both the word and the custom. The point being that the Lord's return for His bride is an "apantesis," and Scripture tells us so:

1TH 4:17 Then we which are alive and remain shall be caught up together with them in the clouds, to **apantesis** the Lord in the air: and so shall we ever be with the Lord.

All agree that 1TH 4:17 is about the Lord coming for the saints. Note that it is an apantesis. So an apantesis is what will take place when the Lord returns. Armageddon will be in progress, and the Lord will appear in the heavens. We will be caught up to meet him in the air, and accompany Him back to Earth in an "apantesis." At the second we are taken to be with the Lord, we are transformed into our glorified bodies. We will then be able to see the brilliant righteousness of the Lord in which we are now clothed, and time for us will be over, REV 10:6-7.

REV 19:7-9 ...the marriage of the Lamb is come, and his wife hath made herself ready. And to her was granted that she should be arrayed in fine linen, clean and white: for the fine linen is the righteousness of saints. And he saith unto me, Write, **Blessed are they which are called unto the marriage supper of the Lamb.**

REV 19:11-18 And I saw heaven opened, and behold a white horse; and he that sat upon him was called Faithful and True, and in righteousness doth judge and make war. His eyes were as a flame of fire, and on his head were many crowns; and he had a name written, that no man knew, but he himself. And he was clothed with a vesture dipped in blood: and his name is called The Word of God. **And the armies which were in heaven followed him upon white horses, clothed in fine linen, white and clean.** And out of his mouth goeth a sharp sword, that with it he should smite the nations: and he shall rule them with a rod of iron: and he treadeth the winepress of the fierceness and wrath of Almighty God. And he hath on his vesture and on his thigh a name written, KING OF KINGS, AND LORD OF LORDS.

What a majestic scene. On those horses will be Enoch, Abraham, Moses, Joshua, Elisha, Zechariah, Paul, John Huss, Hudson Taylor of the China Inland Mission, the slaughtered saints of all ages, and everyone else who has longed for His appearing, from the beginning of time until now. That great army will even include little old no accounts like you and me.[91] It will be the most radiant army that has ever been, or ever will be. The only reason any of us will be there is because we are clothed in the brilliant righteousness of Him whose robe was dipped in blood. Those righteous acts of the saints are the ones accomplished through the imputed righteousness of Jesus. "All our righteousness is as filthy rags."

The dead in Christ of all time and we "who are alive and remain" are they who meet the Lord in the air, and we "are the birds in midheaven!" How can we possibly know that?

From 1TH 4:17 we know that when the Lord returns, we will be caught up in the clouds to meet Him in the air. In this life we are just betrothed. It is after we are taken to be with the Lord that the marriage supper of the Lamb takes place. When we are ready to remain with Him forever we become the bride. The marriage supper precedes our eternal union with Jesus. Rev 19:9 tells us of this marriage supper. In that same passage of Scripture, REV 19:17, we read about the birds in midheaven (i.e. the sky) who are invited to "the great supper of God." So we ask, how many great suppers is the Lord telling us about in REV 19? Does He have one for the saints, and one for the fowls? Is a supper for our feathered friends of sufficient importance to be called "the great supper of God?" Not likely. The greatest supper of all time is the marriage supper of the Lamb, so the birds in midheaven is an allegory of all those who have been caught up to be with the Lord. Separated by only eight verses, "the marriage supper of the Lamb" and "the great supper of God" are the same supper! Astonishing as it may sound, the marriage supper of the Lamb is not a meal, but an event. The saints will have the awesome privilege of taking part in the Lord's final and total defeat of His enemies. What could be more humbling than that? How gracious our loving Savior is to permit these lumps of clay to be part of such an event. "Know ye not that ye shall judge angels?" This is the beginning of that judgment:

---

[91] The author has often wondered what those spiritual horses really are. They must be an allegory of something, but what?

REV 19:17-21 And I saw an angel standing in the sun; and he cried with a loud voice, **saying to all the fowls that fly in the midst of heaven, Come and gather yourselves together unto the supper of the great God; That ye may eat the flesh of kings, and the flesh of captains, and the flesh of mighty men, and the flesh of horses, and of them that sit on them, and the flesh of all men, both free and bond, both small and great.**

And I saw the beast, and the kings of the earth, and their armies, gathered together to make war against him that sat on the horse, and against his army. And the beast was taken, and with him the false prophet that wrought miracles before him, with which he deceived them that had received the mark of the beast, and them that worshipped his image. These both were cast alive into a lake of fire burning with brimstone. **And the remnant were slain with the sword of him that sat upon the horse, which sword proceeded out of his mouth: and all the fowls were filled with their flesh.**

Oh my God, were it not for Your great mercy and loving kindness, that would be the end of me, too. If You had not known me before the foundation of the Earth. Were it not for the blood of Your dear Son. If You had not cared enough. If You had not said...

EZE 16:4-6  ...None eye pitied thee...to have compassion upon thee; but thou wast cast out in the open field, to the loathing of thy person, in the day that thou wast born. And when I passed by thee, and saw thee polluted in thine own blood, I said unto thee when thou wast in thy blood, Live; yea, I said unto thee when thou wast in thy blood, Live.

The Lord in eternity saw us hopelessly in our sin, unloved by any but Himself, and cast out; and He sent His Son and said, "Live!" Will we be ashamed at His coming? Yes. When we see His perfection and look back at our lives, we won't see the successes. All we will see is the times we have failed Him. Will He wipe away all tears? Yes, that sorrow will be but for a moment, then comes eternal life with Him in His Holy City.

Here is one of the most blessed understandings in Scripture. Whose city is it? It is the Lord's. This city was made by Him, and for Him, and through Him, and He has been preparing it for 6000 years. When He returns it will be complete, and He will dwell in it.

> REV 21:2-3   And **I John saw the holy city, new Jerusalem, coming down from God out of heaven, prepared as a bride adorned for her husband.** And I heard a great voice out of heaven saying, Behold, the tabernacle of God is with men, and he will dwell with them, and they shall be his people, and God himself shall be with them, and be their God.

> REV 21:9   And there came unto me one of the seven angels which had the seven vials full of the seven last plagues, and talked with me, saying, **Come hither, I will shew thee the bride, the Lamb's wife.** And he carried me away in the spirit to a great and high mountain, **and shewed me that great city, the holy Jerusalem,** descending out of heaven from God,

John was carried away "in the spirit." That "in the spirit" is one of the signs of allegorical language. All agree that Jesus is the Bridegroom, and the church is the bride. Notice that the Holy City is dressed as a bride. The city is not adorned as the dwelling place of the bride, but the bride herself. This city is 1500 miles to a side. It must be allegorical, not because God couldn't make a square city 1500 miles to a side, but because the mountain would have to be hundreds of miles tall to see it. God could also make a thousand mile high mountain, but like the rest of Revelation, this chapter is in pictorial language, so the Holy City is a probably a spiritual picture of something. What can it mean? The clue is in the text itself. "I will show you the bride; and he showed me the Holy Jerusalem." He did not say I am going to show you where the bride is going to live, but I am going to show you the bride herself. He showed me the bride: the New Jerusalem. Bride = New Jerusalem. The Holy City is not a place for us to stay, it is us! The Holy city is the sum total of all the redeemed. What a shock, the Holy city, the New Jerusalem is all the saved from Adam to the final martyr.

You see, we've had it backwards all along. We have been looking at that city from man's viewpoint. We have seen this heavenly city as some big gilt and tinsel place for us to dwell in, and that is not it at all. God has been preparing a place where He will dwell. It is His Holy City, His dwelling place, and He will dwell among men. Can we show that from the Bible? Sure:

> REV 21:12-14 And had a wall great and high, and had twelve gates, and at the gates twelve angels, and names written thereon, which are the names of the twelve tribes of the children of Israel: On the east three gates; on the north three gates; on the south three gates; and on the west three gates. And the wall of the city had twelve foundations, and in them the names of the twelve apostles of the Lamb.

Remember the 24 elders in REV 5 and elsewhere. There are 24 of them, because that is how many elders there are of the twelve tribes of Israel, and how many apostles there are in the church. Twelve of each, and they are the gates and foundations for all the redeemed. The sons of Israel are the gates, while the twelve apostles are the foundation stones. Now this verse does not say these are "like" the twelve apostles, but that the foundation stones have their names "in them," so those stones are the apostles themselves. They are not the rock Christ Jesus, but little stones like Peter, MAT 16:18. In REV 21:17 the wall is shown as 144 cubits high. Another 12 x 12. Again showing the twelve elders of Israel and the Apostles, and an indirect reference to the 144,000 of REV 7 and 14.

> REV 21:15-16 And he that talked with me had a golden reed to measure the city, and the gates thereof, and the wall thereof. And the city lieth foursquare, and the length is as large as the breadth: **and he measured the city with the reed, twelve thousand furlongs. The length and the breadth and the height of it are equal.**

Remember the 12,000 of all the tribes of Israel? The 12,000 x 12 of REV 7:4-8? Now we have a new equation because the Apostles and the Church are added, 12,000 x 12,000 x 12,000. Multiply that out and you get a monumental 1,728,000,000,000! That is a number that boggles the mind. If taken literally it would be more people than could live on this planet in another 8640 years. LUK 21:24 declares that we don't have that much time. "This generation shall not pass away." So that number must also be an allegorical reference to the complete number of the redeemed.

Covered with His blood, the Lord sees His Church without spot or blemish, and she is shown as twelve of the most beautiful jewels, REV 21:17-21. It is the Lord's dwelling place, and no sin or defilement may enter, only those who are covered in Jesus' blood. It is His city, miraculously made by Him out of sinful flesh, and He tabernacles with man. Not a soul who has not accepted Jesus as their Savior can be a part of it. If we are not totally cleansed by the Lamb, we may not enter.

> REV 21:22-27 And I saw no temple therein: for the Lord God Almighty and the Lamb are the temple of it. And the city had no need of the sun, neither of the moon, to shine in it: for the glory of God did lighten it, and the Lamb is the light thereof. And the nations of them which are saved shall walk in the light of it: and the kings of the earth do bring their glory and honour into it. And the gates of it shall not be shut at all by day: for there shall be no night there. And they shall bring the glory and honour of the nations into it. And there shall in no wise enter into it any thing that defileth, neither whatsoever worketh abomination, or maketh a lie: but they which are written in the Lamb's book of life.

Once we understand that the Holy city is really people, then we start to look at Babylon, the wicked city of REV 18 in a different way. Is Babylon of REV 18 the other side of that coin? Might it be the sum total of all the unsaved people who have ever lived?

> REV 18:24 And in her was found **the blood of prophets, and of saints, and of all** that were slain upon the earth.

Notice that the blood of "all" who have been slain is in Babylon. The prophets were Old Testament believers, the saints are the New Testament church, and that "all" is pretty inclusive. All means everyone! So the deaths of all who have suffered for Jesus through all time are laid at Babylon's door, from the blood of Able to the last tortured saint. The Lord could care less about the bricks and mortar in that evil city.

He is concerned with the people. It was not the buildings of Babylon that killed the saints, but the wicked people within the buildings. Babylon of REV 18 is not New York or Moscow, but all the evil people who have ever lived, and have turned away from God. It is Satan's kingdom on Earth shown as a city of trade, even trading in "the souls of men," REV 18:13, KJV. At the beginning this chapter, the Lord tells us how we should relate to the wickedness in the world, and what will happen to us if we don't do it His way:

> REV 18:4-5   And I heard another voice from heaven, saying, **Come out of her, my people, that ye be not partakers of her sins, and that ye receive not of her plagues.** For her sins have reached unto heaven, and God hath remembered her iniquities.

It is almost over, now. The Lord inspired Revelation in such a way that every generation thought it was applicable to them, and spiritually it was. Revelation is the only book in the Bible which promises a blessing to those who read and obey it. But, how merciful the Lord is. How would the brethren have stood while they were being tortured and burned if they had known that the Lord's return was 1000 or more years away? The way Revelation fits history was hidden through the ages because some of the events needed to decipher it were in the future. They have happened now, and this final book of the Bible is open. From current events, it is apparent that almost all of Bible prophecy is already fulfilled. The man of sin is here, the great apostasy is here, the final beast is here, the new nation of Israel is here, and prophetically, all we need to look for are the final trials of the church, and Armageddon. That could begin overnight. But, as the Bible declares, we will think it is a time of peace, and "in an hour ye think not, the Son of man cometh..."

> REV 22:10-19   And he saith unto me, Seal not the sayings of the prophecy of this book: for the time is at hand. He that is unjust, let him be unjust still: and he which is filthy, let him be filthy still: and he that is righteous, let him be righteous still: and he that is holy, let him be holy still. And, behold, I come quickly; and my reward is with me, to

give every man according as his work shall be. Blessed are they that do his commandments, that they may have right to the tree of life, and may enter in through the gates into the city. I Jesus have sent mine angel to testify unto you these things in the churches. I am the root and the offspring of David, and the bright and morning star. And the Spirit and the bride say, Come. And let him that heareth say, Come. And let him that is athirst come. And whosoever will, let him take the water of life freely.

But Lord, now Your church falters. Many shepherds no longer teach the truth. They tear the hoofs off Jesus' sheep, so they can no longer walk the Christian walk. The great cathedrals of Europe are empty now. The church is also dying here; and few sigh and groan over the abominations committed in our midst. You told us that night was coming when no man could work. Is it not here? As You asked, will the faith be on the Earth when You return?

Oh Lord, we need You now. How can anyone stand, when there are so few left to stand with. Please come quickly, Lord. Are we not Your purchased possession? The prophets of today are declaring that we will have peace in this place; but your Word doesn't say so. Please open the eyes of your people, Lord; we haven't got much time left.

# Chapter 27

# *A Look Ahead*

A verse by verse exegesis of all the Scripture supporting what we have discussed in this book would be an interminable project. It would take a much longer book, and I don't think we have the time. With our own eyes, we are probably watching the marshalling of forces for Armageddon.

There are so many things we haven't covered. We haven't discussed the Seven Churches, the Seven Seals, the Seven Trumpets,and the Seven Bowls. At the end of Book 2 there was an outline of the Seven Churches, and at the end of this chapter, is a brief study outline of the Seven Seals, the Seven trumpets, and the Seven Bowls. It appears that the Seven Bowls of REV 16 are an end-time intensification of the plagues of the Seven trumpets, with the geographic locale set in the Middle East. *(Chart No.25)*

Earlier we mentioned that we would discuss the so-called millennium, the theoretical 1000 year reign of Jesus between the end of the Christian Era and the eternal Kingdom of God. This pre-millennial view came into the church, late in the 17th Century, through Jean de Labadie of the Dutch Reformed Church. At the time, it was considered heresy by a majority of the brethren; and Labadie was ousted from the church.[92] Since then, however, his view has gained immense popularity. Some churches even make the pre-millennial view an article of faith, allowing no readings by authors who hold a differing opinion. That is truly sad...

Revelation is provably an allegorical book. Every other prophecy it contains is allegorical, so why are we required to interpret this one prophecy literally? Who knows; to be consistent with the rest of Revelation, REV 20 should also be looked at allegorically.

Understanding that there is no more time after the last trumpet, REV 10:6-7; REV 20 can no longer be placed after

---

[92] E. H. Broadbent, *The Pilgrim Church,* Pickering & Inglis Ltd. 1931, pp255-263.

the saints are taken to be with the Lord. Consequently, REV
20, the so-called 1000 year millennial kingdom of Jesus, must
take place before the second coming. 2TH 1:7-10 also supports
this conclusion, **declaring that the judgment of the wicked
takes place on the same day as the saints are glorified!**
It might be good to review the graph of that chiasm from
"More Parallels." The first **A** is about Israel, the second is
about the church. REV 20 is the second **A** of the second
chiasm. Both appear to take place in the Christian Era.

| | | | |
|---|---|---|---|
| **(A)** | ch.12 | Woman with 12 Stars | Israel |
| **(B)** | ch.13 | Leopard, Lion, Bear Beast | Satanic Kingdom |
| | ch.14 | 144,000 & The Gospel | The Saved Within It |
| | ch.15 | Song of Moses and Lamb | Victory for Redeemed |
| **(C)** | ch.16 | Bowls of Wrath | Wrath for the Wicked |
| **(B)** | ch.17 | Seven Headed Beast | Satanic Kingdoms |
| | ch.18 | Babylon | Satanic System |
| | ch.19 | King of Kings | Destruction of Wicked |
| **(A)** | ch.20 | The Thousand Years | The Church |

REV 20 can easily be interpreted as an allegory of the
Christian Era. To show how, below it is quoted in full. Text
is in bold face, while supporting verses and comments are
inserted in light face. For ease of understanding, the chapter
is broken into appropriate sections. Section headlines were
inserted by the author, and do not appear in Scripture:

### THE FINISHED WORK OF CHRIST

**REV 20:1 And I saw an angel come down from heaven,** (that angel
is Jesus. "Who hath ascended into heaven and descended?" and REV
10:1 "And I saw another mighty angel come down from heaven, clothed
with a cloud: and a rainbow was upon his head, and his face was as it
were the sun, and his feet as pillars of fire...") **having the key of the
bottomless pit** (Jesus has been given the keys of Hades, REV 1:18) **and
a great chain in his hand. REV 20:2 And he laid hold on the dragon, that old serpent, which is the Devil,** ("Now the ruler of this world
shall be cast out," JOH 12:31, spoken before the Cross) **and Satan, and**

**Satan, and bound him** ("How can anyone enter a strong man's house and carry off his property unless he first bind the strong man?" MAT 12:29. Spoken when Jesus was casting out demons. When we were lost in our trespasses and sins we were Satan's property, and in his kingdom. Jesus is now plundering Satan's house through the church.)

## THE CHRISTIAN ERA

**...a thousand years,** (the Greek word translated thousand here, and throughout the rest of the chapter, is "chilioi," Strong's 5507, the indefinite PLURAL form for thousand. Thus it could mean one thousand or many thousands.) **REV 20:3 And cast him into the bottomless pit, and shut him up, and set a seal upon him, that he should deceive the nations no more,** (note that the binding was Scripturally limited to deceiving nations. Through the whole Christian Era, the Western nations have been nominally Christian. Kings have been crowned; and wars have been fought in Jesus' name. Thus the nations were not deceived that Jesus is Lord.) **till the thousand years should be fulfilled: and after that he must be loosed a little season.** (See REV 12:12 for another mention of this "little season." By context we can pin the beginning of that "little season" to 1948-1967. It is since that time that the Western nations have turned away from the Lord. Satan is loose and we are in an apostasy unequaled in the Christian Era.) **REV 20:4 And I saw thrones, and they sat upon them, and judgment was given unto them:** (Refer to the 1PE 2:5,9 and REV 1:6 and 5:10, quoted earlier, which state that we reign with Christ right now, today.) **and I saw the souls of them that were beheaded for the witness of Jesus,** (thousands of saints have been beheaded in the Christian Era, see Fox's Book of Martyrs.) **and for the word of God, and which had not worshipped the beast, neither his image, neither had received his mark upon their foreheads, or in their hands;** (Satan is the beast, and he has struck his mark on the foreheads of his servants throughout time.) **and they lived and reigned with Christ a thousand years.** (Do we not reign with Christ right now, 1PE 2:5-9, REV 1:6, 5:10?) **REV 20:5 But the rest of the dead** (those who were unsaved) **lived not again until the thousand years** (the Christian Era) **were finished. This is the first resurrection.** How many resurrections are there? Jesus said, "I am the resurrection and the Life." Jesus is the firstborn of the dead, and there is no other resurrection in Scripture.) **REV 20:6 Blessed and holy is he that hath part in the first resurrection: on such the second death hath no power,** (Blessed indeed are those who have part in the resurrection of Jesus our Lord! Indeed, they are the born again, and over them the second death has absolutely no power, praise God.) **but they shall be priests of God and of Christ, and shall reign with him a thousand years.** (REV 1:6

and 5:10 states that we have been made priests and reign with Jesus, right now!) **REV 20:7 And when the thousand years** (as an indefinite plural this "thousand" can refer to the Christian Era regardless of duration.) **are expired,**

## THE END TIMES

**Satan shall be loosed out of his prison,REV 20:8 And shall go out to deceive the nations,** (Since 1948 and 1967 there is a general falling away of the church unprecedented in the Christian Era. We have the second rise of the Islamic States. Parallel the following verse with other descriptions of Armageddon in REV 6,9,12,14,and 19.) **which are in the four quarters of the earth, Gog and Magog: to gather them together to battle** (how many Armageddons and fulfillments of EZE 38-39, are we going to have? Note the details of this battle here parallel other descriptions of Armageddon in the Bible which we have already studied. When we understand the repetitive chiasmic structure of REV, this ceases to be a problem.) **the number of whom is as the sand of the sea.** (REV 9:16 states 200,000,000) **REV 20:9 And they went up on the breadth of the earth, and compassed the camp of the saints about, and the beloved city:** (is this not parallel to JOE 2-3, which all equate with Armageddon?) **and fire came down from God out of heaven, and devoured them.**

## THE ETERNAL KINGDOM OF GOD

**REV 20:10 And the devil that deceived them was cast into the lake of fire and brimstone, where the beast and the false prophet are, and shall be tormented day and night for ever and ever. REV 20:11 And I saw a great white throne, and him that sat on it, from whose face the earth and the heaven fled away; and there was found no place for them. REV 20:12 And I saw the dead, small and great, stand before God; and the books were opened: and another book was opened, which is the book of life:** (There are two sets of books here. The book of deeds, and the book of life. When the Lord blotted out our transgressions, what do you suppose He blotted them out of? The book of the deeds, of course. Since all of our righteousness is as filthy rags, if even one deed, no matter how "good" or "sanctified" remains in that book we are going to the lake of fire. To eat of the tree of life, our names must first be written in the book of life, "...Blotting out the handwriting of ordinances that was against us, which was contrary to us, and took it out of the way, nailing it to his Cross." COL 2:14.) **and the dead were judged out of those things which were written in the books, according to their works. REV 20:13 And the sea gave up the dead which were in it; and**

death and hell delivered up the dead which were in them: and they were judged every man according to their works. **REV 20:14 And death and hell were cast into the lake of fire. This is the second death. REV 20:15 And whosoever was not found written in the book of life was cast into the lake of fire.** (COL 1:13-17 "Who hath delivered us from the power of darkness, and hath translated us into the kingdom of his dear Son: In whom we have redemption through his blood, even the forgiveness of sins: Who is the image of the invisible God, the firstborn of every creature: For by him were all things created, that are in heaven, and that are in earth, visible and invisible, whether they be thrones, or dominions, or principalities, powers: all things were created by him, and for him: And he is before all things, and by him all things consist." Amen and Amen!)

God gave the Earth to Adam. Adam was made the ruler of the Earth and all it contained. Gen 1:28. When Adam fell, he handed his God-given authority over the Earth to Satan. That included us. As head of the family of man, Adam contracted us all into slavery. We legally became Satan's possession, LUK 4:6. This is why, through Adam, that all died. Satan owned us. When "We were bought with a price," that was not just some theoretical acquisition. We were purchased from Satan's kingdom by Jesus' precious blood. We were transferred "out of the domain (kingdom, NASB) of darkness **into the kingdom of His dear Son,**" COL 1:13. Are we looking for the kingdom age? There it is, in COL 1:13, right where the Bible has been telling us it is, all along. We've been in the Lord's spiritual kingdom ever since Jesus was glorified.

### SOME END-TIME NEWS FLASHES...

There is adequate Bible support for the next few pages, but the verses we cite could be interpreted differently. They could apply to a later conflict in this same geographic area (if there is time for one). Because Revelation paints our future picture with a broad brush, details are somewhat speculative. If they fail to come to pass, filling in too many details can risk your credibility. Keeping those reservations in mind, the fulfillment of day-years in our time appears to position many of the Bible's end-time predictions to our own time. The author claims no gift of prophecy; but he does check to see what the Bible has to say about current events in the Middle East. As of this writing, here is how things appear to fit:

In Daniel, the order in which the beasts appear is: Lion, then Bear, then Leopard, DAN 7:4-6. Those beasts are in that order for a reason. The Babylonian, Medo-Persian, and Greek empires came to power in that order. In Revelation they are reversed. The order of the beasts is changed to Leopard, then Bear, then Lion. Is this change of order because end-time nations are going to come into authority in this new sequence? If so, look at what's happened since Israel took back Jerusalem in 1967.

1st. **Leopard** is probably Syria. In the 70's, Syria was the central Islamic nation to come against Israel; and various terrorists called Damascus their home. Syria was a prime mover behind the 1967 and 1973 wars. They encouraged the instability in Lebanon. Hafez el Assad supported the terrorists in Lebanon, and many of them operated out of Syria.

2nd. **Bear** is Iran. In the 80's, Iran was the major power against Israel and the West. In that decade it was the Iranians who were most influential with the terrorists. The Iranian mullah, Ali Akbar Mohtashemi was (and is) their secret leader. He engineered many atrocities against Israel and the West, including the bombing of the marine barracks in Beirut, and the downing of Pan Am flight 103 over Lockerbie, Scotland. The Iranians even seized the American Embassy; and the Ayatollah was suddenly on the front page of every newspaper as public enemy No. 1.

But we quickly forgot, and again try for peace initiatives with satanic regimes. All Europe is again trading with Iran, and business is brisk. Ten horns giving their power to the beast.

A disquieting possibility is that non-christian elements gaining power in this country could neutralize or lead the United States itself to come down against Israel. Today, 14% of our immigrants are Mohammedan, and Islam is taking hold in the inner cities. If that trend continues, and the church continues to decline at its present rate, by the year 2000 the Mohammedans will be the largest religious voting block in the country.

Over the last 40 years, the United States has gained a reputation for betraying its allies. Unbelievable as it may sound, this could also happen to our relationship with Israel. In a search for peace in the Mid-East, our own government might be willing to sacrifice Israel on the altar of expediency. One fears to think of what the Lord would then allow Satan to do to this country. If that does take place, the "one stick" of Ephraim and Judah of EZE 37:15-19 would not be Israel and the United States, but Israel and what little is left of the true Church. Then look up, for Jesus is at hand.

3rd. **Lion is Iraq.** In the 90's, Iraq is the prime enemy against Israel and the West; and the international terrorists now roost with Saddam Hussein in Baghdad. It is interesting to note that these terrorists always camp out in the country which is the most strongly against Israel.

Now Saddam Hussain has had a "dream" in which Mohammed has supposedly given him new instructions. That his guns should not be trained on United State troops in Arabia, but on Israel. That is exactly what Scripture predicts:

REV 12:13 And when the dragon saw that he was cast unto the earth, **he persecuted the woman** (Israel)which brought forth the man child.

REV 12:17 **And the dragon was wroth with the woman** (Israel), **and went to make war with the remnant of her seed,** which keep the commandments of God, and have the testimony of Jesus Christ.

As you remember from our study of the day years, the woman of REV 12 is Israel. These latter day enemies of Israel and the West have appeared in the 1st-Leopard, 2nd-Bear, 3rd-Lion order of REV 13. If this is what Revelation's new beastly order means, it would lead us to believe that this present conflict is the last phase of the Leopard-Bear-Lion Beast; and Armageddon could be started by Iraq!

Another important possibility to consider is that the Leopard-Bear-Lion Beast could be regionally rather than nationally interpreted! Babylon, Medo-Persia and Greece all ruled from within the Tigris and Euphrates Valley. Even Alexander the Great ruled the Greek empire from Babylon. Consequently, it may be wrong to designate precise national boundaries for the Leopard-Bear-Lion Beast. LBL could represent the Middle East as a religious entity, rather than specific geographic areas within it. This may seem like hair splitting, but if Syria remains against Iraq until the very end, it is a vital point!

The Middle East was the cradle of western civilization, and it will be its deathbed. Looking at the big picture, it all began there (with the tower of Babel) and it will all end there (with Armageddon)!

At this very moment, United States troops are in Arabia; and our ships are in the Mediterranean and the Persian Gulf. Nobody's there because they want to be; God is drawing all the nations out...

> EZE 38:8 (NASB) ...**in the latter years you will come into the land that is restored from the sword**, whose inhabitants have been gathered from many nations to the mountains of Israel...

> JOE 3:9-10 **Proclaim ye this among the Gentiles; Prepare war, wake up the mighty men, let all the men of war draw near**; let them come up: Beat your plowshares into swords and your pruninghooks into spears...

Hussein of Iraq has seized Kuwait. Even if he retreats, is this the beginning of what EZE 38-39 is all about? The author is not sure; however, these events seem to fulfill a whole series of verses which appear to be about the final war. Some have been quoted earlier, but now we can look at them with new eyes. Even if the first shots of that battle are still in the future, these verses show that the final national alignments are in the making:

> EZE 38:5 ...**Persia, Ethiopia, and Libya with them**; all of them with shield and helmet: Gomer, and all his bands; the house of Togarmah of the north quarters, and all his bands: and many people with thee...

> DAN 11:41 He shall enter also into the glorious land, and many countries shall be overthrown: but **these shall escape out of his hand, even Edom, and Moab, and the chief of the children of Ammon.**

> DAN 11:43 ...**and the Libyans and the Ethiopians shall be at his steps.**

Right now, Iraq has only two firm allies in the Middle East: Ethiopia and Libya, just as DAN 11:43 states. But EZE 38:5 adds Persia. That's Iran, and just a few days ago, Iran dropped its longstanding feud with Iraq. Those two countries have now exchanged envoys; and Iran is again calling for a holy war against the West. As of this writing Jordan (Ammon) is semi-neutral. From DAN 11:41, Jordan, and possibly some Arabians, may not suffer greatly in the coming conflict, no matter which side Jordan finally takes. Egypt and Syria are standing against Iraq. That appears to be in line with:

ISA 19:23-24 In that day shall there be a highway out of Egypt to Assyria, and the Assyrian shall come into Egypt, and the Egyptian into Assyria, and the Egyptians shall serve with the Assyrians. **In that day shall Israel be the third with Egypt and with Assyria, even a blessing in the midst of the land:**

Admittedly, these verses confuse the author, as well they might. They are in a prophecy which seems to be about the end-times; but they could be historic to us: fulfilled by the Coptic Church, which covered that whole area fifteen hundred years ago.

On the other hand, they could be happening before our eyes. Last year, if anyone had suggested that Syria, Egypt, and Israel would have the same view on anything, he would have been committed to an institution as a raving lunatic! These three enemies being on the same side is extraordinary. How long will this last? Who knows? Syria's Hafez el Assad is as cunning and ruthless a power broker as exists in the Middle East, with his own private agenda. He or a successor could still emerge as a major end-time figure, or he could join Iraq and Iran. But if Syria remains with Israel and Egypt, it could be an indication that Leopard-Bear-Lion should be interpreted regionally rather than nationally. We will have to wait and see.

Cuba, China, North Korea, and a few others have declared that they will not honor the United Nations embargo against Iraq; and Turkey might join them, at least as far as food and other commodities are concerned. Many supplies will probably reach Iraq through their new friend, Iran. This appears to at least partially fulfill:

REV 16:12 And the sixth angel poured out his vial upon the great river Euphrates; **and the water thereof was dried up, that the way of the kings of the east might be prepared.**

Iraq and Iran are separated by the Euphrates river. Now the division between Iran and Iraq is over, and China claims they will be sending supplies. Interesting. The militant Mohammedans claim there are 200,000,000 of them. China has the capability of fielding an army of almost 200,000,000 men! For the second time in the Christian Era, unified militant Mohammedans threaten the Christian world, and they now have powerful Eastern friends. That 200,000,000 men should ring a bell:

REV 9:16 **And the number of the army of the horsemen were two hundred thousand thousand (200,000,000)...**

But there is another important factor. Note that the above are horsemen. Revelation is a spiritual book, and speaks at length of spiritual forces. All over Scripture, angelic forces are shown as horsemen, 2KI 2:11, 6:15-18, 7:6; ZEC 1:8, 6:2-6; REV 6:2-8, 9:16, 19:14. There is no reason to exclude these unseen spiritual armies from this number. They are very real, and very powerful. Satan and his angels are thrown to the Earth sometime before Armageddon, REV 12:9. From context, probably around 1948AD.

The Bible does not tell us how large a force Satan has, but fallen angels are one third of the angels in heaven, REV 12:4. The angelic forces on both sides could represent a major portion of that 200,000,000. As a result, we can't count the size of troop deployments to determine which war is the last one. Most of that army may not be visible to human eyes.

The prophecy about the Leopard-Bear-Lion beast has already been gone into at great length, but the following verse probably applies to him. Here we are shown three unclean spirits from the Middle East. These are probably those same satanic princes we saw earlier in DAN 10:20. This quote (within the Bowls of Wrath) shows that the second rise of Islam is one of the major reasons that Armageddon will take place:

> REV 16:13-14  And I saw **three unclean spirits like frogs come out of the mouth of the dragon, and out of the mouth of the beast,** and out of the mouth of the false prophet. For they are the spirits of devils, working miracles, **which go forth unto the kings of the earth and of the whole world, to gather them to the battle of that great day of God Almighty.**[93]

Only a couple of years ago, if anyone had suggested the collapse of the Communist world, he would have been drummed out of any prophetic school in the country as a heretic. Remember? All the church's prophetic voices were saying that Russia was the No.1 enemy!

In the prophecy of Leopard-Bear-Lion, God knew all along that communism was not the major final enemy. If someone had stated that unlikely nations from all over like Australia, Canada, New Zealand, France, and Holland, would be sending warships into this area, he would have been drummed out, too; yet the Lord also knew this:

> JOE 3:1-11  (excerpts) ...**when I shall bring again the captivity of Judah and Jerusalem, I will also gather all nations**...the Gentiles; Prepare war...let all the men of war draw near...and thither cause thy mighty ones to come down, O LORD.

The United Nations forces in Arabia are South of Leopard-Bear-Lion, and Turkey is to the North. Though Turkey is now our ally, because it is a Moslem state, it is unlikely that they will remain so. They are also part of the old Greek empire, and could be part of the Leopard.

---

[93] Some liberals claim that the Mohammedans have another road to heaven. The above verse shows who they worship, so it isn't true! Jesus is the only mediator between God and man, 1TI 2:5, the only door to the sheepfold, JOH 10:7.

DAN 8:23-25 And in the latter time of their kingdom, **when the transgressors are come to the full**, a king of fierce countenance, and understanding dark sentences, shall stand up. And his power shall be mighty, but not by his own power: and he shall destroy wonderfully, and shall prosper, and practise, and shall destroy the mighty and the holy people. **And through his policy also he shall cause craft to prosper in his hand; and he shall magnify himself in his heart, and by peace shall destroy many: he shall also stand up against the Prince of princes; but he shall be broken without hand.**

DAN 11:40-44 (excerpts) **And at the time of the end shall the king of the south push at him: and the king of the north shall come against him like a whirlwind, with chariots, and with horsemen, and with many ships**; and he shall enter into the countries, and shall overflow and pass over. **He shall enter also into the glorious land**...But tidings out of the east and out of the north shall trouble him: **therefore he shall go forth with great fury to destroy, and utterly to make away many.**

Russia is also North of Leopard-Bear-Lion, and claims to be on our side in this present conflict. From EZE 38-39 we believe the USSR will be at Armageddon, but whose side will she be on? From the above verses it appears she will be with us; but they have a serious problem which no one is discussing. There are some 50,000,000 Shiite Moslems in Southern Russia! Only the Lord knows how they will figure in the final equation, but it is unlikely they will be willing to fight against their Mohammedan "brothers" to the South.

The USSR's internal problem makes their future role in world events somewhat puzzling. However, other prophecies, not to mention those 50,000,000 Mohammedans, make it appear that they, too, will come down on the side of the enemy. The uttermost parts of the North are clearly spoken of in EZE 38-39, and in that passage, powers from the North appear to be coming against Israel. Again, we will have to wait and see.

Major military forces are now being moved into place by many countries. Ships, men, aircraft: all the weapons of modern warfare. Visible or invisible, it takes time to mobilize the 200,000,000 horsemen that are going to be at Armageddon. But mobilization begins with a few thousand troops here, and a million or so there, just like now. Even now, we are in too deep to pull out. The stakes are being raised, and before you know it, a wall of fire will engulf us. "Please return soon, Lord Jesus. If this is it, please bring it on speedily."

Note from the above verses: At the end, in a fit of rage, an evil king from East of Israel will attack God's people.[94] During that battle, with the voice of the Archangel and the Trump of God, Jesus will stand on Zion as the Messiah of His people.

Oh, will they be glad to see him, as will we. They have been waiting for Him, many centuries more than we have. "Oh, Lord, the pain, the sin and suffering, the death...they will all be over for us, won't they? How we long to be free from body of this death: when that which is mortal shall have put on immortality."

---

[94] If you draw a little map of the Middle East, and overlay it with DAN 11:44, it is apparent that this would-be conquorer of Israel has to come from Syria, Iran or Iraq. Russia is to the North, Arabia and Egypt is to the South. The Mediterranean is to the West of Israel, so this final king must come from Israel's East, the location of Leopard-Bear-Lion.

## The Great Image
### DAN 2:31-45

DAN 2:31-45 (excerpts). Thou, O king, sawest, and behold a great image...This image's head was of fine gold, his breast and his arms of silver, his belly and his thighs of brass, His legs of iron, his feet part of iron and part of clay, Thou sawest till that a stone was cut out without hands, which smote the image upon his feet...and brake them to pieces.

(1) "Thou art this head of gold."

(2) "And after thee shall arise another kingdom inferior to thee,"

(3) "and another third kingdom of brass, which shall bear rule over all the earth."

(4) "And the fourth kingdom shall be strong as iron: forasmuch as iron breaketh in pieces and subdueth all things: and as iron that breaketh all these, shall it break in pieces..."

And as the toes of the feet were part of iron, and part of clay, so the kingdom shall be partly strong, and partly broken...they shall mingle themselves with the seed of men: but they shall not cleave one to another, even as iron is not mixed with clay.

And in the days of these kings shall the God of heaven set up a kingdom, which shall never be destroyed: and the kingdom shall not be left to other people, but it shall break in pieces and consume all these kingdoms, and it shall stand for ever.

NOTE: This prophecy was given to a Gentile king at the beginning of "the time of the Gentiles" to show us that there would be only four major world empires (and their descendants) who would rule over the Holy Land during the "time of the Gentiles". This prophecy is repeated to Daniel in the form of "Four Beasts" - Dan. 7:1-24. To show this vision parallels the day=years time line is included.

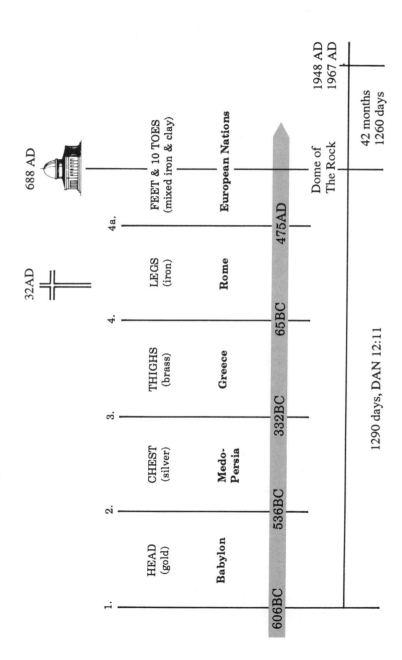

688 AD

1948 AD
1967 AD

32AD

FEET & 10 TOES
(mixed iron & clay)

European Nations

42 months
1260 days

Dome of
The Rock

4a.

475AD

LEGS
(iron)

Rome

65BC

THIGHS
(brass)

Greece

332BC

CHEST
(silver)

Medo-
Persia

536BC

HEAD
(gold)

Babylon

606BC

1290 days, DAN 12:11

1.    2.    3.    4.

## Chart No.22

## The Four Beasts
### DAN 7:1-24

DAN 7:3-24 (excerpts)  And four great beasts came up from the sea, diverse one from another. The first was like a lion...And behold another beast, a second, like to a bear...After this I beheld, and lo another, like a leopard...After this...behold a fourth beast, dreadful and terrible, and strong exceedingly; and it had great iron teeth: it devoured and brake in pieces...and it was diverse from all the beasts that were before it; and it had ten horns...there came up among them another little horn, before whom there were three of the first horns plucked up by the roots. I beheld then because of the voice of the great words which the horn spake: I beheld even till the beast was slain, and his body destroyed...As concerning the rest of the beasts, they had their dominion taken away: yet their lives were prolonged for a season and time.

These great beasts, which are four, are four kings, which shall arise out of the earth...The fourth beast shall be the fourth kingdom upon earth, which shall be diverse from all kingdoms, and shall devour the whole earth, and shall tread it down, and break it in pieces.

And the ten horns out of this kingdom are ten kings that shall arise: and another shall rise after them; and he shall be diverse from the first, and he shall subdue three kings.

NOTE:  The parallel day=year time line is shown under the kingdoms of DAN 7. DAN 7:12 "As concerning the rest of the beasts, they had their dominion taken away: yet their lives were prolonged for a season and time." After the Nazi regime was destroyed there has been no dominant central European power! Through their petroleum, "the rest of the beasts", the Leopard, Bear, Lion (the Mohammedan powers) now influence world economies. Note that the beasts in REV 13 are in the reverse order of the beasts in DAN 7.

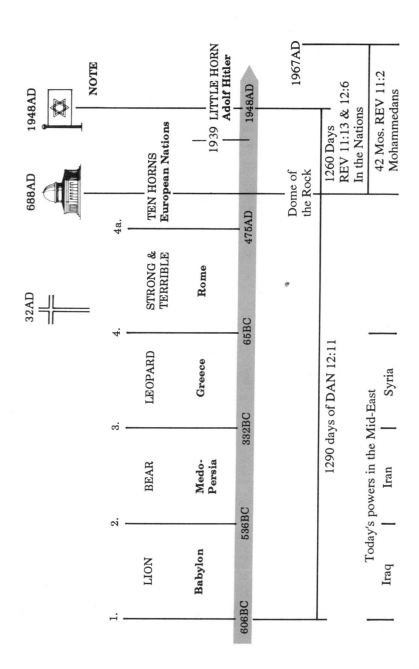

## The Beast To Come
### REV 17:8-11

REV 17:8 The beast that thou sawest was, and is not; and shall ascend out of the bottomless pit, and go into perdition...and they shall wonder...when they behold the beast that was, and is not, and yet is. (and will come, NASB)

REV 17:10-11   And there are seven kings: five are fallen, and one is, and the other is not yet come; and when he cometh, he must continue a short space. And the beast that was, and is, and is not, even he is the eighth, and is of the seven, and goeth into perdition.

| 1 | 2 | 3 | 4 | 5 | 6 | 7 | 8 |
|---|---|---|---|---|---|---|---|
| Egypt | Assyria | Babylon | Medo-Persia | Greece | Rome | Hitler | Eighth |

John's Lifetime

Five Are Fallen

ONE IS

One is Not Yet Come... Remain a Little While

?? (under 1/Egypt)

?? (under 8/Eighth)

**NOTE:** To correctly interpret this prophecy, we must stand in the historic position of the prophet. This prophecy was given to John by Jesus in 95AD, so the kingdom that is, is Rome! The five that are fallen are the kingdoms that had world dominion before John.  Kingdoms seven and eight are after John.

*Chart No.24*

**AFTER THE TRIBULATION**
MAT 24:21-31

MAT 24:21 For then shall be great tribulation, such as was not since the beginning of the world to this time, no, nor ever shall be.

MAT 24:29 Immediately **after the tribulation** of those days shall **the sun be darkened, and the moon shall not give her light, and the stars shall fall from heaven,** and the powers of the heavens shall be shaken:

MAT 24:31 And he shall send his angels with a **great sound of a trumpet,** and they shall gather together his elect from the four winds, from one end of heaven to the other.

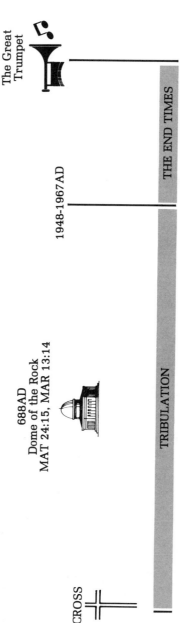

The Great Trumpet

1948-1967AD

688AD
Dome of the Rock
MAT 24:15, MAR 13:14

CROSS

TRIBULATION

THE END TIMES

v.21 "there shall be great tribulation . . ."

v.29 ". . . after the tribulation . . ."

## Seals, Trumpets & Bowls

Though the Four Horsemen of the Seven Seals can be spiritually applied, they probably refer physical trials on man during the Christian Era. The Seven Trumpets are parallel. The Seven Bowls are probably spiritual, and about the end-times, They are placed in the Middle East. This chart is only intended to be a study guide. Different interpretations are possible. Nevertheless, because of the last trumpet, and REV 10:6-7 and 11:15, all three sevens must take place before the return of the Lord for the church.

---

### The Seven Seals

| | | |
|---|---|---|
| 1st Seal | * *White Horse* | Conquerors, World Leaders, and Rulers |
| 2nd Seal | * *Red Horse* | Warfare among Nations. |
| 3rd Seal | * *Black Horse* | Rich get richer, and the Poor get poorer. |
| 4th Seal | * *Ashen Horse* | Natural disasters and murders. |
| 5th Seal | *Altar of God* | Dead in Christ now with Jesus |

**We are here...**

| | | |
|---|---|---|
| 6th Seal | *Earthquake* | Armageddon |
| 7th Seal | *Silence* | Eternal Kingdom of God |

* These Four Horsemen are probably the same four destructive angels that appear in REV 7:2.

---

### The Seven Trumpets

| | | |
|---|---|---|
| 1st Trump | *Earth Polluted* | Physically and spiritually. |
| 2nd Trump | *Ocean Polluted* | Physically, and people in false religions. |
| 3rd Trump | *Water Polluted* | False doctrines in the church. |
| 4th Trump | *Sky Polluted* | One third of the church falls way. |

**Beginning of Three Woes**

| | | | |
|---|---|---|---|
| 5th Trump | *Star Falls* | 1st Woe. | Mohammedans, and the 1st Jihad. |

**We are Here...**

| | | | |
|---|---|---|---|
| 6th Trump | *Angels Released* | 2nd Woe. | Armageddon. |
| 7th Trump | *God Reigns* | 3rd Woe. | The Eternal Kingdom of God. (which is a woe to the wicked) |

---

### The Seven Bowls of Wrath

Unlike the Seals and Trumpets, the Seven Bowls give us a geographic location for these final trials, REV 16:12-4. The River Euphrates. That is the Middle East, and the domain of Leopard-Bear-Lion, the Mohammedan World. Since these are the "final" plagues, they probably refer to the end-times.

1st Bowl    Death and disease on the servants of Satan.
2nd Bowl    Few Christians are left in the world.
3rd Bowl    Gospel of truth greatly polluted with false doctrines.
4th Bowl    Because of God's Word, many natural disasters happen to man.
5th Bowl    Spiritual darkness covers the Mohammedan World.

**We are Here...**

6th Bowl    Armageddon. Islam again released to scourge the Earth.
7th Bowl    Judgment on the Wicked, and The Eternal Kingdom of God.

# *Epilogue*

Some Technical Matters

It has been over ten years since the Lord drew the author into a concentrated study of the prophetic books. Much of what you have read here are deductions drawn from lengthy cross referencing of Scripture and history. If all the lines of reasoning which led to these conclusions had been spelled out in this one book, it would look like Strong's Concordance. So instead, we are trusting the Lord to lead you down the scriptural lines He wills.

As always, the Holy Spirit is He who leads us into all truth, through the Word of God, JOH 14:26. By a few dear brethren, and in my heart, that same Spirit affirms that what is written here is true. Now that you have read this book (if the Holy Spirit has opened your eyes) you know it too. Don't be upset if some brethren don't hear. Remember Jesus' parable of the new wine and old wineskins? How Jesus was just as concerned about bursting the old wineskins as he was in losing the new wine? New wine is for those who need a clearer vision of what is ahead, and are aware that there are some tough times coming. It is for those who need a fresh view of God's Word to spur them on in what little time is left to us.

We are aware that this work is a radical departure from the traditional norm, and that it could make sweeping changes in our end-time positions. As more and more brethren start to reconcile additional scriptures with this doctrinal skeleton, one wonders what the final picture will be like. Scholars in history or archeology could introduce new data that could amplify or modify this initial structure.

However, the evidence for the historic fulfillment of the prophetic day=years is virtually unassailable. Once those day=years are pinned to the new nation of Israel, the rest of end time prophecy falls into place like a grand processional.

God tells us in Isaiah that learning from Him is "line upon line, and precept upon precept, a little here, a little there." We believe that once you understand the day=years (do your homework, and are honest with the Word) that you will come to the same basic, if not the identical, conclusions that we have. The day=years is the key.

Some would argue that the third year of Cyrus could be two or three years earlier than the 533BC date used by the author. However, the 536BC dating for the 1st year of Cyrus is accepted by most conservative authorities. The historic events of 688AD, 1948AD and 1967AD cannot be challenged.

Interestingly enough, the interpretation of 1290 days of DAN 12:11 is pinned to the beginning of the reign of Nebuchadnezzar, and few argue about the 606BC or 605BC dating of that event. That the time of the Gentiles is over is a declaration of Scripture, LUK 21:24. That we are in the "end times" is easily concluded from that verse and DAN 12:4,9.

It cannot be biblically argued that the church will be taken to be with the Lord at some trumpet other than the very last trumpet of all time. Consequently, any position that requires trumpets after the last trumpet of 1CO 15:52 is opposed to Scripture.

That the Two Witnesses are churches is proven from within Revelation itself. That they are scripturally defined as the Jews and the Gentile Church is established from ROM

11:24-25. The scriptural support for the election of the faithful Jew of the Christian Era is extensive.

That the beasts, heads, and horns of Revelation 13 and 17 are empires and kingdoms, rather than the antichrist and his followers, has abundant scriptural foundation. That the final enemies of the church will come from the Mohammedan world is beyond reasonable doubt.

That there will be a final leader of the 8th beast who will lead Satan's forces against Israel is scriptural. However, a final "antichrist" who will rule from Jerusalem cannot be supported from the Bible. Neither can the traditions about his rise to world power during the end times.

That there will be a Seven Year Great Tribulation at the end of this era is suppositional. That the church will be taken to be with the Lord before all things are fulfilled is against open declarations of Scripture.

One could argue against the "time, times, and half a time" being 2500 years, because the Greek word "hemera" is ambiguous; and the 1st year of Belshazzar cannot be pinned to 552BC by primary evidence. However, many authorities accept that date, and there are three examples of the 2500 year prophetic time frame in Scripture. They all fit world history to the year. Consequently, the mathematical probability of this interpretation being in error is very low!

That the Western Church contains the descendants of the ten northern tribes is a logical extension of all the above, and though there is strong support for this thesis, it also is arguable. Unfortunately, this view is also held by some of the church's more radical splinter groups. As a result, identifying lost Israel with the Western Church might be used by some folks as a springboard to attempt to discredit the rest of "Hidden Beast." We considered leaving it out. However, identifying the Western Church with Ephraim has had so much affirmation of the Spirit (from those dear brethren who have read the manuscript) that we believe it to be of the Lord. We have to be careful not to ignore data just because others could use it against us; or because some radicals also happen to include it in their body of doctrine. The biblical and historic evidence itself was sufficient to warrant including the concept.

The chiasms in the first half of both Daniel and Revelation are very clear. It is doubtful that they could be successfully argued against. However, the structure of the second half of both books is less certain. Daniel 8 through 12 could be a simple **A-B-A**, or **AB-BA** with ch9 the first "B" and ch10 the second. Revelation 12 through 20 could be **ABC-CBA**, ch15 being the first "C" with ch16 the second. It is interesting to note that the central thought in the 1st chiasm, REV 7, is about all the redeemed, both Jew and Gentile, while the central thought of the 2nd chiasm, REV 16, is judgment on all the lost. The redeemed are divided into two groups, Israel, REV 7:4-8; and the church v9. The lost, of REV 16, are just the lost, there are no divisions. There are no partly lost, or those who have done good works get a better break. Revelation teaches that you either are under the blood of Jesus, REV 7:14, and included in the redeemed; or your fate will be that of the Seven Bowls of Wrath of REV 16:19, the final war of REV 19:19-20, and the final judgment of REV 20:13-15.

The author does not, by any means, believe that his conclusions are the final answer to the study of chiasms in the prophetic books, or the final answer on anything else, for that matter. There are specialists in structural criticism and history who might be able to define complex areas far more clearly.

Authorities disagree on a couple of dates related to the Babylonian captivity. Some question whether a zero point between BC and AD should be counted. To further complicate matters, Old Testament dates are arrived at from king lists (which are pinned to astronomical phenomenon) and other archeological evidence. Some of that evidence is confusing or contradictory. As a result, there is a one to three year ambiguity in OT dating.

Regardless, the prophecies we show as fulfilled in day=years all fell within the three year window accepted by scholars. When there was disagreement, the author accepted the conservative position. Interestingly enough, the numbers fit perfectly when conservative dates were used. Prophetic confirmation that conservative dating is correct.

In conclusion, the author took the responsibility of writing a work on the Word of God very seriously. We fear God too much to willfully, or through carelessness, become just another heretic who has led the church astray. Consequently, great care has been taken to be as historically accurate as possible, and to handle the Word of God with honor, reverence, and humility. Besides, the author pales at the thought of having a millstone tied around his neck, and being thrown into the depths of the sea.

Reconciling the Scriptures for some of these concepts has been so extensive that it would have been an easy matter to have overlooked some relevant passage of Scripture. This could have lead to incorrect conclusions. We trusted the Holy Spirit to protect us from omission or excess. Nevertheless brethren, be Bereans, ACT 17:10-11. Study the Word to see if these things are so. We claim no prophetic gift; and "in the multitude of words there lacketh not sin," PRO 10:19. So check this book against the straightedge of Scripture.

If error is found, say so right out loud for all to hear, 1CO 14:29; and please write the author, so he can make corrections in the next edition (time on this present Earth permitting). If none is found, thank you Lord for your guidance and protection. To the Eternal God our Father and to His only begotten Son, the Lord Jesus, goes all the Glory.

# A Personal Note

I am the son of missionary parents, raised in the Scripture
from my mother's knee. My early teens were spent in
Westervelt Homes, a school for missionary children. There I
learned the tenets of the faith, and hundreds of Scripture
verses by heart. After serving in the Navy during WW2, I
married, and attended Columbia Bible College, Columbia, SC.
After college, I abandoned my calling, and was in the business
world for the next thirty years. Sin deceived me, and I
wallowed in it like the prodigal son I had become. The Lord
could have left me there to founder. I surely deserved it. But
He saved me from a life of immorality and excess. Then He
cleaned me up and made me a servant.

"Oh Lord, thank You from the depths of my heart for the
unfathomable love and mercy You have poured out on me
through Your dear Son."

I had no idea what His plan was for me then, but He led
me to study His prophetic books (eight to ten hours a day) for

over four years. This study continued (shorter hours) for several more years. Along the way, little miracles would take place. A borrowed magazine or browsing in a bookstore would reveal some necessary little piece that fit His prophetic puzzle. The Lord did not do all this just so the church could hear another lie. Matter of fact, my prayer during all that time was, "Father, please let me know the truth. Please don't let me teach anything that is not of You." I pray that same prayer still.

It is now about 2AM, on September 14, 1990. I am again sitting in my little workroom, thinking back over the past ten years. That is how long I have understood what is in this book. I have just finished the 2nd edition of Hidden Beast, and am naming it Hidden Beast 2. As current events opened new Scriptures, a 2nd edition was needed. If there is time, this edition may need updating too. I believe that this book, and the three earlier works, are what the Lord had in mind for me to do with my life all along.

Because of this knowledge, I have almost become a spiritual casualty. I have fought this fight until I am weary of soul. It is time to pass the baton to others. The author isn't anyone big or important, just a lump of clay that the Lord set in front of a typewriter. Even so, I was led of the Spirit to go from church to church to share these truths with the brethren. Most of the pastors met me with coldness or indifference. Some greeted me with outright anger and hostility. There were a few blessed exceptions, or I would not have been able to go on.

As church doors closed, the Lord led me to teach Bible prophecy in the homes of various brethren. During those studies, the brethren would say: "Why don't you explain this to the church pastors and teach it in all the churches? This is renewing our interest in the Bible, and drawing us closer to the Lord!"

As God is witness, I tried to. I went to about 350 churches within a 100 mile radius of home, but they could not hear. Most of the pastors didn't care. They kept asking me what denomination I belonged to, and whether I was pre-mill or pre, mid, or post-trib rapture. When I said: "None of the above," the interview was over. The possibility of a new opening of God's Word was of little interest to them. I left a copy of an earlier book on prophecy at every church. Many churches were closed and locked, but I could sometimes find the pastor at his home. I was continually urged by the Spirit to get these truths before the brethren so that we could prepare for the coming time of trial, and the subsequent return of the Lord. I coveted no man's pulpit, and never asked for money to teach, even though sometimes we had very little.

With church doors barred by indifference, there was little left to do but write it all down as best I could. To go to the brethren directly. The first Hidden Beast, and this 2nd edition are the results. Let's call it a "to the saint it may concern" letter. I have asked the Lord to put this work in the hands of every Christian He wants to read it (wherever you are), not one more, and not one less. If we pray according to God's will He hears us, so obviously you are on His "read this book" list. May God richly bless you, my dear brother or sister in the Lord.

Now the church grows smaller, not in numbers so much, but in those who are really Jesus' sheep. Those who look to the Lord with their whole heart; prayerful saints, willing to fellowship over the Bible, and obey it. It gets lonelier out there; few evangelize, and fewer yet come to the foot of the Cross. Jeremiah had it right: If you stand against the lethargy and false doctrines in the church (because of what the Bible says) you will become an outcast. But, praise God, and stand anyway! Remember whom we serve. The Lord is returning soon, and His reward is with Him. His true servants have always been outcasts, HEB 11:36-38, and it is a privilege to be numbered among them. Encourage your heart with the beautiful words of this elder brother who has gone on before us:

JER 15:15-21 (excerpts, NASB) O LORD...know that for Thy sake I endure reproach. Thy words were found and I ate them, and Thy words became for me a joy and the delight of my heart; for I have been called by Thy name, O LORD God of hosts. I did not sit in the circle of merry-makers, nor did I exult. Because of Thy hand upon me I sat alone, for thou didst fill me with indignation...Wilt thou indeed be to me like a deceptive stream, with water that is unreliable?

Therefore, thus saith the LORD, "If you return, then will I restore you - before Me you will stand; and if you extract the precious from the worthless, you will become my spokesman. They for their part may turn to you, but as for you, you must not turn to them. Then I will make you to this people a fortified wall of bronze; and though they fight against you, they will not prevail over you; for I am with you to save you and deliver you," declares the Lord.

Maranatha brethren, the Lord is at hand.

# *A Word From Fish House*

This book was published by a small handful of Christian brethren who have only three concerns:

1. To see Jesus glorified.
2. To prepare the brethren for the troubled times ahead.
3. To prepare us for the most awesome event of all time: the return of the Lord at the head of the heavenly hosts.

If Hidden Beast 2 has been of spiritual benefit to you, please share the truths it contains with others. You (not someone else) are the light of the world. Then, please write Fish House, P.O. Box 453, Fort Myers, FL 33902, or call us at (813) 694-0080. We have no denominational or church support, so your calls and letters will be all the encouragement we will get. The author can also be reached through Fish House, and he personally answers all the mail he can. Just address your mail to E. H. Skolfield in care of Fish House, using the above address.

Mr. Skolfield is also an independent, conservative Bible teacher with a special ministry in Daniel and Revelation. He teaches a detailed study of Bible prophecy in a prepared lecture series. This series is usually comprised of seven three hour talks held on seven consecutive evenings. Longer or shorter engagements can be arranged. If you would like him to visit your church or group, please call or write for schedule openings.

If your bookstore does not carry Hidden Beast 2, or you are having difficulty obtaining more copies, please fill in the form and mail directly to Fish House. We will immediately send you as many books as you need.

We have had a few requests for a time chart, and a loose-leaf teaching outline. If their is sufficient demand, we will publish one. Price will be about $7.95 each, plus shipping and handling. Please check if interested.

# ORDER FORM

TO:        FISH HOUSE
P. O. Box 453
Fort Myers, Florida  33902

Please send the following:

| Quantity | Item | Price Each | Total |
|---|---|---|---|
| | **Hidden Beast 2** | 9.95 | |
| | Loose-leaf Teaching Outline | 7.95 | |
| | Time Chart | 7.95 | |

TOTAL: ☐

Name_____

Address_____

City_____ State_____ Zip_____

Prices include postage and handling.  Please enclose check or money order *(make payable to FISH HOUSE)*.  As publishers we have no facilities to accept credit cards.

# NOTES